THE MIRACULOUS
GOSPEL OF JOHN

THE MIRACULOUS
GOSPEL OF JOHN

WITH COMMENTARY BY

Jim Hockaday

Published by Jim Hockaday Ministries, 8516 East 101st Street, Suite E, Tulsa, Oklahoma 74133

Definitions of key words for each chapter are from:

"Thayer's Greek Lexicon," Electronic Database. Copyright © 2000 by Biblesoft)

"Greek-English Lexicon Based on Semantic Domain." Copyright © 1988 United Bible Societies, New York. Used by permission.)

Louw and Nida Greek-English Lixicon of The New Testament (United Bible Societies, 1988) ISBN: 0826703437 NT: 3875

All Scripture quotations, unless otherwise indicated, are taken from the New King James Version. Copyright © 1982 by Thomas Nelson, Inc. All Rights reserved.

Other Scripture references are from the following sources:

The Holy Bible, New International Version (NIV). Copyright 1973, 1978, 1984. International Bible Society. Used by permission of Zondervan Bible Publishers.

THE AMPLIFIED BIBLE, Old Testament copyright © 1965, 1987 by the Zondervan Corporation. The Amplified New Testament copyright © 1958, 1987 by the Lockman Foundation. Used by permission.

The King James Version of the Bible (KJV).

Worldwide English New Testament, by Annie Cressman, Soon Publications, India 1969

Richert Translation, Freedom Dynamics, The Thinker, Big Bear Lake, CA 1977

Riggs Translation, James Stevenson D.D., The Gospel of John; In Explanatory Translation, Spirit to Spirit Publications, Tulsa, OK 1982

Way, Arthur S., The Letters of St. Paul and Hebrews. The Moody Press, Chicago, 1950

ISBN: 1-893301-23-0

Printed in the United States of America
05 06 07 08   9 8 7 6 5 4 3 2 1

CONTENTS

ACKNOWLEDGEMENTS

I believe that the Lord in His wisdom has directed me to write this commentary to the miraculous Gospel of John. I am confident that He knows the significance and importance of this project. I believe that thousands will be saved and instructed to effectively work the works of God.

For these reasons, I am honored to acknowledge our Chief Commander in the army of the Lord, the master mind, with the strategy to reap the harvest.

I am grateful to those who encourage me to continue to be creative with the call of God on my life. Lord Jesus, You are my hero and the inspiration for every word written.

To my wife Erin, and our three girls, Alli, Drew, and Chloe: just your presence in my life is a great strength which empowers me to always do my best.

To Dave Hail and Larry Keefauver, experts in their fields: you continue to graciously encourage and remind me, a novice, that my ideas and talents are from God.

And to all those who read this work: may your lives resemble in every way the love and power of our Lord Jesus Christ. Until He comes we are God's best in the earth to effectively tell the world that Jesus is still alive.

INTRODUCTION

As you read the gospel of John expect to receive an impartation from the life and anointing of our Lord Jesus Christ. Through the timeless truths of John, you will see with Jesus's eyes, hear with His ears and think His thoughts in order to *live in the miraculous*. The gospel of John reveals the awesome consciousness of our Lord.

The apostle Paul said in Philippians 2:5, "Let this mind be in you, which was also in Christ Jesus." All the thoughts of Jesus can be adopted by every Christian as their own. Jesus the Man, anointed by the Holy Spirit as the Christ, developed His thoughts from His youth until with such great dominion over His soul, that He conquered death before dying on the cross. I am challenging your mind-set with God's thoughts. Solomon wrote in Proverbs 23:7, that as a man "thinks in his heart, so is he." The outcome of

Think the way Jesus thinks.

You cannot live in the miraculous as long as you think and act in the commonplace.

your actions will be the sum total of your thoughts.

Think the way Jesus thinks. How exciting it is to think as Jesus thinks. When God spoke to Isaiah saying, "For as the heavens are higher than the earth, so are My ways higher than your ways, and My thoughts than your thoughts" (Isaiah 55:9), He wasn't trying to discourage us. On the contrary, God was inviting us to think His thoughts and act just like Him so to others it would be apparent that we have been in God's presence.

Act the way Jesus acts. Not only will you be able to think His thoughts, you will be empowered to act as He acts. You will act in faith trusting all He said and did. Your obedient actions will not be religious, that is, done out of duty, fear, or obligation. Rather, your obedience will arise out of loving God—heart, mind, body, and soul. In John's gospel, you will discover how

Jesus has given His Spirit to you so that your life can be lived, as He lived—full of power, grace, glory, and truth!

Jesus promised in John 14:12-13, "Most certainly I say to you, he who believes in Me, the works that I do he will do also; and greater works than these he will do, because I go to My Father. And whatever you ask in My name, that I will do, that the Father may be glorified in the Son."

What an awesome promise from the Lord! You are empowered to think His thoughts and do His actions so that the lost are found, the sick are healed, and the oppressed are delivered in His name.

As you read through this gospel, allow the commentary to inspire the miraculous in you. By faith, apply your thoughts, perspectives, mind-set and actions to those of Jesus. Set aside your opinions and mind-set that do not agree with the gospel. Remember that you cannot live in the miraculous as long as you think and act in the commonplace.

Living in the miraculous is living, speaking, thinking, and acting like Jesus. His example is ours. His words are life and Spirit for us. Follow Jesus into all of life's questions, situations, and problems. He will not only "get you through," Jesus will empower you to claim victory and walk in His power and grace.

CHAPTER 1

¹In the beginning was the Word, and the Word was with God, and the Word was God. ²He was in the beginning with God.

³All things were made through Him, and without Him nothing was made that was made. ⁴In Him was life, and the life was the light of men. ⁵And the light shines in the darkness, and the

1:1 We know from 1:14 that, "The Word became flesh," indicating that Jesus was the divine personality of the Godhead mentioned. Jesus was in the beginning, with God and was God. However, Jesus referred to Himself as the Son of Man at least ninety times in the Gospels validating that He walked on the earth as a man. Unlike other religious prophets and teachers, Jesus the man, was and is God.

1:2 Again, John separates Jesus from the great minds and theologians of the world. As preposterous as it may sound, the union and relationship between Jesus and God neither started nor evolved; it always existed in eternity. Indeed the man, Jesus, is divine.

Jesus the man, was and is God.

1:3 Everything created originates in Jesus. Since all things were made through Him, the actions of Jesus on the earth become crucial for our lives if we desire to see miracles manifested as He did. Remember, John is not only singling out the supreme authenticity of Jesus as God, he also intertwines His existence to ours. If Jesus, the second person of the Trinity, spoke and the world came into existence,

then we must learn to speak to our world if we are to see His will manifested.

1:4 Luke spoke of Jesus in Acts 3:15 as the Prince of life. Jesus is the originator or author of life *(zoe)*: the Life of God vs. existence *(bios)*. Life is the very divine reality of God Himself, His nature, and the substance of His being—the nuts and bolts behind the very existence of God. This life comes only from God through Jesus and is given to all who trust in Him. For human beings to possess in any measure the life of God would potentially alter and enhance every fiber in their being. In fact, temporal existence is transformed into immortality by *zoe*. By receiving life, a person begins to grow supernaturally—spirit, soul, and body—through the power of God's life in Christ.

1:5 Describing the action of the Life of God, John refers to its ability to shine as a light. This light represents the growth of God's ability throughout a person's life. It not only affects his spiritual stature and nature, but challenges and enlightens his thinking. As an eternal substance, it supports and sustains his physical body. Notice that this life is not passive, but active. The activity of the Life of God shapes our every word and act.

1:5b Light, development, and ability are all the workings of God's Life. Darkness

darkness did not comprehend it.
⁶There was a man sent from God, whose name *was* John. ⁷This man came for a witness, to bear witness of the Light, that all through him might believe. ⁸He was not that Light, but *was sent* to bear witness of that Light.

⁹That was the true Light which gives light to every man coming into the world.
¹⁰He was in the world, and the world was made through Him, and the world did not know Him. ¹¹He came to His own, and His own did not receive Him.

---

always exists wherever light isn't. Isn't it wonderful to know that God is light, and in Him is no darkness at all? No matter how hard darkness tries to put out the light of God's Life, it will fail. A person's understanding of eternal life will bring revelation that pierces the darkness of the world's system, nullifying its effect upon our lives. Never is a person defeated when eternal life is engaged and its influences known.

No matter how hard darkness tries to put out the light of God's Life, it will fail.

1:6-7 John the Baptist was sent on a mission to give testimony to the coming Christ. We also have been sent by God to preach the gospel message about the Christ. Jesus said in Mark 16 that this message will not only save those who will receive it, but it will demonstrate itself through signs and wonders. Understanding our assignment to speak and act like Jesus launches our life's journey of ongoing, victorious success.

1:8 John the Baptist had a particular purpose in God's divine plan; so do we. Jesus came on purpose to destroy the works of the devil (1 John 3:8). John's revelation of

Jesus Christ comprehended the greatness of God's plan. God, the eternal existence of all light, sent His Son, Jesus, to be the Light of the world, so that those who receive Him would immediately become "lights" that shine in the world. When the light shines, it reveals things otherwise hidden. As we bear witness to the truth, the world will see Jesus.

1:9 Satan masquerades himself as a light, yet is full of darkness. Read 2 Corinthians 11. On the other hand, Jesus is the one and only God, the true Light. Without Him there is no light in the world. Jesus desires for us to walk as children of light in the midst of a dark world. The biblical way to demonstrate to others who you are inwardly is to shine outwardly with the light of Christ. If the world is to see Jesus, then we must represent Him as true lights.

The biblical way to demonstrate to others who you are inwardly is to shine outwardly with the light of Christ.

Jesus manifested works of light by words and deeds through signs, miracles, and wonders to show forth light and thus used the results of successful living to declare His place in God.

¹²But as many as received Him, to them He gave the right to become children of God, to those who believe in His name: ¹³who were born, not of blood, nor of the will of the flesh, nor of the will of man, but of God.

¹⁴And the Word became flesh and dwelt among us, and we beheld His glory, the glory as of the only begotten of the Father, full of grace and truth.

1:12 Everything that John writes is to persuade people to receive Christ. The single most significant event in a person's life is to receive Christ.

The moment you receive Christ, you are given the power and privilege to become someone you weren't before. The amazing thing about transformation is that you can then portray who you are in Christ. You are empowered as a child of God and authorized to represent Jesus in the earth.

1:13 I like how John writes. He first covers the familiarities of our flesh, showing us all the reasons why we can't relate any longer to our past. Being born again is a grand discovery of our present status in Christ, fueling our great expectancy for tomorrow. As Paul writes, "old things have passed away; behold all things have become new" (2 Corinthians 5:17). We know that God's mercies are new every morning. As such we can arise with hope and expectancy knowing that God is at work in and through us to overcome darkness with light, sickness with health, doubt with faith, poverty with prosperity, and bondage with freedom.

1:13b Proper identity is one of the greatest needs in the church. We are no longer governed by problems relating to our family bloodline. All sickness and disease are forever defeated by our new life. There are no desires of the flesh or other people that will ever manipulate or control us. Even among Christians, the majority of problems come from family heredity, yielding to the flesh and/or the pressures of men. Never did a little word such as, "of" mean so much. The phrase "of God" completely identifies and commissions our lives to be lived as God does His. We owe the quality of the life that we now possess to God.

1:14 Notice the divine exchange between verses 12 and 14. When we believe and receive Jesus as Lord, we become sons of God. Yet in order for this to happen, the Son of God had to become flesh. We call this God-man, Jesus. The power of God's Word, which is living and powerful, has the ability to sanctify us—spirit, soul, and body. The Word of God will do for us everything that Jesus did in His time on earth. If God can be manifested inside of the flesh of Jesus, then His Word can come to live in our bodies and manifest itself in the world around us.

As an eyewitness, John describes the life of Jesus as glorious. The power of God was visible through the outward demonstrations Jesus performed. Herein lies the bedrock of our trust in Christ. He was and is the fullness of truth and grace. Every element of His life portrayed what was and is real and available for all.

¹⁵John bore witness of Him and cried out, saying, "This was He of whom I said, 'He who comes after me is preferred before me, for He was before me.' "
¹⁶And of His fullness we have all received, and grace for grace. ¹⁷For the law was given through Moses, *but* grace and truth came through Jesus Christ. ¹⁸No one has seen God at any time. The only begotten Son, who is in the bosom of the Father, He has declared *Him.*

¹⁹Now this is the testimony of John, when the Jews sent priests and Levites from Jerusalem to ask him, "Who are you?"
²⁰He confessed, and did not deny, but confessed, "I am not the Christ."

²¹And they asked him, "What then? Are you Elijah?" He said, "I am not." "Are you the Prophet?" And he answered, "No."

²²Then they said to him, "Who are you, that we may give an answer to those who sent us? What do you say about yourself?"
²³He said: "I *am*
'The voice of one crying in the wilderness:
"Make straight the way of the LORD," '
as the prophet Isaiah said."
²⁴Now those who were sent were from the Pharisees. ²⁵And

Our lives in Christ are being transformed from glory to glory (2 Corinthians 3). That transformation continually fills us with hope (Colossians 1:27). We walk by faith in hope-filled expectancy to see God's Spirit through Christ move in and through us to accomplish mighty things all around us for His glory.

1:16 Jesus was the divine expression of God. Having received Jesus we also have received the fullness of God. The image of God in which we were created (Genesis 1:26-27) is being restored by His Spirit in us.

This great impartation qualifies us to live in and release the fullness of His divine expression. Ephesians 3:19b-20a declares, "that you may be filled with all the fullness of God. Now to him who is able to do exceedingly abundantly above all that we

ask or think according to the power that works in us . . . "

The purpose of the Bible is to show that we are capable to express the will of God as Jesus did. Having received His fullness is to have received as much of God as is possible. This thought is backed up by the phrase "grace for grace." Grace is God's ability in such overflowing measure that living the life of Christ is every bit possible.

1:18 Jesus told Philip in John 14 that he knew the Father. Philip replied, "Show us the Father." Jesus said, "He who has seen Me has seen the Father." This was the assignment of Jesus. He was to declare, or introduce to the world, the heart and responsiveness of the Father. The world was to see and hear of the influences of the Father. This is our assignment today.

they asked him, saying, "Why then do you baptize if you are not the Christ, nor Elijah, nor the Prophet?"

²⁶John answered them, saying, "I baptize with water, but there stands One among you whom you do not know. ²⁷It is He who, coming after me, is preferred before me, whose sandal strap I am not worthy to loose."

²⁸These things were done in Bethabara beyond the Jordan, where John was baptizing.

²⁹The next day John saw Jesus coming toward him, and said, "Behold! The Lamb of God who takes away the sin of the world! ³⁰This is He of whom I said, 'After me comes a Man who is preferred before me, for He was before me.' ³¹I did not know Him; but that He should be revealed to Israel, therefore I came baptizing with water."

³²And John bore witness, saying,

"I saw the Spirit descending from heaven like a dove, and He remained upon Him. ³³I did not know Him, but He who sent me to baptize with water said to me, 'Upon whom you see the Spirit descending, and remaining on Him, this is He who baptizes with the Holy Spirit.' ³⁴And I have seen and testified that this is the Son of God."

³⁵Again, the next day, John stood with two of his disciples. ³⁶And looking at Jesus as He walked, he said, "Behold the Lamb of God!"

³⁷The two disciples heard him speak, and they followed Jesus. ³⁸Then Jesus turned, and seeing them following, said to them, "What do you seek?" They said to Him, "Rabbi" (which is to say, when translated, Teacher), "where are You staying?"

³⁹He said to them, "Come and see." They came and saw where

1:29-34 John the Baptist, a forerunner to the ministry of Jesus, was a personal eyewitness who authenticated the life and ministry of Jesus. As John baptized Jesus in the Jordan River, the Spirit of God descended upon Jesus. John saw this and experienced for himself the truth that Jesus was and is the Son of God. The power of your witness hinges on the reality that you have seen for yourself and experienced Jesus as the Son of God.

1:35-51 It's very significant that John wrote about Jesus choosing His staff supernaturally. Jesus didn't tell them everything that was going to happen. When we accept our responsibility to walk with Jesus, we will do so by faith. Each step that we take will be obedience to what we know at the present. The rest will be shown us. Jesus imparted supernatural words and

He was staying, and remained with Him that day (now it was about the tenth hour).

40One of the two who heard John *speak,* and followed Him, was Andrew, Simon Peter's brother. 41He first found his own brother Simon, and said to him, "We have found the Messiah" (which is translated, the Christ). 42And he brought him to Jesus. Now when Jesus looked at him, He said, "You are Simon the son of Jonah. You shall be called Cephas" (which is translated, A Stone).

43The following day Jesus wanted to go to Galilee, and He found Philip and said to him, "Follow Me." 44Now Philip was from Bethsaida, the city of Andrew and Peter. 45Philip found Nathanael and said to him, "We have found Him of whom Moses in the law, and also the prophets, wrote—Jesus of Nazareth, the son of Joseph."

46And Nathanael said to him, "Can anything good come out of Nazareth?" Philip said to him, "Come and see."

47Jesus saw Nathanael coming toward Him, and said of him, "Behold, an Israelite indeed, in whom is no deceit!"

---

insight into the lives and hearts of His followers. We should expect nothing less.

1:50 Jesus questioned Nathanael because he was so astounded by the supernatural experience that Jesus presented. Jesus seemed to make light of this experience in comparison to what He would eventually see. The course and path that Jesus took were immersed in the supernatural. This didn't shock Jesus, He actually anticipated it. He did, however, endeavor to get Nathanael to anticipate it as well.

Anticipate the miraculous! Expect Jesus to use you in power to manifest His presence and glory. Walk in faith not fear or doubt.

1:51 This is an exceptional verse because it is the first place in the gospel of John

that the phrase "Son of Man" is used. Jesus referred to Himself as a man, who would very naturally experience the supernatural continually. As a man, Jesus spoke of angels ascending and descending upon Him. The man, Jesus, from this point on, shows us that His ministry will be marked by the supernatural. This fact was already settled in His soul.

To what degree do we accept this truth for ourselves? Determine to see the invisible and feel the intangible. The supernatural is really quite natural to you as well. God will never fail you.

Determine to see the invisible and feel the intangible.

⁴⁸Nathanael said to Him, "How do You know me?" Jesus answered and said to him, "Before Philip called you, when you were under the fig tree, I saw you." ⁴⁹Nathanael answered and said to Him, "Rabbi, You are the Son of God! You are the King of Israel!" ⁵⁰Jesus answered and said to him, "Because I said to you, 'I saw you under the fig tree,' do you believe? You will see greater things than these." ⁵¹And He said to him, "Most assuredly, I say to you, hereafter you shall see heaven open, and the angels of God ascending and descending upon the Son of Man."

JOHN 1 KEY WORDS

🗝 **Word** (*logos* λόγος NT: 3056) The Greek meaning for *logos* communicates the concept of word(s) spoken by a living voice in conversation. In other words, that which God speaks is intended to be heard and obeyed by faith. So He speaks, and creation comes into being communicating revelation of who He is. Thus Jesus as the Word communicates who the Father is with the intention that we will "hear and see" the Father and respond in faith and obedience.

Logos is also the mandates, instructions, decrees, and orders of God. As the Word, Jesus's life isn't simply an example of how we should live but also a mandate for His life to be lived in and through us. So the *logos* empowers us to live in obedience to the life He lived. Our response to the *logos* is more than admiration; it's surrender, submission, and love for the truth that we have received.

🗝 **Power** (*exousia* ἐξουσία NT: 1849) Meaning power or authority. The same word used in Matthew 28:18 (KJV) when Jesus said, "All power is given unto me in heaven and earth." The same power and authority in Christ has been imparted to the believer to live in the miraculous. *Exousia* refers to the right to exercise authority. As such, the believer has the right or permission to exercise the same power as Christ in obedience to the will of the Father.

𝟶 Life (*zoe* ζωή NT: 2222)
Life is more than physical existence. After physical birth, we must be born of the Spirit (John 3) through faith in Christ so that we have life both abundantly (John 10:10) and forever (John 6:51, 58). The only source of *zoe* is Jesus (John 14:6). Life is the very nature and power given by the living God through faith in His Son, Jesus, to experience the supernatural and the miraculous every day.

𝟶 Light (*phos* φῶς NT: 5457)
Quantum physics has discovered what Scripture has revealed since the beginning. The basic building block of the universe is light. All matter is energy and all energy derives from light. The source of all light is God (1 John 1:5) and His light dispels all darkness, sin, and death. Light and darkness cannot occupy the same space at the same time. Hence, whenever *phos* appears, darkness must flee. *Phos* also refers to "fire." The believer can declare the Word, "You, O LORD, keep my lamp burning; my God turns my darkness into light" (Psalm 18:28 NIV).

𝟶 Believe (*pisteuo* πιστεύω NT: 4102) To have faith. The noun form of *pisteuo* is *pistis* which is the Greek word for "faith." To have faith or to believe is to place one's trust in someone or something. Such trust is complete and total surrender (Romans 10:1-13; 12:1-2). To believe on His name is to trust Jesus Christ totally and to receive not just His words or teaching, but to "receive Him." By His Spirit, we receive the life of Christ in us and have the power and authority to live His life as the sons of God.

Trusting faith (*pisteuo*) includes what we believe but isn't limited to just true thoughts, creeds, or doctrines. Believe is an action. Faith focuses on total trust in the person of Jesus and includes total surrender and obedience to everything He speaks. To believe (*pisteuo*) is to act upon and live in obedience to what is believed. So Jesus confirms in John 15:10, "If you keep My commandments, you will abide in my love, just as I have kept My Father's commandments and abide in His love."

Faith trusts Jesus so completely that it acts in loving obedience knowing that whatever Jesus promised will be done.

JOHN 1 SUMMARY

John wastes no time in his opening remarks to reveal and authenticate Jesus as the Son of God. The uniqueness of the Christ is found in His origin of existence. As the living Word of God, Jesus participated in the creation of all things that are made. We get a glimpse into the partnership of the Godhead and how they worked as a team to create all things. Jesus is the spoken Word and the incarnate Word of God. All things were made through Him. The Word [the eternal Christ] spoke in Genesis 1:3 and said, "Let there be light." These words were openly manifested by the working of the Holy Spirit who was hovering over the waters in anticipation of creation.

Jesus continued to work with the Father and the Holy Spirit in His time on earth. He acted on the words and deeds that He received from His Father in complete dependence on the empowering of the Holy Spirit to manifest these results. This is a great revelation for the body of Christ. If we will boldly act on the words of Scripture, which to us are the words and deeds of the Father, then we can expect the working of the Holy Spirit to accompany us with the necessary manifestations. Great confidence comes as we view properly our position as representatives of Christ.

I love reading Genesis 1, because it reveals to us how accurate, full, and complete God was in His creation. Everything that He set out to create was created. There were no failures or delays. Is it possible that our lives can be as accurate and successful?

Jesus is the true light that has come into the world to bring development and power to man. The contrast of light to darkness is the great battle between the forces of evil and the power of God. Jesus revealed that light easily conquers all darkness without question. Our confidence is in His overcoming victory as the light of the world. The Good News for us is that we don't just have a great hero who stands alone as the One who conquered and lives victorious. Jesus has provided complete renovation and ultimate change of status for those who will receive Him. His victorious power is released into the lives of believers who receive instantly positions as children of God. Suddenly, the work of the Lord has life-changing implications in our lives.

Can it be that these sonship privileges transmit to the believer the ability to live life to its fullness as Jesus gave us example? As we will discover in the chapters of John's gospel, Jesus accomplishes His mission, paving the way for us as children of God to do the same.

MEDITATIONS FOR SUCCESS

- Jesus was one with God; look at what He did. You also are one with God.
- The devil can try to overcome you all he wants. Jesus is your light and your salvation. Light always wins.

- Calling yourself a Christian is indicating that you know you have received His power.
- You are "of God." Dare to think of the possibilities!
- Everything that Jesus did, the Word of God will do for you today.
- "Of His fullness we have received." Believe that there is nothing that you lack, and you will see evidence of His miraculous power that you have never known or experienced.
- Jesus declared truth and introduced everyone to the Father. We must do the same in His power.

CHAPTER 2

[1]On the third day there was a wedding in Cana of Galilee, and the mother of Jesus was there. [2]Now both Jesus and His disciples were invited to the wedding.

[3]And when they ran out of wine, the mother of Jesus said to Him, "They have no wine."

[4]Jesus said to her, "Woman, what does your concern have to

2:1 Mary, Jesus's mother, is mentioned as being present for this wedding. This has significance for she is the one who involves Jesus in a predicament for which He is not responsible. Her belief that Jesus can solve even this trivial matter can teach us about how we too can live in the miraculous!

2:2 As invited guests, Jesus and His

disciples must have known the couple to be married.

[Mary] involves Jesus in a predicament for which He is not responsible. Her belief that Jesus can solve even this trivial matter can teach us about how we too can live in the miraculous!

do with Me? My hour has not yet come."

⁵His mother said to the servants, "Whatever He says to you, do *it*."

⁶Now there were set there six waterpots of stone, according to the manner of purification of the Jews, containing twenty or thirty gallons apiece. ⁷Jesus said to them, "Fill the waterpots with water." And they filled them up to the brim. ⁸And He said to them, "Draw *some* out now, and take *it* to the master of the feast." And they took *it*. ⁹When the master of the feast had tasted the water that was made wine, and did not know where it came from (but the servants who had drawn the water knew), the master of the feast called the bridegroom. ¹⁰And he said to

---

2:3 As we can see, the absence of wine was an issue for Mary. She immediately consulted with Jesus for a solution. My question is: "Why is Mary concerned with something that is not her responsibility? Or is it?" At least she looked to Jesus when the lack of wine could have been solved by going into town and purchasing more wine. This would have been time-consuming and costly, yet it could have been done.

2:5 The fact that Mary could speak to someone's servants with such forcefulness may mean that Mary had authority to do so. Mary may have had something to do with the planning of the wedding. This would account for her concern. Mary's command to the servants constitutes the prescription for miracles. Notice that Mary did not tell Jesus what to do. Rather, she instructed the servants to do what Jesus said. Too often, we use our relationship with Jesus to try to manipulate Him into doing what we want. Rather, we should always desire what He wants. Our prayer of consecration is, "Not my will, but thy will be done." We, too, should live quickened by the words of God for decisive actions.

The miracles you need for today may well arise from something you already have in hand.

2:6 Jesus looked for a natural vehicle through which the miracle would occur. Many times in the Old Testament the prophets would use something natural as a means to releasing a person's faith for the miracle. The miracles you need for today may well arise from something you already have in hand. "The miracle is in the house." Don't be surprised by how simple and practical God's ways can be.

2:7 Jesus wasn't opposed to helping Mary, for He wasted no time in giving the command of faith for the miracle. Jesus gave the servants something that they could do for faith to be initiated. The power of God will work with what you have and through your willingness to use what you have His way. Notice that the servants filled the pots up to the brim. They must have been so convinced by how Jesus presented Himself, that they acted wholeheartedly.

him, "Every man at the beginning sets out the good wine, and when the *guests* have well drunk, then the inferior. You have kept the good wine until now!" ¹¹This beginning of signs Jesus did in Cana of Galilee, and manifested His glory; and His disciples believed in Him.

¹²After this He went down to Capernaum, He, His mother, His brothers, and His disciples; and they did not stay there many days.

¹³Now the Passover of the Jews was at hand, and Jesus went up to Jerusalem. ¹⁴And He found in the temple those who sold oxen and sheep and doves, and the money changers doing business. ¹⁵When He had made a whip of cords, He drove them all out of the temple, with the sheep and the oxen, and poured out the changers' money and overturned the tables. ¹⁶And He said to those who sold doves, "Take these things away! Do not

---

If you will believe the word of the Lord and act upon it in spite of your doubts or past, you will experience the miraculous.

2:8 Jesus tested the faith of the servants, which would be the catalyst for the miracle. He asked them to take of what was in the pot and give it to the master of the feast. Well, the servants knew exactly what was in the pot; it was water. The servants had to trust that Jesus knew what He was doing in order to obey the command. Their prior natural experience and senses didn't confirm what Jesus was doing. At some instant from the water pots to the master's cup, the water became wine. This passage is encouraging to those who need a miracle. Step out in faith. If you will believe the word of the Lord and act upon it in spite of your doubts or past, you will experience the miraculous.

2:11 The purpose of glory is for demonstrations and manifestations that will cause people to believe. This is where the out-

ward evidence of God's anointing became visible in the ministry of Jesus. Notice the purpose of the anointing—to bring God glory by producing results.

The purpose of glory is for demonstrations and manifestations that will cause people to believe.

2:12-13 Jesus went into the temple and found unlawful things going on. He revealed His attitude toward the temple.
2:14-15 When Jesus made a whip to remove the people, He exhibited the Father's eagerness to remove all obstacles that stand in the way of our receiving His presence. Paul said that we are the temple of God (1 Corinthians 3; 6). God will not tolerate competition for His heart. God's presence will not occupy the same place with anything or anyone else.
2:16 Jesus relates the temple to the Father's house. Jesus only seeks to eliminate the wrong from the house; He

make My Father's house a house of merchandise!" ¹⁷Then His disciples remembered that it was written, "*Zeal for Your house* has eaten Me up."

¹⁸So the Jews answered and said to Him, "What sign do You show to us, since You do these things?"

¹⁹Jesus answered and said to them, "Destroy this temple, and in three days I will raise it up."

²⁰Then the Jews said, "It has taken forty-six years to build this temple, and will You raise it up in three days?"

²¹But He was speaking of the temple of His body. ²²Therefore, when He had risen from the dead, His disciples remembered that He had said this to them; and they believed the Scripture and the word which Jesus had said.

²³Now when He was in Jerusalem at the Passover, during the feast, many believed in His name when they saw the signs which He did. ²⁴But Jesus did not commit Himself to them, because He knew all *men*, ²⁵and had no need that anyone should testify of man, for He knew what was in man.

---

doesn't condemn the house. Likewise, God loves you. However, He hates sin. James said that the Spirit yearns after us. Another way of saying this is: The Spirit is intolerant of rivalry. Sin, bondages, and strongholds must go; God's Kingdom ruled by His Spirit must take control of our every thought, feeling, decision, and action.

2:17 God, through His love, is consumed with His temple. We should be encouraged to trust Him to eliminate those things that hinder the functioning of our temple. The attitude of God's love toward us and His zeal to remain the first love (Revelation 2:4) in our lives is crucial in our development.

2:22 "They believed the Scripture and the word which Jesus had said." In other words, Jesus took the Old Testament scripture and applied it to their situation. When you know the Word of God, then the Holy Spirit, given to you by Jesus to teach you all truth, will reveal what you are to believe and how you are to act. Memorize and meditate on Scripture (Psalm 1). The sword of the Word cannot be used by you unless it's in you. Hide God's Word in your heart (Psalm 119:11).

2:23 "Believed in His name." Read John 1:12. The power in Jesus's name invoked His ability to save, heal, and deliver. Those who believed in Him and operated in the authority of His name, would have the *dunamis* power to work the same signs (Mark 16:17).

2:23-25 Signs and wonders produced in the ministry of Jesus again provide people with a reason to believe in Him. The reason Jesus did not commit Himself to men is that He understood their intentions. I believe that Jesus, led by the Holy Ghost, had great discernment into the heart intentions of men. As we persuade men to believe, there is great benefit in knowing how to position someone for the miraculous. Jesus was a master at saying and doing the right thing to open the heart of an individual to receive His miracles.

JOHN 2 KEY WORDS

🔑 **Sign** (*semeion* σημεῖον NT: 4592) This is the primary Greek word that the apostle John uses in referring to miracles in his gospel. Each of Jesus's miraculous signs in John gives the reader major revelation about who Jesus is, both as the Son of Man and the Son of God (John 2:11, 18, 23; 3:2; 4:54; 6:2, 14, 26, 30; 7:31; 9:16; 10:41; 11:47; 12:18, 37; 20:30).

Semeion points or directs the person to God. Hence, a sign is a pointer, guide, or signpost to the glory of God being manifest in time and space. A sign is an event that has special and significant meaning or revelation. Jesus uses signs to authenticate His authority as the Son of Man to reveal the power as well as the loving heart of the Father. A sign is more about the one doing it than the one receiving it. Thus, in the case of this miraculous sign in John 2, we never learn the names of those for whom the wine is created, but we certainly see the revelation of the Creator of the wine.

🔑 **Glory** (*doxa* δόξα NT: 1391) It's appropriate to first mention the Old Testament use of the word "glory" (*kabod* כָּבוֹד OT: 3519) which refers to the outer garment, weight, or covering of splendor and light. God's iridescent light and the profound weight of His presence is His glory. God's glory is resident in Jesus (John 1:14) and once we trust Him, His glory is transforming us (2 Corinthians 3:18).

Doxa refers to the supernatural power of God that deserves one's respect and honor. *Doxa* is the excellence and majesty of God that demands our praise. So when Jesus does a miracle, it's a sign pointing to the majesty, honor, and excellence of God that has been revealed so that persons might give Him praise. Glory brings to light God's presence and power which dispel all darkness—sin, sickness, and bondage. In the presence of His glory, all that is not of His glorious nature must flee (Psalm 104:31-35).

🔑 **Temple** (*hieron* ἱερόν NT: 2411) When Jesus refers to *hieron* in John 2, He not only speaks of Herod's temple, the physical location of the second temple and its surroundings, but Jesus also uses the word symbolically to refer to his body (John 2:19, 21). His broken temple or body would be sacrificed on the cross for our sins.

Hieron refers to that house in which God's presence or Spirit dwells. So later in the New Testament, a temple would be a person indwelt by God's Spirit (Acts 7:48, 17:24; 1 Corinthians 3:16-17, 6:19; Ephesians 2:21-22).

℘ Name (*onoma* ὄνομα NT: 3686) Name refers to a specific person and also includes that person's lineage. In Hebrew culture, a person's name linked him to all his forefathers, tribe or clan, and heritage. A name invoked the covenants and blessings of the past as well as spoke of the destiny to come.

In Jesus's name (read Matthew 1:1-16; Luke 3:23-38), every promise and covenant of God from the past made to Adam, Abraham, and David were realized. Every future promise of God would be fulfilled (2 Corinthians 1:20). Power, life, and authority were in His name (Mark 16:17; John 1:12; Acts 2:38; 3:16; 4:7-12; 10:43-48; Romans 1:5). His name gave

those called by His name the same authority and power to live in the miraculous.

℘ Scripture (*graphe* γραφή NT: 1124) *Graphe* refers to a particular verse or passage while the plural (*graphai*) refers to the whole of the Old Testament. The Scripture functions in two ways for Jesus's ministry. First, He fulfilled Old Testament prophecy in demonstration that He was the Messiah. Secondly, Jesus interpreted the Scriptures so that God's ways might be properly understood within the context of living life righteously, fully, and abundantly. He spoke of the Old Testament with authority (Mark 1:22) not with simply insight or discernment.

So, the disciples combined His Word (*logos*) with the authority by which He applied Old Testament scripture (*graphe*) and believed Him (John 2:22). We live and operate in the same manner. His words (John 6:63) to us grounded in the authority of the whole of God's Word (2 Timothy 3:16) become the powerful sword of the Spirit (Ephesians 6:17) which we wield in prayer to bring the Father's will in heaven to earth (Matthew 6:10) and live in the miraculous.

JOHN 2 SUMMARY

Chapter 2 begins with the first miracle of the ministry of Jesus. Before commenting on the method of this miracle, verse 11 gives us the purpose. Soon after His baptismal service in the river Jordan where Jesus received the power of the Holy Spirit, Jesus begins His ministry with a miracle. He did so to manifest His glory that His disciples might believe. It took the entire three and a half years of Jesus's ministry for Jesus to prove to His disciples that He was the Son of God.

If it was important for Jesus to produce miracles to authenticate His place in God, then it should be just as important for us, the body of Christ, to do the same. There are many nice people in the world who do not know Jesus as Lord. Being kind is good, but not enough to reveal to the world that Jesus lives. Jesus was not only loving and kind, but He also healed the sick, fed the multitudes, cast out devils, revealed His dominion over the elements of the world. In addition to all His other marvelous works, Jesus gave His life for all of humanity.

Is it any wonder that Jesus waited until He received the power of the Holy Spirit to begin His ministry? John the Baptist said in John 3 that unless a man receives something from God, he has nothing godly to give. Jesus told the church to wait until they received the power of the Holy Spirit in the book of Acts. He obviously knows the necessity of this wonderful endowment of power. Jesus manifested His glory to His disciples to train them for what they could expect from this power when it was time for them to receive it. Remember that we can learn much about the working of miracles from watching the Master at work.

Being kind is good, but not enough to reveal to the world that Jesus lives.

Knowing that the miracle at the wedding feast of Cana was the first miracle in the ministry of Jesus, it is interesting to note that Jesus seemed extremely natural about the supernatural. God uses the supernatural very naturally.

We miss many opportunities for God to move because we're looking for something spectacular instead of paying attention to many natural promptings of the Holy Spirit. For Jesus not to hesitate, act fearful, or question His ability in this first miracle shows us that He was already prepared through His time of meditation in the Word that He studied. Jesus didn't wait until confronted with this miracle to begin a process of considerations that it would be possible. He already found Himself in the Scriptures years before and had contemplated the great destiny that God would fulfill through Him.

> *We ought to note that our preparation is not to get us to a place of authority that we don't already occupy.*

We ought to note that our preparation is not to get us to a place of authority that we don't already occupy; it's simply becoming aware of what God has qualified us to do so that we will dare to do it.

Jesus's love for people, seeing them as God's temples, was His motivation for stepping beyond His comfort level. He never missed an opportunity to show the heart of His Father. In fact, there was a great zeal for God's best that consumed Jesus. To be consumed like the Master is to accept every opportunity given to put God on display.

MEDITATIONS FOR SUCCESS

- Prepare for success; know who you are.
- You are anointed because God said so. The purpose of the glory is for the manifestations that will honor God and bring the world to a saving knowledge of Christ.
- Using the anointing is acting on truth, even when it appears not to be. If the water has to turn into wine at the last second, it can be no other way.
- You are God's prize. You are the temple of God. Turn God loose in your life by believing Him to work the miraculous through you. God has sanctified you to be a pure and clean vessel—an instrument for His glory and miracle-working power.
- Whether it's a scripture or a word from God, you can go your way rejoicing, for the battles are won. The moment you receive His Word, the victory is yours.

CHAPTER 3

¹There was a man of the Pharisees named Nicodemus, a ruler of the Jews. ²This man came to Jesus by night and said to Him, "Rabbi, we know that You are a teacher come from God; for no one can do these signs that You do unless God is with him."

³Jesus answered and said to him, "Most assuredly, I say to you, unless one is born again, he cannot see the kingdom of God."

⁴Nicodemus said to Him, "How can a man be born when he is old? Can he enter a second time into his mother's womb and be born?"

⁵Jesus answered, "Most assuredly, I say to you, unless one is born of water and the Spirit, he cannot enter the kingdom of God. ⁶That

---

3:1-2 A ruler of the Jews and a prominent man, Nicodemus was curious enough to approach Jesus because of the signs and wonders He produced. He didn't understand who Jesus was, yet there was no mistaking that God was with Him. Every person must also individually approach Jesus. Your relationship with God is personal, intimate, and transparent. Nothing can be hidden from Him.

3:3 Jesus spoke to Nicodemus's heart by saying a man cannot be supernaturally empowered in this life unless he is reborn from above. Fallen man cannot just be forgiven. Every person needs a complete spiritual (*pneuma*) transformation. Being born again is the central issue of salvation. A man must accept God's way of salvation through Jesus Christ in order to experience the kingdom of God. The establishment of the kingdom of God both corporately and individually is the central issue in Jesus's teaching. Jesus declares here that this is not just a messianic and an eschatological issue, it's also an issue of the individual's heart.

3:4-5 Nicodemus lacks the spiritual comprehension to effectively see his need for transformation. He understands the kingdom of God as simply an earthly kingdom.

3:6 The flesh births flesh, and the Spirit births spirit. There is no natural kingdom through the efforts of flesh which will supercede the importance of the spirit of man being born again. The kingdom of God represents the authority, love, and blessings of God. Without spiritual access, man continues to live under the limitations of the flesh.

For the Jewish mind, the concept that everyone can receive of the Holy Spirit is new. In the Old Testament, only certain individuals had an encounter with the Holy Spirit. For example, the Holy Spirit came upon certain persons like Samson and David, but did not permanently indwell people. Here, Jesus is revealing the plan of God the Father. Everyone "born of the Spirit" will experience within the wonder-working power (*dunamis*) of God.

which is born of the flesh is flesh, and that which is born of the Spirit is spirit. [7]Do not marvel that I said to you, 'You must be born again.' [8]The wind blows where it wishes, and you hear the sound of it, but cannot tell where it comes from and where it goes. So is everyone who is born of the Spirit."

[9]Nicodemus answered and said to Him, "How can these things be?"

[10]Jesus answered and said to him, "Are you the teacher of Israel, and do not know these things? [11]Most assuredly, I say to you, We speak what We know and testify what We have seen, and you do not receive Our witness. [12]If I have told you earthly things and you do not believe, how will you believe if I tell you heavenly things? [13]No one has ascended to heaven but He who came down from heaven, *that is,* the Son of

---

Everyone "born of the Spirit" will experience within the wonder-working power (dunamis) of God.

3:7 We must be fathered from above. This second birth is the divine exchange necessary to reidentify man with God. Jesus partook of man's sin so that we can partake of God's nature and love.

3:8 This experience is something that the spirit of man in being reborn can discern. The flesh gains the benefits of the real inner man coming in contact with God. However, the flesh has nothing to do with contacting God. It is the born-again spirit of man that connects with the Spirit of God. We might not be able to see the wind, yet we can surely see the effect of the wind. The Spirit of God is invisible, yet powerful to visibly transform a person into a child of God and to empower him as the wind empowers a sailing vessel to move forward.

3:9-10 Jesus is shocked to find Nicodemus so spiritually ignorant. Jesus

thoroughly expected Nicodemus to know these truths. When we study the Word of God just for information, we miss the power to transform. Paul said this then becomes a religion that denies the power (2 Timothy 3:5).

3:11 Jesus reveals the authority behind all that He says and does. The Spirit of seeing and knowing was in great operation in Jesus's life. This supernatural insight into the Scriptures and the mind of God is available to all who believe. The Holy Spirit will illuminate the Word of God to our conscience and through fellowship reveal the heart of the Father for each day. Staying supernaturally connected to the will and mind of God is a believer's empowerment for great boldness.

3:12 Paul commented in 2 Corinthians 4:18 that we must look at or be conscious of things that are not seen, instead of being mindful of the seen world. Here Jesus separates the two worlds in which we live. Our physical being (body or flesh) contacts the earthly realm, and our spirit contacts

Man who is in heaven. ¹⁴And as Moses lifted up the serpent in the wilderness, even so must the Son of Man be lifted up, ¹⁵that whoever believes in Him should not perish but have eternal life. ¹⁶For God so loved the world that He gave His only begotten Son, that whoever believes in Him should not perish but have everlasting life. ¹⁷For God did not send His Son into the world to condemn the world, but that the world through Him might be saved.

¹⁸"He who believes in Him is not condemned; but he who does not believe is condemned already, because he has not believed in the name of the only begotten Son of God. ¹⁹And this is the condemnation, that the light has come into the world, and men loved darkness rather than light, because their deeds were evil. ²⁰For everyone practicing evil hates the light and does not come to the

---

the spirit realm. Only dwelling in the earthly or physical realm means that all our solutions to problems must also be earthly or visible. Jesus embodied reality in the physical world ("the Word became flesh"). We are continually astounded by Jesus's uncanny astuteness to the spiritual realm. Naturally and effortlessly, Jesus confronted every possible problem with the answers from heaven. Without fail, He always prevailed supernaturally.

3:13 This is the essence of Jesus's success. He descended from heaven to dwell on earth while still being connected to heaven. Very simply this means that while Jesus walked on the earth, He lived out of heaven. Jesus drew His strength, insight, information, and power from heaven— from God Himself. We too can know this powerful lifestyle.

3:14-15 As the children of Israel were wandering through the wilderness, their continual complaining brought devastation upon them (Numbers 21). God's protection was released as snakes commenced to kill thousands of Israelites. God's provi-

sion for safety was to erect a pole with a serpent on it so that all who gazed upon it would be healed and live. This snake represented the curse that Jesus would become for all mankind. As Jesus hung upon the cross, He took unto Himself the full weight of the curse upon mankind.

Salvation, physical healing, and all forms of deliverance are available to those who look to and call upon the name of the Lord. Even as the Israelites were instructed to give undivided attention to the curse which He overcame, so must we give our undivided attention to God if we are to experience the liberty that Jesus provided through the cross.

Salvation, physical healing, and all forms of deliverance are available to those who look to and call upon the name of the Lord.

3:16 God's sacrificial love was so great that He offered up the best that He had, His Son. God demonstrates that real love will provide complete answers whether or

light, lest his deeds should be exposed. ²¹But he who does the truth comes to the light, that his deeds may be clearly seen, that they have been done in God."

²²After these things Jesus and His disciples came into the land of Judea, and there He remained with them and baptized. ²³Now John also was baptizing in Aenon near Salim, because there was much water there. And they came and were baptized. ²⁴For John had not yet been thrown into prison.

²⁵Then there arose a dispute between *some* of John's disciples and the Jews about purification. ²⁶And they came to John and said to him, "Rabbi, He who was with you beyond the Jordan, to whom you have testified—behold, He is baptizing, and all are coming to Him!"

²⁷John answered and said, "A man can receive nothing unless it

---

not it is deserved. The merit of the provision is rooted in the heart of the provider.

When God sent Jesus, He was the only begotten Son. In the epistles (Ephesians 1; Colossians 1), Paul received the revelation that the great plan of God was to reproduce in man the privilege of sonship. There, Jesus is referred to as the firstborn Son. We are Jesus's brothers and sisters. God's love is more than the emotional feeling that comes with great passion. It is a calculated plan to restore to man the dominion he had lost, by providing a substitute to purchase our legal right of possessing the kingdom of God.

To believe in Jesus is more than mental assent. Knowing that Jesus is the way, the truth, and the life is only the first step to acceptance. Next, there must be a surrendering to this truth by an open confession and declaration of Jesus as Lord (Acts 2:38). The moment someone accepts Jesus as God's true provision to their needs and submits to His lordship, they are born again. The most amazing transformation happens at this moment. Eternal

life replaces the nature of sin and reassigns that soul into the kingdom of God. Eternal life is simply the quality and degree of life (*zoe*) that God Himself enjoys.

3:17-18 God's eternal purpose is exemplified through Jesus, to bring eternal *life* and replace all condemnation. Condemnation is something that all men face because of their status as eternally lost. God's life restores man's hope, power, position, and heart.

3:19-21 The condition of the world is indeed grievous. Normality is living in sin and a consciousness of condemnation without recognizing its consequences. God's normality is living in the miraculous. The moment His light comes to our existence, it exposes the deceptions of Satan and reveals our true need of Him. If those practicing evil consistently produce results of sin, then how much more should we, the children of God, become extremely effective at manifesting God's goodness! When we discern correctly between earthly and heavenly things, we then have God's ability to establish truth. Whenever

has been given to him from heaven. ²⁸You yourselves bear me witness, that I said, 'I am not the Christ,' but, 'I have been sent before Him.' ²⁹He who has the bride is the bridegroom; but the friend of the bridegroom, who stands and hears him, rejoices greatly because of the bridegroom's voice. Therefore this joy of mine is fulfilled. ³⁰He must increase, but I *must* decrease. ³¹He who comes from above is above all; he who is of the earth is earthly and speaks of the earth. He who comes from heaven is

---

we act on things that are real in God, we always have God's manifested change in the earth. The important question to ask at this point is, "what is real?" Is it those things merely physically visible or God's promise of things unseen?

3:27 John made a wonderful observation: receiving from God is always in proportion to what it is that God has given. "Receive" and "given" are the two operative words in this text. God loves us so much that He gave us the answer to all of life's problems. Once received, His answer then becomes our possession. What is in our possession then becomes usable based on His spiritual authority at work in us.

3:31-33 Heavenly things have and always will have the supremacy over earthly things. John indicates that those who are earthly are conditioned to speak and respond with earthly means. Verse 32 declares that Jesus hears and sees things from above. This is so because He is from above. Our first insight from this passage is that Jesus accessed heavenly information as a man. He learned through prayer and the Word to cultivate a relationship that would supply Him with important information for each day. Next we understand the relationship between "being from above" and "having access to things

from above." Each believer has access to God. When we are born again, we are born from above. This entitles us to all that heaven has. Our willingness to exercise our faith with diligence for God's promised advantages will determine our level of success. The testimony that one has who knows God and regularly makes withdrawals on His provisions, prosperity, and privileges is always manifested in the visible. The world will have to admit that God is the source.

Our willingness to exercise our faith with diligence for God's promised advantages will determine our level of success.

3:34 We know that One who is from above has the privilege to hear and see things from above. Jesus's mission from God entitled Him to speak certain words and perform certain acts. Jesus is heaven's representative. The Spirit "without measure" is simply the ability of God to abundantly and infinitely perform the responsibilities given. Jesus said to His disciples that "as the Father has sent Me, I also send you" (John 20:21). Those who are saved also have the same ability as Jesus to perform their responsibilities. In the end, the Father is magnified by much fruit.

above all. ³²And what He has seen and heard, that He testifies; and no one receives His testimony. ³³He who has received His testimony has certified that God is true. ³⁴For He whom God has sent speaks the words of God, for God does not give the Spirit by measure. ³⁵The Father loves the Son, and has given all things into His hand. ³⁶He who believes in the Son has everlasting life; and he who does not believe the Son shall not see life, but the wrath of God abides on him."

JOHN 3 KEY WORDS

Sign (*semeion* σημεῖον NT: 4592) *Semeion* points or directs the person to God. Hence, a sign is a pointer, guide, or signpost to the glory of God being manifest in time and space. A sign is an event that has special and significant meaning or revelation. Jesus uses signs to authenticate His authority as the Son of Man to reveal the power as well as the loving heart of the Father. A sign is more about the one doing it than the one receiving it.

Born again (*gennethe* γεννηθῇ NT: 1080 *anothen* ἄνωθεν NT: 509) Being "born again" is to experience a complete change so that one moves from mere existence into true life in Christ which is birthed of the Spirit (*pneuma*) and lasts forever.

Jesus answers the ongoing question of "why?" in human existence, "Is there life after birth?" One's physical birth occurs when one is begotten (*gennethe*) from flesh. But true life in Christ who is the Life can only happen by being birthed by the heavenly Father through His Spirit.

Being "born again" also means being "born from above." A natural father births a natural child; but the heavenly Father deposits His Spirit into a person who believes in Jesus (Romans 10:9) so that being "born again" refers to being indwelt by the Holy Spirit. God's only Son was conceived by the Spirit. So too, we can be birthed by the Spirit by becoming His children (John 1:12-13) and empowered to do even greater works than Jesus did (John 14:12).

ℱ **Kingdom of God** (*basileia* βασιλεία NT: 932 *tou theou* τοῦ θεοῦ NT: 2316) The kingdom of God is the realm in which He rules supremely and absolutely. One of Jesus's primary preaching themes in the Gospels is the kingdom of God or the kingdom of Heaven. The citizens of His kingdom are "born again" and trust Jesus as Lord and Savior. The Law of His kingdom is God's will, and the power and authority of His kingdom are given to those who follow Jesus as His disciples.

ℱ **Flesh** (*sarx* σάρξ NT: 4561) The flesh refers in Jesus's teaching as the physical body. Later in the New Testament, the apostle Paul will refer to flesh as the realm of sin in the soul that wars against the Spirit and needs to be sanctified (Galatians 5). For Jesus, the flesh represents the physical or natural world of our senses. This visible, physical world is real but there is a greater reality—the realm of the Spirit which is invisible.

ℱ **Water** (*hudatos* ὕδατος NT: 5204) In this passage, water refers to the rite of passage as one obediently enters the kingdom of God by faith. The faithful believer submits to the water of

baptism giving witness outwardly of what God's Spirit has done inwardly. Read Matthew 28:19; Acts 2:38; Romans 6; 1 Peter 3:21; 1 John 5:5-10.

ℱ **Spirit** (**wind**) (*pneuma* πνεῦμα NT: 4151) The Hebrew word (*ruach*) for Spirit as well as the Greek word *pneuma* means "breath, wind." The wind or breath of God is His Spirit. Jesus uses a play on words interchangeably using wind and Spirit in this passage. Through God's Spirit, just as the wind is invisible, we can witness its effects. The effect of the Spirit entering our beings is to create within us new life as we are "born of the Spirit."

ℱ **Believe** (*pisteuo* πιστεύω NT: 4100) To believe or have faith, *pisteuo* involves more than mental assent which acknowledges truth but does not act upon it. True faith completely trusts Jesus. Trust surrenders self-reliance and has total faith in His ability to work and do in and through us as He desires. Trusting Jesus is active faith that lays ultimate claim to eternal life through Him.

ℱ **Love** (*agapao* ἀγαπάω NT: 25) God's unconditional love in giving His Son, Jesus, could not be merited or earned. Rather, God's nature is love (1 John 4:7-8). God initiated a loving relationship for us to enter into by faith or trust in Jesus. His love neither judges nor condemns. *Apape* accepts the believer as he is and begins to transform the believer into who Christ is.

🗝 **World** (*kosmos* κόσμος NT: 2889) Though "world" can refer to the total universe, in this context Jesus is speaking of God loving the earth and, in particular, those inhabiting the earth. God's love is so expansive that He offers salvation by faith through His Son to all—Jews and Gentiles, male and female, slave and free. The notion that God's saving love was available to everyone may have surprised Nicodemus, a Jew who would have believed that the Jews were God's chosen people for salvation.

🗝 **Only Begotten** (*monogenes* μονογενής NT: 3439) This critical term means "unique" or "one of a kind." God's only Son gave His life for all humanity. Jesus is not birthed or created. Rather, He is "of the nature" of God. As such, whatever He says and does, God speaks and effects. Jesus came as the unique and only expression of God's love who could die for our sins and save us. No other sacrifice for our sins was possible as the perfect expression of God's love for the world.

🗝 **Condemn (Judge)** (*krino* κρίνω NT: 2919) *Krino* speaks of a judgment by God that would finally and ultimately condemn a soul to damnation or hell. While we deserved such a judgment, Jesus came as God's representation to take our sin upon Himself.

🗝 **Save** (*sozo* σώζω NT: 4982) To save is to deliver or rescue from harm, disaster, or evil. In saving us, Jesus rescued us from the wages of sin which resulted in death and eternal judgment. He also saved us for eternal life, health, and freedom from every curse. Salvation isn't just *from* all that is evil but *for* all that is good.

🗝 **Evil** (*poneros* πονηρός NT: 4190) Evil doesn't just refer to that which is bad or ungodly. It specifically connotes "that which is sick or diseased." In saving us from evil, Jesus not only removed the curse of sin from us but also put the mantle of health and wholeness on us, clothing us with His anointing for healing power.

𝄞 **Made Manifest** (*phaneroo* φανερόω NT: 5319) To manifest is to bring into the light, to appear and become visible. Evil loves darkness. But truth brings light into darkness. The light of truth reveals whatever is not of God.

𝄞 **Give** (*didomi* δίδωμι NT: 1325) God's giving is an act of grace prompted not by what we deserve but rather by His giving nature. God's gift provides us with the opportunity to receive or grasp something that is eternal.

𝄞 **Receive** (*lambano* λαμβάνω NT: 2983) To receive is not to passively get something. Rather, receiving is "grasping, taking hold of" something with assertiveness. When one receives from God, that person has literally grabbed that which God offers and refuses to relinquish it.

JOHN 3 SUMMARY

For God so loved the world. What exactly does this mean? For many, love is an emotion. Thank God He wasn't just emotional when He sent Jesus. What if His emotions were to change, like most people driven by how they feel?

For many, love is a convenience. However, sending your only begotten Son to die is not convenient. Some actually try to move love over into the action realm through lip service. Yet this would mean that God never really sent Jesus into the world, He just talked about it.

God's love was the supreme action and sacrifice based on His benevolent heart that was and is disposed to showing favor or grace. God created us for the highest kind of fellowship possible between the Creator and His creation. God's heart, always disposed to do good, could not pass up the opportunity to redeem mankind, even if it cost Him His only begotten Son.

God just loved us too much to leave us the way we were—sinners hopelessly without redemption.

From God's exalted position, salvation is the only thing that makes sense. It's the best way for God to restore humanity back to its rightful place of supremacy on the earth and humanity's rightful duty to serve and honor the Creator. God just loved us too much to leave us the way we were—sinners hopelessly without redemption.

As a man, Jesus shows us how important it is to become a master of spiritual things. His development of spiritual discernment in seeing and hearing the Father's heart is the reason why He did what no other had done before.

When Jesus encountered a ruler of the synagogue who questioned Him concerning spiritual things, Jesus revealed to him the love plan of the Father. The summation of why Jesus did the things He did was to lead humanity into the experience of being born again. The supreme need in the heart of sinful man is to be born from above. As plain as it sounds to us, Jesus had to simplify it for this man to understand. That which is born of the flesh is flesh, yet that which is born of the Spirit is spirit.

Man didn't need to be forgiven, that would leave him a forgiven sinner. Man needed to be created anew on the inside where sin abounded. This could only come from an experience in the Spirit. Jesus was well versed in these areas.

Man didn't need to be forgiven, that would leave him a forgiven sinner. Man needed to be created anew on the inside where sin abounded.

Nicodemus tried to understand what Jesus was explaining from his experience and through his natural mind. He simply spoke of religion—the knowledge of what is visible. Religious people have knowledge, yet no supernatural power to back up what is preached. Jesus revealed that in order to experience the spiritual world, one had to access it through the Spirit, not natural experience. This then becomes the reason why God the Father would send Jesus. Where sinful man failed to find access to God based on human effort, God, by sending Jesus, would pave the way for us all. Jesus then became the substitute for sinful man, the perfect sacrifice.

Thus His light would expose the evil intentions of man, making opportunity for the surrender of the heart. Only those who would accept the path that Jesus would provide would have acceptance with the Father.

John the Baptist would herald this message as loudly as he could as a forerunner to the ministry of Jesus: "Behold the Lamb of God, which takes away the sin of the world." John understood the difference between earthly man and God's heavenly Man. Jesus was blessed with what was necessary to accomplish His mission.

All of us should realize that God would not send anyone into the world on assignment without fully equipping them for complete success. Jesus was no exception. The Father filled Jesus with the Spirit of power to fulfill all that His heart intended. God does the same for us. What makes God's heart of love so special? We can see in the gospel of John that the Father was backing Jesus up each step of the way.

> *The Father filled Jesus with the Spirit of power to fulfill all that His heart intended. God does the same for us.*

You too can have the satisfaction of having God with you every step of the way. Make Jesus the Lord of your life, and get ready for God to back you up with His abundance.

MEDITATIONS FOR SUCCESS

- Spirit births spirit. Since you were created as a spiritual being, you can access God through faith in Christ.

- "Born again" means being fathered from above. You have been birthed by the Spirit of God. To be supernatural is now normal.

- Heaven is now your new home. Thinking heavenly with a renewed mind is how you find your answers for life.

- Jesus came to give you life—something beyond mere existence. It's a full and abundant life that never ends. Begin to consider that you have everything you need to live in the power and Spirit of God. What He speaks and does supernaturally through your spirit, you can manifest in the natural for all those around you to witness. They will see God living in and through you!

CHAPTER 4

¹Therefore, when the Lord knew that the Pharisees had heard that Jesus made and baptized more disciples than John ²(though Jesus Himself did not baptize, but His disciples), ³He left Judea and departed again to Galilee. ⁴But He needed to go through Samaria.

⁵So He came to a city of Samaria which is called Sychar, near the plot of ground that Jacob gave to his son Joseph. ⁶Now Jacob's well was there. Jesus there-fore, being wearied from *His* journey, sat thus by the well. It was about the sixth hour.

⁷A woman of Samaria came to draw water. Jesus said to her, "Give Me a drink." ⁸For His disciples had gone away into the city to buy food.

⁹Then the woman of Samaria said to Him, "How is it that You, being a Jew, ask a drink from me, a Samaritan woman?" For Jews have no dealings with Samaritans.

¹⁰Jesus answered and said to her,

4:1-7 To avoid conflict with the Pharisees, Jesus traveled through Samaria on His way to Galilee. Here at Jacob's well, He met a woman of Samaria. Such a meeting nor-mally would never have taken place between a Jewish man and a Samaritan woman. The Samaritans were a mixed race of people. When Samaria was taken captive by the Assyrians many foreigners were brought in to settle the land. These foreigners intermarried with the Jews of that region. This is why the Samaritans were thought to have betrayed their people. Therefore, they were hated and despised. Just the fact that Jesus would go through Samaria proves that He had a love and desire to meet the needs of the world, not just the Jewish nation.

4:7-8 As you can see from the journey that Jesus was on, He was tired and thirsty. Though we often endeavor to make everything in the Word spiritual, I believe that Jesus's request for water was purely natural. I don't see in these statements any preconceived notions that Jesus had to win this woman's heart for God. It is important for us to see that Jesus took advantage spiritually of a natural situation.

4:9 Even though the Jews had no deal-ings with the Samaritans and would have frowned on a rabbi speaking directly to a Gentile woman, Jesus was not bound by prejudice, race, or gender. The gospel is for everyone.

4:10 This verse presents four important revelations Jesus had: (1) Jesus knew that He was God's gift to the world—a gift to be experienced by those to whom it is given. (2) Jesus knew who He was. So much wasted time is spent dealing with insecurity. To know whose you are and who you are to the world will release you

"If you knew the gift of God, and who it is who says to you, 'Give Me a drink,' you would have asked Him, and He would have given you living water." [11]The woman said to Him, "Sir, You have nothing to draw with, and the well is deep. Where then do You get that living water? [12]Are You greater than our father Jacob, who gave us the well, and drank from it himself, as well as his sons and his livestock?" [13]Jesus answered and said to her, "Whoever drinks of this water will thirst again, [14]but whoever drinks of the water that I shall give him will never thirst. But the water that I shall give him will become in him a fountain of water springing up into everlasting life." [15]The woman said to Him, "Sir, give me this water, that I may not thirst, nor come here to draw." [16]Jesus said to her, "Go, call your husband, and come here." [17]The woman answered and said, "I have no husband." Jesus said to her, "You have well

---

to be effective for the Lord. (3) Jesus knew that He possessed eternal living water. Eternal life is the solution for every problem in the world. Jesus came with the intention of using eternal life to solve life's problems and then distribute His life (*zoe*) to all who would accept Him. (4) Jesus knew that He could give this life away. What you possess and are conscious of will always be the thing that you effectively use. Jesus knew that this life would solve this woman's problems.

Realizing who you are in Christ, what you possess, and your authority to give life away will make you a champion in any situation.

These four simple revelations can change the way we live and benefit the lives of others we come in contact with. Realizing who you are in Christ, what you

possess, and your authority to give life away will make you a champion in any situation.

4:7-11 Jesus paralleled this woman's natural responsibility for drawing water to a water that freely flows and will never dry up. At this point the woman was curious yet unaware of the spiritual significance of the One who was before her. Very naturally, Jesus had prepared this woman for the power of God.

4:16-19 Prompted by the Holy Spirit, Jesus received a word of knowledge which transformed the entire conversation with the woman. Jesus revealed her past and present circumstances as evidence to His spiritual authority and to confront this woman's need to repent. It is very interesting to see her spiritual journey unfold. From a purely natural need for water to quench one's thirst to a special revealing of this woman's heart condition, the objective was met. The more confident we

said, 'I have no husband,' ¹⁸for you have had five husbands, and the one whom you now have is not your husband; in that you spoke truly."

¹⁹The woman said to Him, "Sir, I perceive that You are a prophet. ²⁰Our fathers worshiped on this mountain, and you *Jews* say that in Jerusalem is the place where one ought to worship."

²¹Jesus said to her, "Woman, believe Me, the hour is coming when you will neither on this mountain, nor in Jerusalem, worship the Father. ²²You worship what you do not know; we know what we worship, for salvation is of the Jews. ²³But the hour is coming, and now is, when the true worshipers will worship the Father in spirit and truth; for the Father is seeking such to worship Him. ²⁴God *is* Spirit, and those who worship Him must worship in spirit and truth."

²⁵The woman said to Him, "I know that Messiah is coming" (who is called Christ). "When He comes, He will tell us all things."

²⁶Jesus said to her, "I who speak to you am *He.*"

²⁷And at this *point* His disciples came, and they marveled that He talked with a woman; yet no one said, "What do You seek?" or, "Why are You talking with her?"

²⁸The woman then left her waterpot, went her way into the city, and said to the men, ²⁹"Come, see a Man who told me all things that I ever did. Could this be the Christ?" ³⁰Then they went out of the city and came to Him.

³¹In the meantime His disciples urged Him, saying, "Rabbi, eat."

³²But He said to them, "I have food to eat of which you do not know."

³³Therefore the disciples said to one another, "Has anyone brought Him *anything* to eat?"

³⁴Jesus said to them, "My food is to do the will of Him who sent Me, and to finish His work. ³⁵Do

---

become of the answers from God that He has given to us the greater will be the inner working of the Holy Spirit for the final outcome which brings glory to God.

4:21-24 As this woman moved her thoughts away from the insight of Jesus, He reminded her that real worship is found not in a location but in the heart. Since God is a spirit, then we also must worship Him out of our spirit. Worship must be truthful—a personal intimacy with God.

4:32-34 Jesus used the need for natural food as an example to relate how spiritual hunger is satisfied by being consumed with and doing the will of God. As important as natural diet is to the physical body, so is a spiritual diet to the spirit.

4:35-38 God is always at work around

you not say, 'There are still four months and *then* comes the harvest'? Behold, I say to you, lift up your eyes and look at the fields, for they are already white for harvest! ³⁶And he who reaps receives wages, and gathers fruit for eternal life, that both he who sows and he who reaps may rejoice together. ³⁷For in this the saying is true: 'One sows and another reaps.' ³⁸I sent you to reap that for which you have not labored; others have labored, and you have entered into their labors."

³⁹And many of the Samaritans of that city believed in Him because of the word of the woman who testified, "He told me all that I *ever* did." ⁴⁰So when the Samaritans had come to Him, they urged Him to stay with them; and He stayed there two days. ⁴¹And many more believed because of His own word.

⁴²Then they said to the woman, "Now we believe, not because of what you said, for we ourselves have heard *Him* and we know that this is indeed the Christ, the Savior of the world."

⁴³Now after the two days He departed from there and went to Galilee. ⁴⁴For Jesus Himself testified that a prophet has no honor in his own country. ⁴⁵So when He

---

us. As laborers, we are continually employed as long as we bring in the harvest; the lost people who need Jesus. Many seeds have been planted into the lives of people all around us. There is such a need to harvest the lives that are ripe and sow seed into the lives that haven't heard. How conscious we are of the work of God will determine how effective we are in finishing our work of harvesting—evangelism. For this reason, the devil continues to divert our attention to worldly things, thereby halting our kingdom progress.

How conscious we are of the work of God will determine how effective we are in finishing our work of harvesting—evangelism.

4:39-42 We must climb out of our infatuation for information and begin to perform with regularity the works of Jesus in order to effectively reach the world. One miracle of any kind, whether a word from God for someone, as Jesus gave to this woman, or a physical healing will affect more people than just preaching alone. The testimony of this woman stirred a whole city. There is at least one miracle waiting on you, no matter where you go. Just as Jesus spoke and acted, you can be His vessel through whom God can pour saving and healing love on someone today.

4:43-45 Jesus realized that a prophet is without honor in his own country. However, as Jesus found out, He was at least tolerated because of the first miracle He performed at the wedding feast of Cana.

came to Galilee, the Galileans received Him, having seen all the things He did in Jerusalem at the feast; for they also had gone to the feast.

⁴⁶So Jesus came again to Cana of Galilee where He had made the water wine. And there was a certain nobleman whose son was sick at Capernaum. ⁴⁷When he heard that Jesus had come out of Judea into Galilee, he went to Him and implored Him to come down and heal his son, for he was at the point of death. ⁴⁸Then Jesus said to him, "Unless you *people* see signs and wonders, you will by no means believe."

⁴⁹The nobleman said to Him, "Sir, come down before my child dies!"

⁵⁰Jesus said to him, "Go your way; your son lives." So the man believed the word that Jesus spoke to him, and he went his way. ⁵¹And as he was now going

A receptive crowd is worth another miracle! **4:46-47** The nobleman came to Jesus and begged Him to come and heal his son because he had heard of the miracle that Jesus performed at the wedding feast of Cana. Living in the miraculous will give you a reputation that will attract those in need to come to you expecting miracles.

Living in the miraculous will give you a reputation that will attract those in need to come to you expecting miracles.

4:48 Jesus understood the human mind and heart better than anyone. He spoke in this verse to our unwillingness to fully believe without seeing the results. Actually the statement should read, "Unless you people see signs and wonders, you cannot and will not believe." God never has had a problem with heralding His message with the miraculous. If the necessary tools for Jesus to complete His work included signs and wonders, wouldn't the Father be an unfair employer to exclude these tools? God has and always will have plenty of ammunition available to complete any assignment given.

4:49-50 Out of desperation, this royal official addressed Jesus as an authority by pleading with Him to heal his son. We must submit ourselves to the authority of God and His Word. Childlike faith (Mark 10:15) simply trusts what is said. Jesus's response was the answer for this man's son, yet it was different from the request. How many would have missed their miracle because they were looking for it by their interpretation? The nobleman didn't flinch in a negative manner at the command of Jesus. Having submitted himself to Jesus, he simply believed and departed for home.

4:51-54 Time and space cannot hinder the God who inhabits all eternity. We learn a great lesson here. The words of Jesus penetrated the sick son of this nobleman some twenty miles away. The man's faith was the catalyst through which this miracle

down, his servants met him and told *him,* saying, "Your son lives!" ⁵²Then he inquired of them the hour when he got better. And they said to him, "Yesterday at the seventh hour the fever left him." ⁵³So the father knew that *it was* at the same hour in which Jesus said to him, "Your son lives." And he himself believed, and his whole household.

⁵⁴This again *is* the second sign Jesus did when He had come out of Judea into Galilee.

---

worked. The teaching of the Word of God is our foundation to Christian living. However, Jesus didn't teach a lesson here, He simply released a command of faith which, when obeyed, produced its desired intention. Notice in verse 53 that the whole household ended up believing. Whole households are waiting today for one miracle. Will you live in the miraculous for their sake?

JOHN 4 KEY WORDS

𝄢 **Baptize** (*baptizo* βαπτίζω NT: 907) To baptize means to immerse in water. The Jews would baptize new converts (proselytes) as an act of ritual cleansing. John baptized people in the Jordan who were repenting of their sins (Matthew 3). Baptism in the early church for followers of Jesus represented both repentance and entry into new life through His death and resurrection (Romans 6). Jesus submitted Himself to baptism as an act of obedience and commanded His disciples to baptize converts.

𝄢 **Gift** (*dorea* δωρεά NT: 1431 and 1434) God is the Father of good gifts (James 1:17). His gifts are not only the visible provisions of grace like food, shelter, and clothing to meet our needs but also invisible gifts like eternal life which Jesus speaks of here in John 4. God's gifts are given freely without being earned or necessary. His supernatural gifts include the Holy Spirit (Acts 2:38; 10:45; 11:17; Hebrews 6:4), grace (Romans 5:15; 2 Corinthians 9:14-15; Ephesians 3:7), eternal life (John 4:9-11), righteousness

(Romans 5:17), and His Son, Jesus the Christ (Ephesians 4:7).

Living Water (*hudor zoe* ὕδωρ ζῶν NT: 5204 and NT: 2198) This is the water of eternal life, true life found only in Christ. Remember the early notes in John 1 and John 3 about life versus existence. Jesus, the true Life *(zoe)* gives living water that satisfies every thirst known to humanity. The water of life flows freely in the heavenly new Jerusalem (Revelation 22:17).

Truth (*aletheia* ἀλήθεια NT: 225) That which really is and really happens in time and eternity is true. The Old Testament word for truth ('*amet*) literally speaks of absolute consistency between the inner and outward man. Truth refers to complete integrity, openness, and transparency.

Spirit (*pneuma* πνεῦμα NT: 4151) The Hebrew word (*ruach*) for Spirit as well as the Greek word *pneuma* means "breath, wind." The wind or breath of God is His Spirit. The human spirit (self) is crucified with Christ (Galatians 2:20) so that the Holy Spirit can indwell our temples (1 Corinthians 3; 6). We are being sanctified in body, soul, and spirit (1 Thessalonians 5:23). Our worship of the Lord is "of the Spirit" as we yield to His Spirit giving praise to Him through us.

Prophet (*prophetes* προφήτης NT: 4396) A prophet is an inspired mouthpiece of God's word spoken to others. The Old Testament prophets heard from God and infallibly spoke that word. A prophet speaks with the authority of having heard directly from God. People often fail to understand, respect, or honor God's prophet because they know the person only in the flesh and not according to the Spirit.

Worship (*proskuneo* προσκυνέω NT: 4352) Worship means to prostrate oneself before God in reverence, awe, and the fear of the Lord. Worship is not just a position of the body but an attitude of a heart filled with love and humility. Worship also implies a singularity of purpose and attention without distraction or ulterior motive.

Christ (Greek form of the Hebrew word "Messiah") (*christos* Χριστός NT: 5547) Literally meaning "one who is anointed." In the Old Testament, priests, kings, and prophets were anointed with oil (symbolizing the Holy Spirit). To be anointed is to be empowered by the Spirit. Jesus came as God's Anointed One to fulfill the mission of saving the world through His death and resurrection.

𝛾ʳ **Work** (*ergon* ἔργον NT: 2041) James emphasizes that "faith without works is dead" (James 2). Jesus came to do the work of the Father. He has no desire or will of His own. Jesus is completely submitted in word and deed to the Father. The primary focus of the Father's work is to reach the lost—sowing and reaping in the harvest of God's kingdom.

𝛾ʳ **Testify** (*martureo* μαρ-τυρέω NT: 3140) To testify is to bear witness and give truthful evidence concerning that of which the witness has firsthand knowledge. The Samaritan woman had personal knowledge and a life-changing encounter with Jesus. Hence, she became an eyewitness to truth. Jesus commands us in Acts 1 to testify as witnesses to

His marvelous salvation and grace so that others will come to salvation through hearing our testimony of the gospel.

𝛾ʳ **Honor** (*time* τιμή NT: 5092) Honor refers to the weight, merit, or worth attributed to someone. Honor also refers to giving praise where praise is deserved. A prophet is honored not because of his merits but because of the One he represents and speaks for. The Israelites over the centuries had persecuted the messenger because they didn't like the message from God. In spite of signs and wonders, Jesus increasingly experienced persecution and rejection from the religious leaders because they rejected both Him and His message from God.

𝛾ʳ **Wonders** (*teras* τέρας NT:5059) This word is often used in conjunction with signs (*seimeon*) to refer to the miracles wrought at the hand of God through God's chosen instruments. A wonder is an unusual sign often in altering nature in an unusual or startling way.

JOHN 4 SUMMARY

Whether preaching to the multitude or reclining by a well out of exhaustion, Jesus remained the answer to life's problems. Put to rest the fantasy that man is anointed to preach, yet he gets to choose how he wants to live the rest of his life. We are always sons of God, whether in work or in play. Certainly the anointing will come on you to preach or witness; however, the anointing is always on you to live as Christ.

> *We are always sons of God, whether in work or in play.*

Jesus shows us how to be what we are even when we may feel extremely natural. We don't need to put on some spiritual air to convince the world that we are spiritual. Just simply being yourself will do, if being yourself means that you access God when needs arise.

Jesus in a very natural way began to meet the needs of the woman from Samaria. He offered no justification or rationale for who He was. Likewise, as His disciples, there is no sense apologizing for who we are. We don't need to answer the world with hyperspiritual responses. On the other hand, if we have the answer, we have an obligation to tell people about it.

Watching the Holy Spirit work with Jesus in this passage, reveals how active He becomes when we approach the need of people out of love with a pure heart.

Is it possible that talking about eternal life will stir up the giftings of the Holy Spirit? Jesus didn't seem to wait on the Holy Spirit to move. Yet, when He initiated His faith in the power of eternal life, the Holy Spirit certainly worked with Jesus to reach this woman and her need.

> *When you have eternal life, you are positioned to give the spiritual answers that will remedy the world's problems.*

When you have eternal life, you are positioned to give the spiritual answers that will remedy the world's problems. Becoming confident with eternal life will come as you continue to remember who you are in Him. You can't see yourself like Jesus for too long until the image of

Christ becomes your vision. Almost unexpectedly, you will hear yourself telling someone that you have something that will meet their need. You may even shock yourself. Half the secret to eternal life is receiving it; the other half is releasing and revealing it to others.

> **Half the secret to eternal life is receiving it; the other half is releasing and revealing it to others.**

The demeanor of Jesus throughout the gospel of John is so authoritative. If we wonder why, maybe it has to do with what He continually immersed Himself in. Jesus said that He had food to eat that we know not of. He was describing the intake of spiritual sustenance.

A regular diet of the Word of God and prayer will consciously endear your heart and soul to the anointing of God. This seems to be the reason why Jesus could send the anointing to the nobleman's son with just a word. When you stay on the side of heaven's truths, you access them with power. This really brings Mark 11:23 to light: "Whosoever says to this mountain, 'Be removed and be cast into the sea,' and does not doubt in his heart, but believes that those things he says will be done, he will have whatever he says." What have you been saying lately?

> **When you stay on the side of heaven's truths, you access them with power.**

MEDITATIONS FOR SUCCESS

- You are supernatural whether you feel like it or not.
- The anointing is potentially available at all times.
- Since you possess eternal life, put it to work by revealing it to others.
- The Holy Spirit will work with you, if you will work with the Holy Spirit.
- Believe in the power of God's words. Believe in the authority and power behind your words.

CHAPTER 5

¹After this there was a feast of the Jews, and Jesus went up to Jerusalem. ²Now there is in Jerusalem by the Sheep *Gate* a pool, which is called in Hebrew, Bethesda, having five porches. ³In these lay a great multitude of sick people, blind, lame, paralyzed, waiting for the moving of the water. ⁴For an angel went down at a certain time into the pool and stirred up the water; then whoever stepped in first, after the stirring of the water, was made well of whatever disease he had. ⁵Now a certain man was there who had an infirmity thirty-eight years. ⁶When Jesus saw him lying there, and knew that he already had been *in that condition* a long time, He said to him, "Do you want to be made well?" ⁷The sick man

---

5:1-4 When Jesus entered into Jerusalem during the feast time, a sizable crowd of sick people had gathered at the pool of Bethesda. A great multitude could be interpreted as hundreds or even thousands. They were all seeking their healing through a spectacular experience where an angel from God would stir the water at the pool. When this happened, the power of God was available for the first one in. On our behalf, Jesus stirred the waters of healing once and for all through His shed blood (Isaiah 53). Thank God for His covenant of continual health.

> *On our behalf, Jesus stirred the waters of healing once and for all through His shed blood.*

5:5-6 The knowledge that Jesus had concerning this man came from God. I'm sure that anyone looking at this crowd could tell that they were sick and that some of them had been in that condition for a long time. Here the actual duration of sickness was mentioned. If we will keep in mind that Jesus performed and functioned on the earth as a man, then we will understand how important it is that Jesus had knowledge from God. Also, know that Jesus didn't make it a regular occurrence to seek out someone for His help. Usually, Jesus would preach His gospel message and men would come in faith to Him. There was no message preached here, this was a definite leading of the Holy Spirit.

5:7-8 When God gives you knowledge about someone, you only need to act on what you know. This is a different situation than when the person needing ministry is already expectant and believing. This man's total focus is on the water. Jesus is standing right there willing to heal, and the man still refers to the source of his healing as different from Jesus—the true source. The body of Christ is largely focusing the

answered Him, "Sir, I have no man to put me into the pool when the water is stirred up; but while I am coming, another steps down before me." ⁸Jesus said to him, "Rise, take up your bed and walk." ⁹And immediately the man was made well, took up his bed, and walked. And that day was the Sabbath. ¹⁰The Jews therefore said to him who was cured, "It is the Sabbath; it is not lawful for you to carry your bed."

¹¹He answered them, "He who made me well said to me, 'Take up your bed and walk.' "

¹²Then they asked him, "Who is the Man who said to you, 'Take up your bed and walk'?" ¹³But the one who was healed did not know who it was, for Jesus had withdrawn, a multitude being in *that* place. ¹⁴Afterward Jesus found him in the temple, and said to him, "See, you have been made well. Sin no more, lest a worse thing come upon you."

¹⁵The man departed and told the Jews that it was Jesus who had made him well.

¹⁶For this reason the Jews persecuted Jesus, and sought to kill Him, because He had done these

---

way this man did. They are hanging around the church waiting for a spectacular stirring of the waters before they would even conceive of believing God. Even if the waters were stirred, they would need someone else to help them step in. This must change!

5:9 The man was immediately made well when Jesus gave him the command to rise and walk. Because the man had no knowledge of Jesus, you couldn't say that he exercised faith in Jesus. This healing account is better explained as a gift of healing as the Spirit of God moved on Jesus. God has reserved the right on the earth to move as the Spirit of God so desires. As we saw in chapter 4, a gift of the Spirit was in operation for Jesus to know about the Samaritan woman's past and present situation. These gifts of the Holy Spirit ought to be in great demon-

stration in the church. How often we put ourselves in the position given in Jesus's command to be a witness to the world will have a great influence on the regular manifestations of these gifts.

5:10-15 The Pharisees were much more concerned with the work of healing being done on the Sabbath than giving God praise for the healing. The law was given through Moses that the Jews should rest on the Sabbath. The Pharisees were professional at adding their interpretation to the law.

5:14 Jesus met the man who was healed and revealed to him the source of his healing. He also instructed the man how to keep his healing by releasing him from the sin that hindered this man's faith.

5:16-17 Whenever you begin yielding to the Great Commission by setting men free, those who are insecure and controlling will try to undermine the work of God.

things on the Sabbath.

¹⁷But Jesus answered them, "My Father has been working until now, and I have been working."

¹⁸Therefore the Jews sought all the more to kill Him, because He not only broke the Sabbath, but also said that God was His Father, making Himself equal with God.

¹⁹Then Jesus answered and said to them, "Most assuredly, I say to you, the Son can do nothing of Himself, but what He sees the Father do; for whatever He does, the Son also does in like manner. ²⁰For the Father loves the Son, and shows Him all things that He Himself does; and He will show

---

Jesus responded by saying that the Father is always working, therefore He is always working. If the highest authority is always working for the good of mankind, then we ought to take every opportunity to work with God.

Great comfort should arise in knowing that God the Father is always working. The apostle Paul mentioned that God is always effectually at work within us, creating and empowering us with desire and ability to work with Him. If the Father is always working, then the only reason why we wouldn't see the same results as Jesus would be if we were not working with Him. When Jesus expressed the revelation that the Father is always working, it was in the context of the gift of healing that raised this man up. If the Father is always working, and gifts are a necessary part of His work, then we should expect them to operate through us as often as necessary if we will only get busy ourselves.

If the Father is always working, then the only reason why we wouldn't see the same results as Jesus would be if we were not working with Him.

5:18 The Jews unknowingly released a very interesting revelation in this verse. When Jesus said that God was His Father, He was saying that He was equal with God. The Jews said that He made Himself equal with God. This is not true. Jesus didn't make Himself equal with God; God did. God made the human flesh called Jesus who was from Nazareth equal with Himself by pouring Himself into that flesh. God has poured His Spirit into our flesh at the new birth and legally became our Father. The fact that God is our Father qualifies us for this revelation as well. His indwelling Spirit empowers us to represent Him by living miraculously on the earth. We are to live life with the mind of Christ (Philippians 2:5-7).

5:19 When your mind considers the depth of your position with God, you will also, as Jesus, have insight into the ways of God. Jesus relates to us the complete submission of His heart to obey everything that He sees His Father do. If we would do the same, then the same miracles would happen. You must think like Jesus in order to conceptualize the possibility.

5:20 If the love of the Father toward the Son is the ingredient for the Son having the

Him greater works than these, that you may marvel. ²¹For as the Father raises the dead and gives life to *them,* even so the Son gives life to whom He will.

²²For the Father judges no one, but has committed all judgment to the Son, ²³that all should honor the Son just as they honor the Father. He who does not honor the Son does not honor the Father who sent Him.

²⁴"Most assuredly, I say to you, he who hears My word and believes in Him who sent Me has everlasting life, and shall not come into judgment, but has passed from death into life. ²⁵Most assuredly, I say to you, the hour is coming, and now is, when

revelation of the Father then we too are included in like manner. Jesus said in John 17:23 that the Father loves us as He loves Jesus. I thank God that He continually reveals and shows us all things, and even greater things than we have experienced thus far, He will show us. If this is true, then how will you act?

5:21 The authority behind being the source of all power is the ability to use it. Jesus, God's Son, is a man anointed by the Holy Spirit who can use God's miraculous power as He wills. When you are sure that you possess a thing, you have control to give it to whom you will. The child's game called "monkey in the middle" is all about who has the ball and who doesn't. If we are to imitate Jesus, then we must of necessity have not only the ability of God, but the authority to give it away. Jesus told the disciples in Matthew 10:8 to raise the dead with the power they received. This kind of power is all one would need to handle any health problem.

Raising the dead would be all the power you need to handle any physical health problem.

5:22-23 If Jesus didn't come into the world to condemn the world, then whom would Jesus judge? John said in his epistles to the church that Jesus came with purpose to destroy the works of the devil. Jesus exposed the devil's lies and judged them with the power of God, even if they were manifest through the lives of people. Concerning people, Jesus came to seek and save that which was lost.

5:24 Immediately see how important it is to hear what is being spoken. As parents, we teach children to hear correctly and respond. When God speaks, we must hear correctly and respond. Faith is our response. One of the most significant thoughts in the Bible is that our believing is the same as having our answer. For he that believes has at that moment what he believes. In that instant, the greatest transformation occurs, we pass from death into life. When you step out of the region of death into God's glorious power of eternal life, just like stepping into a pool of water, you are wonderfully changed, both in this lifetime and in the one to come.

5:25 Just as those who hear the voice of the Son of God will live, even so, those

the dead will hear the voice of the Son of God; and those who hear will live. 26For as the Father has life in Himself, so He has granted the Son to have life in Himself, 27and has given Him authority to execute judgment also, because He is the Son of Man. 28Do not marvel at this; for the hour is coming in which all who are in the graves will hear His voice 29and come forth—those who have done good, to the resurrection of life, and those who have done evil, to the resurrection of condemnation. 30I can of Myself do nothing. As I hear, I judge; and My judgment is righteous, because I do not seek My own will but the will of the Father who sent Me.

31"If I bear witness of Myself, My witness is not true. 32There is another who bears witness of Me, and I know that the witness which He witnesses of Me is true. 33You have sent to John, and he has borne witness to the truth. 34Yet I do not receive testimony from man, but I say these things

---

who hear His voice through you will live. The world needs to hear your voice.

5:26-27 The life that is in the Father is the inherent life that exists only in God. It originates in the Father and is distributed by Him also. The Father not only gave this life to the Son, but authorized Him to exercise His will over this life. As verse 27 indicates, the Son of God mentioned in verse 26 is the Son of Man. As a man, just like the first Adam, Jesus was granted the possession and right to govern the life and nature of God on the earth. This privilege was the authority to execute judgment. As stated earlier, Jesus didn't come to judge people, but the devil. John records in 1 John 3:8 that Jesus came with the express purpose of destroying the works of the devil. God's life and light are the cure and power to destroy the works of the devil. What the Father passed on to Jesus, He passed on to us.

If understood correctly, these verses eliminate all fear and empower the believer to stand toe to toe with the works of the devil and prevail. Life in Jesus conquered death; we now have become recipients of God's life. With this life come position and status and accessibility in the realm of the spirit. We are God's representatives of all that is good, just as Jesus.

5:28-30 Jesus displayed great control in that though He had such glory and power He used it only in accordance with His Father's will.

5:31-38 Jesus understood the importance of a witness for verification. John the Baptist witnessed concerning Jesus, yet Jesus said that the witness of man is not what He seeks. The witness of His Father and the miracles He was sent to perform are the greater witness. It's interesting that Jesus told the disciples that when the Holy Spirit would come upon them, they

that you may be saved. ³⁵He was the burning and shining lamp, and you were willing for a time to rejoice in his light.

³⁶But I have a greater witness than John's; for the works which the Father has given Me to finish—the very works that I do—bear witness of Me, that the Father has sent Me. ³⁷And the Father Himself, who sent Me, has testified of Me. You have neither heard His voice at any time, nor seen His form. ³⁸But you do not have His word abiding in you, because whom He sent, Him you do not believe. ³⁹You search the Scriptures, for in them you think you have eternal life; and these are they which testify of Me. ⁴⁰But you are

not willing to come to Me that you may have life.

⁴¹ "I do not receive honor from men. ⁴²But I know you, that you do not have the love of God in you. ⁴³I have come in My Father's name, and you do not receive Me; if another comes in his own name, him you will receive. ⁴⁴How can you believe, who receive honor from one another, and do not seek the honor that *comes* from the only God? ⁴⁵Do not think that I shall accuse you to the Father; there is *one* who accuses you—Moses, in whom you trust. ⁴⁶For if you believed Moses, you would believe Me; for he wrote about Me. ⁴⁷But if you do not believe his writings, how will you believe My words?"

---

would become witnesses of Him.
5:37 Jesus was committed to pleasing the Father. Jesus not only had the Father's approval, He also spent time in actual communion with Him. There is no reason why we, also, cannot see and hear the

Father just like Jesus.
5:39-44 The approval or disapproval of men meant nothing to Jesus. The approval of the Father was the priority of our Lord. We would do good to have such fear of God that the opinions of man meant nothing.

JOHN 5 KEY WORDS

Infirmity (*astheneia* ἀσθένεια NT: 769) Disability, weakness, or disease. Jesus takes upon Himself

our infirmities (Matthew 8:17). The source of healing resides in Him not in the wonder or the sign sought for by a person in need. So instead of saying, "I need healing" or "I need a miracle," one infirmed might more appropriately declare, "I need Jesus" in whom resides the power through the Holy Spirit.

☞ **Whole** (*hugies* ὑγιής NT: 5199) To be made whole, complete, sound, or well. The root word for the English is *hygiene*. *Whole* means being restored back to the original state which God intended.

☞ **Made Well** or **Cured** (verse 9) (*therapeuo* θεραπεύω NT: 2323) The root for the English, *therapy*. To be healed or cured or to recover health. In this instance, Jesus cures whatever the root to the man's infirmity is. The cause of the infirmity is removed by the root when God cures.

☞ **Healed** (verse 13) (*iaomai* ἰάομαι NT: 2390) This word for healing means to cause someone to become well again after being sick. Those who made contact with Jesus experienced healing (*iaomai*) (Mark 6:56; Luke 6:18-19). In Luke 6:17, the crowds came to hear Jesus and be healed.

☞ **Sin** (*hamartano* ἁμαρτάνω NT: 264) To sin literally means to miss the mark. In that sense, one is separated from God. That separation causes one to err, fail, transgress His law and not hear His voice. Separation from Him also brings disease, sickness, and death. The wages of sin is death. Jesus's sacrifice bridges the gap and spans the separation between us and the Father. Being connected by faith to the Father through the Son empowers us in the Spirit to walk in wellness, salvation, and health.

☞ **Work** (*ergazomai* ἐργάζομαι NT: 2038) With the Father, Jesus worked to accomplish His will. Likewise, we labor with, work with, and minister with the Father to accomplish His work on earth according to His will. In this work we expend great effort and engage in committed activity. In other words, the believer is actively at work with God expending significant effort, for as James 2:26 tells us, "faith without works is dead."

Some want living in the miraculous, walking in health, and ministering to others to be effortless. Actually, great commitment is required as we become willing vessels for His power and anointing to flow in and through us. Every relationship requires commitment and dedication including our relationship with the Father. It is granted by grace; after receiving it, walking by faith in relationship with God requires our ultimate trust in the finished work of Jesus.

JOHN 5 SUMMARY

The gospel presents Jesus's ministry of healing in two ways. First, Jesus healed individually and second, He healed the masses. We learn much from the individual cases of healing. There are nineteen individual cases of healing singled out by the gospel writers. This case presents a side of ministry concerning healing that relied on the work of the Holy Spirit to accomplish the result. As we can see, because the man didn't know who Jesus was, there couldn't have been faith on his part. Jesus was led by the Holy Spirit to meet with this man and set him free.

Usually those who were sick would come to Jesus for help. As you minister to the sick, it will be to your advantage if the sick person is calling you for help. This way they are interested in what you have to say and the way you feel led to minister. James addresses this very point by saying that those who are beyond help for themselves should call for the elders of the church for prayer. For Jesus to go to this man without the man's permission meant that the Holy Spirit revealed information to Jesus about this man and provided a work of healing for the result.

When Jesus told this man to take up his bed and walk on the Sabbath, things became interesting. Even though the man was healed, the Pharisees became indignant because this man was doing work on the Sabbath. When they questioned Jesus about what He had done, His reply to them was an insult. Jesus said that His Father was working, indicating that the Father always sought to meet the needs of people. He also said that He was working with the Father.

Oh, that we might understand the heart of the Father to work His miraculous wonders in the lives of people.

If we would only work as Jesus did, then there would be tremendous results. Jesus continued to show us how important it is to have the mind of God for everything we do. God is endeavoring to reveal His heart and will in every confrontation we encounter. Jesus said that the Father wants to take the limits off our immediate expectations and lift us into greater expectations. Jesus mentions eternal life being given to those who believe, thus including the believer in the same work that He Himself accomplished.

Eternal life is the most dominating force the world will ever know. This is the nature and being of God, imparted into the spirit of man. This makes man a ruler over the forces of darkness; he becomes an authority in the earth. Man is not independent of God, but completely one with Him so that everything done is in cooperation with God. As Jesus reveals, then the very works that are accomplished give witness to our union with God.

According to Jesus, all the study in the world is irrelevant if it doesn't lead you to a relationship with God that in the end produces results for the Kingdom of God.

MEDITATIONS FOR SUCCESS

• When you are led to minister to someone, do so with the confidence that God has provided you with the tools that will complete the assignment.
• The Father is always working. Partnering with God will always produce results.
• Believe big! God desires you to be unlimited in thought and deed.
• Eternal life is the divine nature of God Himself. You receive His quality of existence the moment you receive Christ.
• Since you possess the life of God, then you can release it at your will for the benefit of God's will being accomplished.
• You have a witness in the Holy Spirit—an agent to produce evidence to the world that Jesus is alive.

CHAPTER 6

¹After these things Jesus went over the Sea of Galilee, which is *the Sea* of Tiberias. ²Then a great multitude followed Him, because they saw His signs which He performed on those who were diseased. ³And Jesus went up on the mountain, and there He sat with His disciples. ⁴Now the Passover, a feast of the Jews, was near. ⁵Then Jesus lifted up *His* eyes, and seeing a great multitude coming toward Him, He said to Philip, "Where shall we buy bread, that these may eat?" ⁶But this He said to test him, for He Himself knew what He would do.

⁷Philip answered Him, "Two hundred denarii worth of bread is not sufficient for them, that every one of them may have a little."

6:1-2 If the ministry of Jesus had not produced results, there would have been no crowds. The fact that so many people followed Him speaks for itself. It should be easy to follow a ministry today for the same reasons—the needs of people are met. In verse 2, the words "followed" and "saw" are in continuous action. The verse could be interpreted that the multitude followed and followed Jesus because they saw and saw and saw the miracles which He performed. The ministry of Jesus is the standard for the church. Anything else is unacceptable.

6:2 The Gospels represent the life of Jesus. They record the three-and-a-half years of ministry Jesus was engaged in before going to the cross. However, if you compressed the Gospels together, you would only have anywhere from twenty to twenty-two days of actual recorded ministry. In that period of time, Jesus produced so many miracles that John said later that the books of the world could not contain the volumes of miracles, signs, and wonders that He did. Unless we see where the standard is, we will never reach for it.

6:3-6 As Jesus beheld the people on the hillside, He saw in His heart what must be done to meet the needs of the people. Spending time in the presence of the Father will provide you with answers to all of life's needs. Either Jesus was given a fresh word from His Father concerning this situation or He simply knew that since this had been done before through the ministry of Elisha, it was available to be reproduced. Actually a combination of these two thoughts more than likely was how Jesus knew what to do. Knowing that God had provided miraculously in the past certainly gave Jesus expectancy for God's power to work in the present. God's past faithfulness is a great catalyst for the miraculous in the *now*.

6:7-9 As a teacher, Jesus continually worked with His disciples to open their consciousness to the possibilities of the

⁸One of His disciples, Andrew, Simon Peter's brother, said to Him, ⁹"There is a lad here who has five barley loaves and two small fish, but what are they among so many?"

¹⁰Then Jesus said, "Make the people sit down." Now there was much grass in the place. So the men sat down, in number about five thousand. ¹¹And Jesus took the loaves, and when He had given thanks He distributed *them* to the disciples, and the disciples to those sitting down; and like-wise of the fish, as much as they wanted. ¹²So when they were filled, He said to His disciples, "Gather up the fragments that remain, so that nothing is lost." ¹³Therefore they gathered *them* up, and filled twelve baskets with the fragments of the five barley loaves which were left over by those who had eaten. ¹⁴Then those men, when they had seen the sign that Jesus did, said, "This is truly the Prophet who is to come into the world."

¹⁵Therefore when Jesus perceived

---

power of God. Here we see that they remained conscious of the natural and their visible ability to feed the crowd. At least the little boy's lunch given sacrificially, would provide Jesus with a vehicle through which a miracle could take place. God only needs our commitment and effort to accomplish much.

6:10-14 When Jesus worked the miraculous, He would always give direction to the place that the anointing was to work. That is how His faith was exercised. For instance, when God instructed Moses to split the Red Sea in Exodus 14, He told Moses to tell the people to go toward the sea first. Faith always sees the end result before it takes a step. The loaves and fish become the vehicle through which Jesus will bring increase. It is a must situation; He has already committed Himself by having the people sit down.

6:11 Notice that God gave the people as much as they wanted. God is only limited by what you can contain. We must enlarge our capacity to receive and release the abundance which God has provided. In the same way it was necessary for Jesus to recognize the supply of increase that waited on the action of faith; even so, we must recognize the supply of anointing that awaits our command of faith.

We must enlarge our capacity to receive and release the abundance which God has provided.

6:14 "This truly is the Prophet who is to come into the world." This word of the Lord was spoken by Moses. Jesus was being recognized as the Messiah. How wonderful it would be if the signs and wonders that we produced caused the world to understand that we are disciples of the Christ.

6:15 The crowd wanting to immediately make Jesus a king on the earth was the

that they were about to come and take Him by force to make Him king, He departed again to the mountain by Himself alone. [16]Now when evening came, His disciples went down to the sea, [17]got into the boat, and went over the sea toward Capernaum. And it was already dark, and Jesus had not come to them. [18]Then the sea arose because a great wind was blowing. [19]So when they had rowed about three or four miles, they saw Jesus walking on the sea and drawing near the boat; and they were afraid. [20]But He said to them, "It is I; do not be afraid." [21]Then they willingly received Him into the boat, and immediately the boat was at the land where they were going.

[22]On the following day, when the people who were standing on the other side of the sea saw that there was no other boat there, except that one which His disciples had entered, and that Jesus had not entered the boat with His

---

reason why Jesus retreated. Notice that He went to the mountains alone. The gospel of John continues to remind us that the miraculous ministry would not exist or be sustained without the intimacy that Jesus maintained with His Father.

6:16-19 These verses record the third miracle that Jesus did concerning water. The first was turning the water into wine; the second was commanding the winds and the sea to become still and now the third. Every step that Jesus took was a manifestation of God's Spirit supporting the action of our Lord. Because this was not the standard procedure for crossing the Sea of Galilee, Jesus must have received word from His Father to do so. Remember, He was in solitary prayer before this miracle. Our time with the Father should also empower us with tremendous ideas where the Spirit of the Lord will make opportunity for the miraculous.

6:20 Jesus never allows fear to rule Himself or others. The ability to face life's biggest trials without fear shows the dominion in the soul of the Lord. This demeanor is the Spirit of faith which is sensed by all in His presence.

6:21 Every miracle that applies to your life will come as you willingly receive Jesus into your boat. The boat, the place where you dwell or the place of buoyancy, connects you to either the opportunities of a lifetime or the situations of despair. Those places are where you willingly receive Jesus. This simply means that you give up the right to control your life. Place your life in the hands of the Lord and immediately receive the reward of your faith. Don't fight the illusion that you are in the middle of the sea battling the waves. Whether it seems like it or not, rejoice that once the Lord was received into your heart, you were placed immediately at shore. You can now rejoice in the answer, instead of yielding to the temptation to wander aimlessly in what seems like your greatest problem.

disciples, but His disciples had gone away alone— [23]however, other boats came from Tiberias, near the place where they ate bread after the Lord had given thanks— [24]when the people therefore saw that Jesus was not there, nor His disciples, they also got into boats and came to Capernaum, seeking Jesus. [25]And when they found Him on the other side of the sea, they said to Him, "Rabbi, when did You come here?"

[26]Jesus answered them and said, "Most assuredly, I say to you, you seek Me, not because you saw the signs, but because you ate of the loaves and were filled. [27]Do not labor for the food which perishes, but for the food which endures to everlasting life, which the Son of Man will give you, because God

the Father has set His seal on Him."

[28]Then they said to Him, "What shall we do, that we may work the works of God?"

[29]Jesus answered and said to them, "This is the work of God, that you believe in Him whom He sent."

[30]Therefore they said to Him, "What sign will You perform then, that we may see it and believe You? What work will You do? [31]Our fathers ate the manna in the desert; as it is written, *'He gave them bread from heaven to eat.'"*

[32]Then Jesus said to them, "Most assuredly, I say to you, Moses did not give you the bread from heaven, but My Father gives you the true bread from heaven. [33]For the bread of God is He who

---

6:26-27 The battle is forever raging; man must fight to keep his thoughts on the Lord and not be absorbed in the natural. We are instructed to seek first the kingdom of God and His righteousness, and then all the things of life will be added unto us. The Lord reminds the people that the effort that is given unto spiritual things will end in the blessing of eternal life.

6:28-29 Great revival will come to those who effectively answer the question given by this crowd. Working the works of God is done with skill and knowledge through the power of the Holy Spirit. Yet Jesus

narrows down the answer to simple trust that we exercise in Him as God's Son.

6:30-37 As signs and wonders are produced, people will be required to make decisions for the Lord. Some will follow just to see another sign, yet their hearts will remain far from God. When Jesus revealed that He was the true bread come down from heaven, He was revealing that He was the Messiah. However, many saw Him without believing. Jesus knew that an impact in the realm of the natural was necessary to convince people that the spiritual power behind it all was from God.

comes down from heaven and gives life to the world."

³⁴Then they said to Him, "Lord, give us this bread always."

³⁵And Jesus said to them, "I am the bread of life. He who comes to Me shall never hunger, and he who believes in Me shall never thirst. ³⁶But I said to you that you have seen Me and yet do not believe. ³⁷All that the Father gives Me will come to Me, and the one who comes to Me I will by no means cast out. ³⁸For I have come down from heaven, not to do My own will, but the will of Him who sent Me. ³⁹This is the will of the Father who sent Me, that of all He has given Me I should lose nothing, but should raise it up at the last day. ⁴⁰And this is the will of Him who sent Me, that everyone who sees the Son and believes in Him may have everlasting life; and I will raise him up at the last day."

⁴¹The Jews then complained about Him, because He said, "I am the bread which came down from heaven." ⁴²And they said, "Is not this Jesus, the son of Joseph, whose father and mother we know? How is it then that He says, 'I have come down from heaven'?"

⁴³Jesus therefore answered and said to them, "Do not murmur among yourselves. ⁴⁴No one can come to Me unless the Father who sent Me draws him; and I will raise him up at the last day. ⁴⁵It is written in the prophets, '*And they shall all be taught by God.*' Therefore everyone who has heard and learned from the Father comes to Me. ⁴⁶Not that anyone has seen the Father, except He who is from God; He has seen the Father. ⁴⁷Most assuredly, I say to you, he who believes in Me has everlasting life. ⁴⁸I am the bread of life. ⁴⁹Your fathers ate the manna

---

6:38 We must follow the example of Jesus by laying down our opinions and sincerely following the heart of God. The reason why Jesus was so successful is that He followed wholeheartedly the will of His Father.

6:41-44 Jesus revealed the hardness of the hearts of the Jewish leaders who continued to question Him with regard to His relationship with the Father. It becomes very difficult to see spiritual truth when

confronted with natural familiarities. Jesus said it takes the work of the Holy Spirit to draw a man unto Himself in order to make correct assessments. Even the apostle Paul prayed that God would open our eyes to properly understand heavenly truth (Ephesians 3:14-21).

6:48 The Jewish people were very familiar with the prophet Moses and the supernatural bread that God sent to sustain them in the wilderness. When Jesus

in the wilderness, and are dead. [50]This is the bread which comes down from heaven, that one may eat of it and not die. [51]I am the living bread which came down from heaven. If anyone eats of this bread, he will live forever; and the bread that I shall give is My flesh, which I shall give for the life of the world."

[52]The Jews therefore quarreled among themselves, saying, "How can this Man give us *His* flesh to eat?"

[53]Then Jesus said to them, "Most assuredly, I say to you, unless you eat the flesh of the Son of Man and drink His blood, you have no life in you. [54]Whoever eats My flesh and drinks My blood has eternal life, and I will raise him up at the last day. [55]For My flesh is food indeed, and My blood is drink indeed. [56]He who eats My flesh and drinks My blood abides in Me, and I in him. [57]As the living Father sent Me, and I live because of the Father, so he who feeds on Me will live because of Me. [58]This is the bread which came down from heaven— not as your fathers ate the manna, and are dead. He who eats this bread will live forever."

[59]These things He said in the synagogue as He taught in Capernaum.

[60]Therefore many of His disciples, when they heard *this,* said, "This is a hard saying; who can understand it?"

[61]When Jesus knew in Himself

---

declared that He was the bread of life, He meant that He was the link to eternal life.

6:49-51 Instead of using the analogy that Jesus gave concerning the bread of life and trusting in Him as Messiah, the Jewish leaders continued to make Jesus a stumbling stone by consenting to natural knowledge. Moses was used by God to reveal that the Messiah was coming who would bring eternal freedom and liberty. What God did through Moses was very temporal. More bread was necessary each day. What God provides through Jesus is eternal.

6:52-59 The words that Jesus used almost sound cannibalistic. Of course you cannot consume the physical flesh and blood of Jesus and live forever. Yet the spiritual understanding of the Jews was not open for such an analogy to be presented. Accepting Jesus as Lord and believing in His substitutionary work at Calvary is the only way to partake of what His blood meant and His flesh provides. Thank God for the shed blood of our Lord that provides eternal life and provision through covenant. Also, we thank Him for His broken body, which brings a continual healing power to our mortal bodies. These thoughts are best described through communion.

6:60-62 It is very interesting that Jesus used the term "Son of Man" when talking

that His disciples complained about this, He said to them, "Does this offend you? ⁶²*What* then if you should see the Son of Man ascend where He was before? ⁶³It is the Spirit who gives life; the flesh profits nothing. The words that I speak to you are spirit, and *they* are life. ⁶⁴But there are some of you who do not believe." For Jesus knew from the beginning who they were who did not believe, and who would betray Him. ⁶⁵And He said, "Therefore I have said to you that no one can come to Me unless it has been granted to him by My Father."

⁶⁶From that *time* many of His disciples went back and walked with Him no more. ⁶⁷Then Jesus said to the twelve, "Do you also want to go away?" ⁶⁸But Simon Peter answered Him, "Lord, to whom shall we go? You have the words of eternal life. ⁶⁹Also we have come to believe and know that You are the Christ, the Son of the living God." ⁷⁰Jesus answered them, "Did I not choose you, the twelve, and one of you is a devil?" ⁷¹He spoke of Judas Iscariot, *the son* of Simon, for it was he who would betray Him, being one of the twelve.

---

about ascending to where He was before. The Son of Man wasn't in heaven before. Jesus completely fused and intertwined His deity and humanity. He became completely confident as the Son of Man to declare His potential as the Son of God.

6:63 Jesus's words were spirit and life. Jesus spoke everything that the Father revealed to Him. This then is the reason why such power was released when He spoke. You will always work with the power of God when you speak the words of God. Paul said that the message of the gospel is the power of God. Words of life! Never be timid again when declaring the words of God. His Word contains the power of spirit and life. Healings and deliverances will come by giving someone the Word of God.

6:68 Simon Peter also recognized that the words of Jesus were indeed the words of eternal life. To leave Him would be in violation to the life they sought.

JOHN 6 KEY WORDS

🗝 **Bread** (*artos* ἄρτος NT: 740) Jesus uses the image of natural bread to speak about the spiritual bread He provides to nurture our spiritual natures. During the feast of Passover and Unleavened Bread, Jesus draws an analogy between His own body or life and spiritual nurture. Jesus is the Living Bread whose words give life and whose sacrifice on the cross brings forgiveness of sin. Bread was the primary staple of physical existence in the Middle East. Likewise, Jesus's words and power give His followers the power to live forever.

King (*basileus* βασιλεύς NT: 935) The crowd wanted to make Jesus their earthly king. Jesus insisted throughout His ministry that His kingdom was heavenly or spiritual, not in the natural realm. Even though He continually acknowledged the natural authority of the rule of Rome, He insisted that humans should focus on God's rule in their hearts. God's kingdom and realm are found in the heart and in obedient relationship with Him.

Take by Force (*harpazo* ἁρπάζω NT: 726) To gain control of; to seize by force; to snatch or take away. In John 6, the crowd was physically trying to grab hold of Jesus and elevate Him to a position of kingship. They wanted to literally crown Him king. Jesus never sought mass popularity. His compassion, not need for power, compelled Him to feed the people.

Disciple (*mathetes* μαθητής NT: 3101) To follow or be a student of someone. This literally means to learn or be instructed. The disciples of Jesus were at His side for the purpose of learning. A disciple isn't simply one who passively learns by seeing and listening but also by doing what Jesus was doing.

Lord (*kurios* κύριος NT: 2962) One of the titles which John uses to describe Jesus is *kurios* which means "one who exercises supernatural authority over humanity." As Lord, whatever Jesus says or does has authority over the believer's life. As Lord, He not only has the power to command a miracle but also to effect it. So when the Lord speaks into your life about living in the miraculous, you have the authority and power to walk in miracles because He is the Lord of all!

The Son of Man (*o huios tou anthropou* ὁ υἱὸς τοῦ ἀνθρώπου) This title which is prominently used in Ezekiel, refers to God's human agent or representative much in the sense of an ambassador. In other words, Jesus is God's agent from heaven on earth to embody the full potential of being human. He is fully human and fully God. As the Son of Man, Jesus had God-given authority to do the Father's will on earth as it is in heaven.

JOHN 6 SUMMARY

God is the God of increase. El Shaddai means "the God of more than enough." Jehovah Jireh means "the God who sees and makes provision before the need." When Jesus was confronted with the need of a multitude who lacked food, He immediately looked to God as the God of provision. Jesus knew by spiritual insight what He would do before He did it.

When you know by the Spirit what to do, it doesn't take faith, it just takes action.

When you know by the Spirit what to do, it doesn't take faith, it just takes action. However, when you don't know what to do, it takes faith to step out and trust God to give you the answer when it's time to know. Applying your faith to the will of God is the reason why you will see the miraculous. Our natural tendency is to wait for God to do something that He actually requires of us.

Paul said in 2 Corinthians 4:18 that we must look not at things that are seen, but at things that are unseen; for the things that are seen are temporary, yet the things that are unseen are eternal. Philip, when asked by Jesus to feed the multitude, responded out of the natural by talking about the food, or substance, not being sufficient. Jesus wasn't looking to the natural, He contemplated the supernatural and its ability when faith is engaged.

Many times Jesus would use something natural as a vehicle through which the anointing would flow to create the miracle. God is very creative. He's the Creator! As Isaiah 55:8-9 says God's thoughts are higher than our thoughts, His ways beyond our ways. We greatly limit God's ability toward us by our lack of creativity and responsiveness to

Him. God operates outside of our boxes. He has a multitude of different ways to accomplish His purposes. Open yourself up to the mind of God; after all, you have the mind of Christ.

God's ability in and through us is limited by our response to Him.

Seeing the results of the Master should stir you up to desire to be used in the same way. The disciples asked the Lord, "What shall we do, that we may work the works of God?" Jesus responded, "Believe in Me." Don't underestimate the significance of this phrase. If you trust everything Jesus said and did, and He indwells you, you can do His works . . . even greater works (read John 14). Limitation no longer exists when God becomes the center of your equation. What you believe about this will determine how well you accept the Great Commission to evangelize the world.

All miracles should point man to the heart of God. Our desire in producing the miraculous is that all come to the saving knowledge of our God. If you are not discerning and wise in living in the miraculous, people will try to use you to receive what they will not believe for themselves. And they will be critical of you when you do not please them.

This certainly doesn't mean that we should back away from the truth and our need for the miraculous. It does mean that we continue to explain and teach people to respect and honor every thing that God has said and done for them. Always direct people to God, the source of the miraculous, and continue to strengthen them in their faith.

MEDITATIONS FOR SUCCESS

- The supply of God's Spirit will be present for the manifestation of His Word wherever and whenever we will act boldly in faith.

- Natural things in life can be used for the supernatural. Don't overlook your miracle.

- You are called to work the works of God. The works of God are awesome, if someone would dare to work them. Only believe!

- There is only one way to experience God's best. Live in His will.

- Jesus is the Bread of Life. When you receive Him, you will begin partaking of His goodness.

CHAPTER 7

¹After these things Jesus walked in Galilee; for He did not want to walk in Judea, because the Jews sought to kill Him. ²Now the Jews' Feast of Tabernacles was at hand. ³His brothers therefore said to Him, "Depart from here and go into Judea, that Your disciples also may see the works that You are doing. ⁴For no one does anything in secret while he himself seeks to be known openly. If You do these things, show Yourself to the world." ⁵For even His brothers did not believe in Him.

⁶Then Jesus said to them, "My time has not yet come, but your time is always ready. ⁷The world cannot hate you, but it hates Me because I testify of it that its works are evil. ⁸You go up to this feast. I am not yet going up to this feast, for My time has not yet fully come." ⁹When He had said these things to them, He remained in Galilee.

¹⁰But when His brothers had gone up, then He also went up to the feast, not openly, but as it were in secret. ¹¹Then the Jews sought Him at the feast, and said, "Where is He?" ¹²And there was much complaining among the people concerning Him. Some said, "He is good"; others said, "No, on the contrary, He deceives the people." ¹³However, no one spoke openly of Him for fear of the Jews.

¹⁴Now about the middle of the feast Jesus went up into the temple and taught. ¹⁵And the Jews marveled, saying, "How does this Man know letters, having never studied?"

¹⁶Jesus answered them and said,

7:1-9 We see that Jesus's brothers struggled with the thought that Jesus was anything special except their brother. Their words were sarcastic and their attitude was jealous. Jesus would not let the pressure even from family persuade Him to do something that was not in the timing of His Father.

7:10-15 Jesus went up to the feast in secret so He could avoid arguing with the religious leaders. He would be more effec-

tive by getting His message to the people, than to debate with those who sought to kill Him. We should be thankful for opportunities to share our faith with others without persecution. Many countries today are searching to persecute Christians for their faith.

7:16 It is so important for each of us to have our doctrine established in our hearts from God and not from man. Jesus received revelation from the Father and so

"My doctrine is not Mine, but His who sent Me. ¹⁷If anyone wills to do His will, he shall know concerning the doctrine, whether it is from God or *whether* I speak on My own *authority.* ¹⁸He who speaks from himself seeks his own glory; but He who seeks the glory of the One who sent Him is true, and no unrighteousness is in Him. ¹⁹Did not Moses give you the law, yet none of you keeps the law? Why do you seek to kill Me?"

²⁰The people answered and said, "You have a demon. Who is seeking to kill You?"

²¹Jesus answered and said to them, "I did one work, and you all marvel. ²²Moses therefore gave you circumcision (not that it is from Moses, but from the fathers), and you circumcise a man on the Sabbath. ²³If a man receives circumcision on the Sabbath, so that the law of Moses should not be broken, are you angry with Me because I made a man completely well on the Sabbath? ²⁴Do not judge according to appearance, but judge with righteous judgment."

²⁵Now some of them from Jerusalem said, "Is this not He whom they seek to kill? ²⁶But look! He speaks boldly, and they say nothing to Him. Do the rulers know indeed that this is

---

should we. Thank God for teachers, but the ultimate source of confirmation for what you hear and read is the Holy Spirit.

Legalism will rob you from the simple truths of scripture that work.

7:17-24 Jesus constantly fought with legalism in the people. This is a good lesson to learn: Legalism will rob you from the simple truths of Scripture that work. Behind every teaching is the spirit or attitude that the teaching represents. Make sure you not only hear what is being said, but also check for the attitude or spirit by which it is said. Something may sound good yet be said out of an attitude of fear. You will subconsciously pick up on that attitude and therefore fail to apply the teaching with success.

7:25-28 In the face of those who desired to kill Him, Jesus spoke with extreme boldness. Bold speaking comes from knowing by revelation that the words you speak are completely true. Why back down from anyone when you have the word of eternal life? Also, boldness comes by the presence of the Holy Spirit. The anointing upon someone as they speak will empower them to be very bold about what they say and do. We read in Acts 4:31 that the early disciples "were all filled with the Holy Spirit, and they spoke the word of God with boldness." Just as the

truly the Christ? [27]However, we know where this Man is from; but when the Christ comes, no one knows where He is from."

[28]Then Jesus cried out, as He taught in the temple, saying, "You both know Me, and you know where I am from; and I have not come of Myself, but He who sent Me is true, whom you do not know. [29]But I know Him, for I am from Him, and He sent Me."

[30]Therefore they sought to take Him; but no one laid a hand on Him, because His hour had not yet come. [31]And many of the people believed in Him, and said, "When the Christ comes, will He do more signs than these which this *Man* has done?"

[32]The Pharisees heard the crowd murmuring these things concerning Him, and the Pharisees and the chief priests sent officers to take Him. [33]Then Jesus said to them, "I shall be with you a little while longer, and *then* I go to Him who sent Me. [34]You will seek Me and not find *Me,* and where I am you cannot come."

[35]Then the Jews said among themselves, "Where does He intend to go that we shall not

---

disciples were filled with the Spirit and spoke boldly, in like manner that same boldness should indwell us.

7:28 Jesus knew what was in the hearts of these individuals as they spoke about Him. Many times when you are delivering the Word of God, God will allow you to understand what is in the mind of those who hear. Of course the reason would be to address their thoughts and bring correction through the Word of God.

"I am sent from above" gives you authority to do what God wants in your life.

7:29 Being conscious of where you are from and what the assignment is that brought you are vital to your success. Remember, we are in the world, but not of

it. We have been born from above. God does things differently in His realm than most do in this one. "I am from above," is the attitude of Jesus that empowers your position in Christ. "I am sent from above" gives you authority to do what God wants in your life. Forget these things and you will aimlessly wander as the powerless lost—in the futility of their own ability.

7:30 Jesus was aware of the timing of His work. He knew that He was not finished until the work was done. Therefore, He showed great resolve and determination to act boldly in the face of opposition knowing that no one would stop Him until He had fulfilled the will of God. Isn't it thrilling to know that the same power that saved us also keeps us?

7:32-36 Knowing that we shall soon see the Lord should inspire us to continue the work of the Lord. John said in his epistle

find Him? Does He intend to go to the Dispersion among the Greeks and teach the Greeks? ³⁶What is this thing that He said, 'You will seek Me and not find Me, and where I am you cannot come'?"

³⁷On the last day, that great *day* of the feast, Jesus stood and cried out, saying, "If anyone thirsts, let him come to Me and drink. ³⁸He who believes in Me, as the Scripture has said, out of his heart will flow rivers of living water." ³⁹But this He spoke concerning the Spirit, whom those believing in Him would receive; for the Holy Spirit was not yet *given,* because Jesus was not yet glorified.

⁴⁰Therefore many from the crowd, when they heard this saying, said, "Truly this is the Prophet." ⁴¹Others said, "This is the Christ."

But some said, "Will the Christ come out of Galilee? ⁴²Has not the Scripture said that the Christ comes from the seed of David and from the town of Bethlehem, where David was?" ⁴³So there was a division among the people because of Him. ⁴⁴Now some of them wanted to take Him, but no one laid hands on Him.

⁴⁵Then the officers came to the chief priests and Pharisees, who said to them, "Why have you not brought Him?"

⁴⁶The officers answered, "No man ever spoke like this Man!"

⁴⁷Then the Pharisees answered

---

that as we expect the day of the Lord is approaching, we should purify ourselves even as He is pure (1 John 3:3).

7:37-38 Jesus was not embarrassed to preach the truth. He cried or shouted with a loud voice. He obviously wanted as many people to hear Him as possible. The word concerning the Holy Spirit would be the single most important information given the church outside of their born-again experience. Jesus was so persistent that He told His disciples in Luke's gospel to wait for this experience. He said that they shouldn't go anywhere without it.

7:39 Not until Jesus was glorified would the world qualify to be empowered by the Holy Spirit. Redemption was necessary for the spirit of man to be born again so that the Holy Spirit would have access into their hearts. Once man received God's divine nature within, they would then become candidates for the infilling of the Holy Spirit. We see this experience through the eyes of the disciples in Acts 2:1-4.

7:46 You will find that the nonreligious pagans will recognize more quickly when someone is telling the truth than those who are religious. Religious people always have things figured out their way. If something differs at all from the way they see it, they struggle to see what is important because their petty innuendos have been upset.

them, "Are you also deceived? [48]Have any of the rulers or the Pharisees believed in Him? [49]But this crowd that does not know the law is accursed."

[50]Nicodemus (he who came to Jesus by night, being one of them) said to them, [51]"Does our law judge a man before it hears him and knows what he is doing?"

[52]They answered and said to him, "Are you also from Galilee? Search and look, for no prophet has arisen out of Galilee."

[53]And everyone went to his *own* house.

JOHN 7 KEY WORDS

𝒱 **Secret** and **Open** (*kruptos* κρυπτός NT: 2927 & *parrhesia* παρρησία NT: 3954 also **bold**) *Kruptos* means to be kept hidden or concealed. Jesus purposely hid the truth of who He was from all but His disciples and even they, at times, did not fully understand who He was. Jesus taught in parables so that the secrets of the kingdom would be understood only by those who truly sought Him with childlike faith. What Jesus hid, He also revealed to those who trusted Him.

Parrhesia means to make public or openly reveal with boldness and courage. When Jesus decided to reveal Himself as the Christ, His boldness and courage stunned and shocked the Jewish religious leaders to the point that they wanted to kill Him (read Matthew 26). In John 7:26, *parrhesia* is translated boldly since whatever is done openly with courage is boldness.

𝒱 **Time** (*kairos* καιρός NT: 2540) *Kairos* speaks of a specific and appointed time in which God invades or enters time with His eternal power and presence. *Chronos* speaks of the general passage of time. Jesus had a specific *kairos* time for the manifestation of His full power as Messiah. That *kairos* would be His resurrection —the ultimate sign that He was the Son of God. Until that *kairos*, both Jews and Gentiles would not fully understand His relationship to the Father.

𝒱 **Doctrine** (*didache* διδαχή NT: 1322) Doctrine means the content of what is taught. Jesus was not speaking of the doctrine of men but the sound doctrine or teaching that comes from God.

Jesus's teaching is rooted in the absolute truth that comes from above. Consider the source of doctrine. If it is from God, then learn from sound doctrine and apply it in making right decisions.

🔑 **Law** (*nomos* νόμος NT: 3551) The Law, or Torah, referred specifically to the books of Moses—Genesis, Exodus, Leviticus, Numbers, and Deuteronomy. The religious leaders had made the letter of the Law more important than the Spirit of God. Jesus came to fulfill the Law and to be an example of how to live righteously not legalistically.

🔑 **River** (*potamos* ποταμός NT: 4215) A river is a flowing, fresh stream or brook that runs continually not just seasonally. When Jesus likens the Spirit to rivers of living (*zoe*) water flowing out of one's heart, He is speaking of the life-giving Holy Spirit who flows without pause or interruption in our lives to empower us to walk and live fully in the miraculous. The implication here is that the flow will never stop or run dry. His Spirit is unlimited and limitless as the resource and power for all we say and do in the Father's will.

JOHN 7 SUMMARY

You've heard the phrase, "Timing is everything!" Jesus walked in divine timing. The Father orchestrated His will in Jesus's life with perfection. Jesus never allowed others to persuade Him to do things that were not of the Father. If we desire to imitate our Lord, then seeking His direction is always in our best interests.

Once Jesus rose from the dead, He made available all the benefits of life that would provide us access to God's highest and best.

We also could say that Jesus waited on His time so that we could live in the time frame of *now*. *Now* faith, *now* salvation, *now* healing, and *now* all the benefits of God are available to us.

Once Jesus rose from the dead, He made available all the benefits of life that would provide us access to God's highest and best. We are God's blue ribbon, His best, that we might show forth the praises of Him to the world. We must learn to walk as Jesus did—on the side of victory all the time. You could say that Jesus didn't need healing because He walked in health. Actually healing was working all the time so that He was never touched by sickness.

We are God's blue ribbon, His best, that we might show forth the praises of Him to the world.

Living in the realm of *now* will certainly challenge the way we so often relegate God's timetable to the future. Anything that He has already provided is available now. God lives in this realm, where there is no time, and all things exist in Him. "How wonderful for Him," we might think. Actually, how wonderful for you, if you are drawn into union with Him. The assets and benefits that we inherit from God are not only additions to what we don't have, they also are liberty from all the negative liabilities that used to limit us.

How is all this possible? Jesus said the Holy Spirit would come upon you, and out of your heart or innermost being would flow rivers of living water. Think of the implications. God the Holy Spirit from heaven saturates your spirit, soul, and body. His Spirit exponentially increases your life from just barely getting by to automatically superseding every known limitation this world has to offer. Instantly, in your Spirit, you are like Christ in nature, substance, and ability. Cooperating with Him means absolute success in all He wills.

This event that Jesus alluded to was to happen after His resurrection. Jesus instructed the disciples to wait for the promised endowment of power from heaven that would come upon them. This power would come by a baptism of the Holy Spirit and His anointing. Jesus waited for this to begin His ministry. In the river Jordan as John the Baptist baptized Jesus, the Holy Spirit like a dove came upon Jesus to remain for supernatural ministry.

If you will surrender yourself as a living sacrifice . . . this wonderful experience of power that came upon Jesus will come upon you too.

If you will surrender yourself as a living sacrifice (Romans

12:1-2), this wonderful experience of power that came upon Jesus will come upon you too. Developing your relationship with the Father will help you to understand the level of confidence in which Jesus walked. If the power has come upon you, then you will only increase its effectiveness by your time spent in the Father's presence.

The ways of the Holy Spirit are diverse and available to you now.

Remember what Jesus said concerning the baptism of the Holy Spirit, that there would be a flow of living water coming out of our heart. Notice the action of the Holy Spirit. He moves like rivers of living water. Not just one river, but many rivers. The ways of the Holy Spirit are diverse and available to you now.

There are many ways of getting the job done. Every flow of the Spirit contains living power. Life always conquers death. Therefore, since we are saturated with His power, every hinderance of the devil is easily removed. This is a great reason for all who

are filled with the Holy Spirit to be praying in other tongues on a regular basis. The more familiar we become with the person of the Holy Spirit, the easier it will be to follow Him.

MEDITATIONS FOR SUCCESS

• Seek God's timing concerning certain events that you desire to see fulfilled. Otherwise, claim right now the benefits to your redemption.

• Be led by God, not man.

• The baptism of the Holy Spirit is for all who believe. According to the Word of God, the experience is followed by speaking in other tongues. Receive by faith this experience for yourself.

• We must take advantage of all the entitlements of power that the Lord has available. He knows best what will assist us in His work.

• Don't compare the flow of the Spirit in your life to others. He may move differently in you than He does in someone else. What matters is that the will of God is accomplished in your life.

CHAPTER 8

¹But Jesus went to the Mount of Olives. ²Now early in the morning He came again into the temple, and all the people came to Him; and He sat down and taught them. ³Then the scribes and Pharisees brought to Him a woman caught in adultery. And when they had set her in the midst, ⁴they said to Him, "Teacher, this woman was caught in adultery, in the very act. ⁵Now Moses, in the law, commanded us that such should be stoned. But what do You say?" ⁶This they said, testing Him, that they might have *something* of which to accuse Him. But Jesus stooped down and wrote on the ground with *His* finger, as though He did not hear.

⁷So when they continued asking Him, He raised Himself up and said to them, "He who is without sin among you, let him throw a stone at her first." ⁸And again He stooped down and wrote on the ground. ⁹Then those who heard *it,* being convicted by *their* conscience, went out one by one, beginning with the oldest *even* to the last. And Jesus was left alone, and the woman standing in the midst. ¹⁰When Jesus had raised Himself up and saw no one but the woman, He said to her, "Woman, where are those accusers of yours? Has no one condemned you?"

¹¹She said, "No one, Lord." And Jesus said to her, "Neither do I condemn you; go and sin no more."

¹²Then Jesus spoke to them again, saying, "I am the light of

8:1-6 It is very evident that the Jewish leaders were trying to set Jesus up to break the Law and alter the commandments of Moses. However, they themselves disregarded the law by bringing only the woman and not the man, who was also caught in adultery. Jesus would not be influenced by their hypocrisy. You can see that Jesus, by stooping to the ground, would check His heart before answering.

8:7 Jesus identified that the Law required that the individual be stoned, yet He brought into the equation the deceit of the leaders. Because of their sin, there was no ground to stand on for the act of stoning. Jesus was not condoning the sin of the woman; He was exposing the greater sin—the hard-heartedness of the leaders.

8:10-11 We see the forgiveness and compassion of the Lord as He dealt with this woman. He was more interested in restoring her than condemning her.

the world. He who follows Me shall not walk in darkness, but have the light of life."

¹³The Pharisees therefore said to Him, "You bear witness of Yourself; Your witness is not true."

¹⁴Jesus answered and said to them, "Even if I bear witness of Myself, My witness is true, for I know where I came from and where I am going; but you do not know where I come from and where I am going. ¹⁵You judge according to the flesh; I judge no one. ¹⁶And yet if I do judge, My judgment is true; for I am not alone, but I *am* with the Father who sent Me. ¹⁷It is also written in your law that the testimony of two men is true. ¹⁸I am One who bears witness of Myself, and the Father who sent Me bears witness of Me."

¹⁹Then they said to Him, "Where is Your Father?"

Jesus answered, "You know neither Me nor My Father. If you had known Me, you would have known My Father also."

²⁰These words Jesus spoke in the treasury, as He taught in the temple; and no one laid hands on Him, for His hour had not yet come.

²¹Then Jesus said to them again, "I am going away, and you will seek Me, and will die in your sin. Where I go you cannot come."

²²So the Jews said, "Will He kill Himself, because He says, 'Where I go you cannot come'?" ²³And He

---

8:12 Jesus revealed that He is the light of the world. The world will continue to walk in the darkness unless God who is light (Isaiah 60:19) grants us light. Jesus is the beacon of light that will lead men to eternal life.

> *Be ready when all others forsake you to stand secure on the authenticity of the Word of God.*

8:13-20 Jesus again entered into a discourse concerning His identity. If we are to lead people to the light, we must of necessity know from where we have come and where we are going. Jesus understood that anything the Father gave Him to do or say had the authority of heaven itself. There is no other higher rule in the universe. The witness of Jesus and the Father God stand alone as true and just. Be ready when all others forsake you to stand secure on the authenticity of the Word of God.

8:23 What are the advantages of knowing that you are not of this world? Each place of origin has with it hierarchy and cultural differences. Coming from heaven means that God is your government and pleasing Him is the cultural guideline. Purpose is a wonderful thing. Fulfilling the purpose of God as Jesus did will cause you to finish your course (read Ecclesiastes 3:1; Philippians 1).

said to them, "You are from beneath; I am from above. You are of this world; I am not of this world. ²⁴Therefore I said to you that you will die in your sins; for if you do not believe that I am *He,* you will die in your sins." ²⁵Then they said to Him, "Who are You?" And Jesus said to them, "Just what I have been saying to you from the beginning. ²⁶I have many things to say and to judge concerning you, but He who sent Me is true; and I speak to the world those things which I heard from Him." ²⁷They did not understand that He spoke to them of the Father.

²⁸Then Jesus said to them, "When you lift up the Son of Man, then you will know that I am *He,* and *that* I do nothing of Myself; but as My Father taught Me, I speak these things. ²⁹And He who sent Me is with Me. The Father has not left Me alone, for I always do those things that please Him." ³⁰As He spoke these words, many believed in Him.

³¹Then Jesus said to those Jews who believed Him, "If you abide in My word, you are My disciples indeed. ³²And you shall know the truth, and the truth shall make you free."

³³They answered Him, "We are Abraham's descendants, and have never been in bondage to anyone. How *can* You say, 'You will be made free'?"

³⁴Jesus answered them, "Most assuredly, I say to you, whoever commits sin is a slave of sin. ³⁵And a slave does not abide in the house forever, *but* a son abides forever. ³⁶Therefore if the Son makes you

Our lives should be a revolving door of godly thoughts with the intent of accomplishing all of them for God's glory.

8:24-30 Jesus never wavered off course from the intent of God. If your desire is always to do those things that please God, then your mind must be fixed on your goal. In order to please your spouse you must think often about him or her and the gesture that will bless your mate. Our lives should be a revolving door of godly thoughts with the intent of accomplishing all of them for God's glory.

8:32 The truth of God's Word will set anyone free. However, knowing the truth is the beginning step to your freedom. Without knowledge your faith has nothing to act on.

8:34 Sin's intent is to enslave you. The power of sin is the inadequacy and hopelessness that one feels. Through Jesus and His shed blood we have absolute freedom from the bondage of sin.

8:36 The words of Jesus are always so

free, you shall be free indeed.

³⁷"I know that you are Abraham's descendants, but you seek to kill Me, because My word has no place in you. ³⁸I speak what I have seen with My Father, and you do what you have seen with your father."

³⁹They answered and said to Him, "Abraham is our father." Jesus said to them, "If you were Abraham's children, you would do the works of Abraham. ⁴⁰But now you seek to kill Me, a Man who has told you the truth which I heard from God. Abraham did not do this. ⁴¹You do the deeds of your father." Then they said to Him, "We were not born of fornication; we have one Father—God."

⁴²Jesus said to them, "If God were your Father, you would love Me, for I proceeded forth and came from God; nor have I come of Myself, but He sent Me. ⁴³Why do you not understand My speech? Because you are not able to listen to My word. ⁴⁴You are of *your* father the devil, and

---

uplifting and encouraging. He doesn't speak to the probability of a thing. He releases the uncompromising reality of a thing which becomes the reason why we can express our faith so boldly. When the Son sets you free, you will without fail be set free. No sense checking your senses, if Jesus said you are free, then you can count on it. Faith is easy when you see the strength of the words of Christ.

8:37-39 There is a difference between the physical descendants of Abraham and the spiritual descendants. Just because you call yourself a Christian doesn't mean you are displaying yourself with the heart and spirit of Jesus. The Jews here were the physical descendants of Abraham yet they acted like the devil. Verse 39 reveals that when you associate with someone, you partake of their whole purpose. Jesus was an exact representation of the Father. The Jews were acting out the role of Satan, their father.

8:42 Remind yourself often that you came from your Father God and you are on a mission to please Him by doing the works of Jesus. You live in the miraculous. Don't allow yourself to think earthly concerning yourself. If you will keep every thought heavenward, your actions will increasingly become godly.

8:44-46 Much wisdom is gained concerning our enemy in these verses. There is no truth in Satan; he embodies the lie. If you desire to live hassle-free from the onslaughts of the enemy, then stand in the truth where Satan isn't. Those things that come to distract you and bring calamity are not as real as they seem. The devil is a master illusionist. He seeks to deceive you into thinking and accepting his evil deeds as truth. The moment you accept his lies as truth, you empower them to be reality. Let's remember that the power of truth will always expose a lie and reveal it for what it is.

the desires of your father you want to do. He was a murderer from the beginning, and does not stand in the truth, because there is no truth in him. When he speaks a lie, he speaks from his own *resources,* for he is a liar and the father of it. ⁴⁵But because I tell the truth, you do not believe Me. ⁴⁶Which of you convicts Me of sin? And if I tell the truth, why do you not believe Me? ⁴⁷He who is of God hears God's words; therefore you do not hear, because you are not of God."

⁴⁸Then the Jews answered and said to Him, "Do we not say rightly that You are a Samaritan and have a demon?"

⁴⁹Jesus answered, "I do not have a demon; but I honor My Father, and you dishonor Me. ⁵⁰And I do not seek My *own* glory; there is One who seeks and judges. ⁵¹Most assuredly, I say to you, if anyone keeps My word he shall never see death."

⁵²Then the Jews said to Him, "Now we know that You have a demon! Abraham is dead, and the prophets; and You say, 'If anyone keeps My word he shall never taste death.' ⁵³Are You greater than our father Abraham, who is dead? And the prophets are dead. Who do You make Yourself out to be?"

⁵⁴Jesus answered, "If I honor Myself, My honor is nothing. It is My Father who honors Me, of whom you say that He is your God. ⁵⁵Yet you have not known Him, but I know Him. And if I say, 'I do not know Him,' I shall be a liar like you; but I do know Him and keep His word. ⁵⁶Your father Abraham rejoiced to see My day, and he saw *it* and was glad."

⁵⁷Then the Jews said to Him, "You are not yet fifty years old, and have You seen Abraham?"

⁵⁸Jesus said to them, "Most assuredly, I say to you, before

8:47 What an encouraging verse. Say this to yourself, "I am from God, therefore I do hear His words. Never again will I doubt that I hear God's voice and understand His Word. If my faith is activated, then the reality is sure to follow."

8:54-55 Jesus said that the very God whom the Jewish people declared to be God is His Father. Jesus revealed His relationship with the Father by saying that He

would be a liar to say that He didn't know God and keep His commands. What an incredible thought that God will honor you for speaking the truth.

8:58 Jesus here said that before Abraham existed, He was. This is one of the most powerful statements that Jesus makes of Himself. Clearly He defines His deity by using the holy name of God as His own. I AM!

Abraham was, I AM."
⁵⁹Then they took up stones to throw at Him; but Jesus hid Himself and went out of the temple, going through the midst of them, and so passed by.

JOHN 8 KEY WORDS

Tempt (*peirazo* πειράζω NT: 3985) To make a trial or test of something. The Jews were trying to trap Jesus into saying something wrong that would disagree with the Law. They were attempting to catch Jesus in a mistake. They actually tried to use God's Law against the Son of God. The Pharisees in Acts 15:4-11 tried also to tempt God. At times our faith is tested and tried, yet during those times, we should never accuse or tempt God. The apostle James writes, "Let no man say when he is tempted, I am tempted of God: for God cannot be tempted with evil, neither tempteth he any man" (James 1:13 KJV).

Condemn (*katakrino* κατακρίνω NT: 2632) To judge someone guilty and assign a sentence or punishment. Condemnation goes beyond discerning sin or conviction of sin—it assigns both a verdict of guilt and punishment. It is accompanied by a condescending and often a critical attitude rooted in self-righteousness. Being saved, we do not live under condemnation (read Romans 8:1-2). Likewise, we are not to condemn others (read Matthew 7:1-2).

Life (*zoe* ζωὴ NT: 2222) Life is more than physical existence. After physical birth, we must be born of the Spirit (John 3) through faith in Christ so that we have life both abundantly (John 10:10) and forever (John 6:51, 58). The only source of *zoe* is Jesus (see John 14:6). Life is the very nature and power given by the living God through faith in His Son, Jesus, to experience the supernatural and the miraculous every day. Read John 1. Following Jesus means that we walk in light and experience the fullness of life in Him.

Light (*phos* φῶς NT: 5457) Quantum physics has discovered what Scripture has revealed since the beginning. The basic building block of the universe is light. All matter is energy and all energy derives from light. The source of all light is God (1 John 1:5) and His light dispels all darkness, sin, and death. Light and darkness cannot occupy the same space at the same time. Hence, whenever *phos* appears, darkness is exposed. *Phos* also refers to "fire." The believer can declare the Word, "You, O LORD, keep my lamp burning; my God turns my darkness into light" (Psalm 18:28 NIV). Jesus as the light of the world overcomes all darkness and sin and gives us direction and power to live abundantly (John 10:10).

🕊 **Testify** (*martureo* μαρτυρέω NT: 3140) To testify is to bear witness and give truthful evidence concerning that of which the witness has firsthand knowledge. Jesus walked in the truth so His life testified or gave witness to the truth that He knew the Father.

🕊 **Remain** or **Abide** (*meno* μένω NT: 3306) To continue in an activity or state of being; to remain or dwell in. When we abide in Christ, and His Word remains or abides in us, then we have the power to walk continually in the miraculous. This speaks of consistency and the ability to continue in the truth

no matter what the situation or circumstance.

🕊 **Truth** (*aletheia* ἀλήθεια NT: 225) That which really is and really happens in time and eternity is true. The Old Testament word for truth ('*amet*) literally speaks of absolute consistency between the inner and outward man. Truth refers to complete integrity, openness, and transparency. God is truth; Jesus is truth. Anyone who disagrees with the Father or the Son is a liar.

🕊 **Lie** (*pseudos* ψεῦδος NT: 5579) A false utterance; a falsehood. No truth exists within a lie. Satan as a liar has no truth in him. Jesus as Truth has no lie in Him. A lie deceives the hearer.

🕊 **Free** (*eleutheroo* ἐλευθερόω NT: 1659) To set free, release, to set at liberty. Freedom from sin and death can only come through Jesus the Messiah. His liberty from every bondage is rooted in truth. When we hear the truth and act in accordance with it, we discover freedom from all control of the flesh. Freedom isn't the independence to do what we want but rather the liberty to live in the miraculous and do what the Father wants.

JOHN 8 SUMMARY

What a joy to know the Father intimately. Through Jesus we have been drawn into union with our heavenly Father. With a heavenly mind-set, Jesus fought the religious mind-set of the Jews. They were not willing to accept that Jesus was God's Son. They endeavored to stone Jesus for His bold accusations concerning His relationship with the Father. Jesus declared that He was not of this world, yet those who opposed Him were from beneath.

We would benefit as well to develop such an awareness of our Father and our heavenly abode. All things that we do should bring honor and pleasure to God. Jesus could declare that all things that He did pleased the Father.

A great theme continues to run throughout the gospel of John. We continue to see through time and effort that Jesus saturated Himself with a consciousness of His calling and purpose. Paul's revelation in Philemon 6 helps to explain what Jesus was doing, "that the sharing of your faith may become effective by the acknowledgment of every good thing which is in you in Christ Jesus."

The things that you talk about the most are the things that you believe the most. Or you could say that the things that you talk about the most are the things that you are most aware of. I have heard science mention that there is a remarkable inner working in our brain which sorts and files our data. This compartmentalization in our brains takes the things that are most important to us and resorts them to the front of our mental files.

The things that you talk about the most are the things that you believe the most.

Once this happens, you will begin to notice what's important to you with regularity. Are you regularly thinking about and recognizing spiritual things? For example, if you get excited about and become endeared to a certain car that you desire to buy, this compartment will make room at the front of your file. The result will be that you will not only be talking about it all the time, you will immediately begin to notice all the cars on the highway that are like the one you want.

Jesus talked about His Father,

the anointing, heavenly things, and through a variety of ways, the will, and assignment of His Father. Could this be the cause for His easy access into those places in God that brought such blessing to man? If there is any truth to these thoughts, then changing our meditations and words will make available experiences that we otherwise would miss.

Jesus backed up His claims by revealing to His disciples that the key to knowing the truth for themselves is to abide in His Word. *Abide* says to continue on a regular basis in the things of God, and they will become more real than the natural. Of course, living for Jesus was never meant to be difficult. Our adversary, along with this world's system, keeps us so distracted that we very rarely have time to clear our minds and concentrate on God.

Abide *says to continue on a regular basis in the things of God, and they will become more real than the natural.*

This may be why Jesus continued to comment to the religious Jews that to reject Him was rejecting the Father God. Accepting the ways of the world is agreeing with Satan. Satan is always a liar; there is no truth in him. As real as it seems when accusations come, at best, they are lies. The only power a lie has is the power you give it by believing it. On the other hand, if you adhere to and believe the truth of God's Word, you empower that truth to release the anointing on that Word.

Everything that God does is bathed in His glory. If anything in the gospel of John sounds too unbelievable, it's simply because the church has accepted such a low level of Christianity for so long that we have lost our point of reference. Through the death, burial, resurrection, and ascension of the Lord Jesus Christ, it is the privilege of every believer to witness demonstrations of God's glory with regularity.

MEDITATIONS FOR SUCCESS

- Don't become religious about your relationship with God.
- In everything find joy.
- As things get worse and worse, look for the lie that's hidden in the circumstances seeking to rob your joy and faith.
- Develop the habit of paying attention to the truth. This empowers you to respond correctly in every situation.

CHAPTER 9

¹Now as *Jesus* passed by, He saw a man who was blind from birth. ²And His disciples asked Him, saying, "Rabbi, who sinned, this man or his parents, that he was born blind?"

³Jesus answered, "Neither this man nor his parents sinned, but that the works of God should be revealed in him. ⁴I must work the

---

9:1-3 God in His great love sent Jesus to deal with the burden of sickness and disease. God could not have expressed Himself any more clearly concerning the subject of whether or not He afflicts or heals. Jesus only brought health. The Riggs Translation of Exodus 15:26 says, "I am the Lord that brings thee only health." He doesn't have any sickness to bring. Ever since the fall, man has contemplated his worth based on the good works he has done. Sin will always be wrong; however, God is not counting up your mistakes. The shed blood of Jesus so purifies your life of sin that God actually believes that you are free from it. His bountiful provision of blessings is always available to keep one in God's perfect peace.

9:3a Jesus's answer draws attention away from speculation and builds faith in God's uncompromised willingness to do good, which reveals the heart of the Father. Notice that the works of God herein included healing the man's eyes. God's works are, however, not visible unless someone manifests them. This is something that God desires. Be confident that whenever you meet those with problems, it is God's desire to meet their needs.

9:3b Ever since the beginning of creation, God has proven His intentions to manifest His work with natural results. If verse 3 says that it is God's intention to manifest the works of God in this man, then you can be confident that God is not withholding physical manifestations. The work that Jesus did was a necessary ingredient for the outcome of physical sight for the man. We are mistaken if we believe we need to wait on God to manifest His promises. God has already confirmed all His promises through the redemptive work of Christ.

> *God has already confirmed all His promises through the redemptive work of Christ.*

It is so significant that we change our thinking in this area and see manifestations of God as a regular occurrence.

9:4 Jesus revealed that the works of God unless worked will not be effective. In John 6:28 the disciples asked the question, how do we "work the works of God?"

works of Him who sent Me while it is day; *the* night is coming when no one can work. ⁵As long as I am in the world, I am the light of the world." ⁶When He had said these things, He spat on the ground and made clay with the saliva; and He anointed the eyes of the blind man with the clay. ⁷And He said to him, "Go, wash in the pool of Siloam" (which is translated, Sent). So he went and washed, and came back seeing. ⁸Therefore the neighbors and those who previously had seen that he was blind said, "Is not this he who sat and begged?" ⁹Some said, "This is he." Others *said,* "He is like him." He said, "I am *he.*" ¹⁰Therefore they said to him, "How were your eyes opened?" ¹¹He answered and said, "A Man called Jesus made clay and anointed my eyes and said to me, 'Go to the pool of Siloam and wash.' So I went and washed, and I received sight." ¹²Then they said to him, "Where

---

Working the works of God has to do with releasing the anointing of God. To engage the power of God takes faith and a working relationship with the Holy Spirit. Jesus saw His place concerning this man as the missing link to solve the problem. We also must take the initiative to work or release the anointing into the problems confronting us if we are to see continual change. There are only two ways to flow with the Holy Spirit—saying and doing.

9:5 Jesus represented the purity and ability of God in the earth. If the world will see God, they must see Him through the life of Jesus. The light of the world symbolizes the wonderful shining presence of God who challenges wrong and brings good works into view. In just the same way that Jesus is the light of the world, we too shine as lights to the world establishing God's will through the power of God.

9:6-11 Jesus said in John 5:19 that He did nothing without seeing what His Father did. Putting the clay to the blind man's eyes was a vehicle for the anointing to work. The command of faith is an opportunity for the blind man to obey and therefore receive the blessing of healing. There were many times in which the anointing of God would work through the command of faith. In this manner, the individual has an opportunity to respond in faith to the working of the anointing. This practice was widely used among the Old Testament prophets. In 2 Kings 4:38-41, Elisha told the men with the poisoned stew to put flour in it. There was nothing special about the flour; its purpose was to be the focus where faith and obedience meet.

9:12-34 It's very obvious in this passage that the Jewish leaders were struggling

is He?" He said, "I do not know." ¹³They brought him who formerly was blind to the Pharisees. ¹⁴Now it was a Sabbath when Jesus made the clay and opened his eyes. ¹⁵Then the Pharisees also asked him again how he had received his sight. He said to them, "He put clay on my eyes, and I washed, and I see."

¹⁶Therefore some of the Pharisees said, "This Man is not from God, because He does not keep the Sabbath." Others said, "How can a man who is a sinner do such signs?" And there was a division among them.

¹⁷They said to the blind man again, "What do you say about Him because He opened your eyes?" He said, "He is a prophet."

¹⁸But the Jews did not believe concerning him, that he had been blind and received his sight, until they called the parents of him who had received his sight. ¹⁹And they asked them, saying, "Is this your son, who you say was born blind? How then does he now see?"

²⁰His parents answered them and said, "We know that this is our son, and that he was born blind; ²¹but by what means he now sees we do not know, or who opened his eyes we do not know. He is of age; ask him. He will speak for himself." ²²His parents said these *things* because they feared the Jews, for the Jews had agreed already that if anyone confessed *that* He *was* Christ, he would be put out of the synagogue. ²³Therefore his parents said, "He is of age; ask him."

²⁴So they again called the man who was blind, and said to him, "Give God the glory! We know that this Man is a sinner."

²⁵He answered and said, "Whether He is a sinner *or not* I do not know. One thing I know: that though I was blind, now I see."

²⁶Then they said to him again, "What did He do to you? How did He open your eyes?"

²⁷He answered them, "I told you already, and you did not listen. Why do you want to hear *it* again? Do you also want to become His disciples?"

²⁸Then they reviled him and said, "You are His disciple, but we are Moses' disciples. ²⁹We know

---

with understanding how such a healing came through Jesus on the Sabbath.

Instead of giving God glory for a work of God, they insisted on their legalistic explanation.

that God spoke to Moses; *as for this fellow,* we do not know where He is from."

³⁰The man answered and said to them, "Why, this is a marvelous thing, that you do not know where He is from; yet He has opened my eyes! ³¹Now we know that God does not hear sinners; but if anyone is a worshiper of God and does His will, He hears him. ³²Since the world began it has been unheard of that anyone opened the eyes of one who was born blind. ³³If this Man were not from God, He could do nothing."

³⁴They answered and said to him, "You were completely born in sins, and are you teaching us?" And they cast him out.

³⁵Jesus heard that they had cast him out; and when He had found him, He said to him, "Do you believe in the Son of God?"

³⁶He answered and said, "Who is He, Lord, that I may believe in Him?"

³⁷And Jesus said to him, "You have both seen Him and it is He who is talking with you."

³⁸Then he said, "Lord, I believe!" And he worshiped Him.

³⁹And Jesus said, "For judgment I have come into this world, that those who do not see may see, and that those who see may be made blind."

⁴⁰Then *some* of the Pharisees who were with Him heard these words, and said to Him, "Are we blind also?"

⁴¹Jesus said to them, "If you were blind, you would have no sin; but now you say, 'We see.' Therefore your sin remains."

9:35-41 Jesus takes the time to secure the healing and win a heart. When Jesus presented Himself to the man as the Son of God, He revealed the heart of the Father to him. Also, it is very important to note that Jesus was just as interested in the lifelong relationship with this man as the healing of his eyes. Salvation is much more than getting your needs met, although this is a wonderful benefit.

Salvation is much more than getting your needs met, although this is a wonderful benefit.

In fellowship with God, we are always filled with purpose, living life to fulfill the plan and mission of God.

JOHN 9 KEY WORDS

🗝 **Work** (*ergazomai* ἐργάζομαι NT: 2038) Jesus worked with the Father to accomplish His will. Likewise, we labor with, and minister with the Father to accomplish His work on earth according to His will. This work engages in committed activity. In other words, the believer is actively at work with God; faith without works is dead.

Some want living in the miraculous, walking in health, and ministering in healing to be effortless. Actually, our work is to become willing vessels for His power and anointing to flow in and through us. Every relationship requires commitment and effort including our relationship with the Father. The effort mentioned is simply learning to stand your ground in faith. We must resist the temptation to submit to the senses and the distractions of the enemy. As long as we remain steadfast in the faith, immovable from God's Word, there is victory. By the grace of God every believer can live successfully in the power and strength of Jesus Christ.

Jesus declared that He must work the works of His Father. That is our mandate as well.

Walking in faith requires initiative on our part. We have to trust, receive, and act upon what the Father commands.

🗝 **Send** (*pempo* πέμπω NT: 3992) Even as the Father sent Jesus, so He sends us into the world to do the work of the Father and to bear witness to His life and truth. As ambassadors into the world, we represent the love of the Father to others. *Pempo* means to cause someone to depart for a particular purpose. The Father sent His Son, Jesus, to manifest and declare His love through the cross in order to accomplish the Father's purpose of salvation. Likewise, the Son sends us (Matthew 28:19-20; Mark 16:15-16) into the world as His representatives with great demonstrations of His power and love so that all the world will know that Jesus is Lord.

🗝 **Anoint** (*chrio* χρίω NT: 5548) *Chrio* means to smear, rub, or anoint. When Jesus applied mud to the blind man's eyes, He was activating the anointing. As the blind man obeyed the instructions of Jesus, the power of God would complete its work. Anoint also means to be appointed to a special task by God (Luke 4:18). When Christ anoints us for ministry, we activate that anointing by going and doing that which He has commissioned.

🖐 **The Son of Man** (*o huios tou anthropou* ὁ υἱὸς τοῦ ἀνθρώπου) This title which is prominently used in Ezekiel, refers to God's human agent or representative much in the sense of an ambas-sador. In other words, Jesus is God's agent from heaven on earth to embody the full potential of being human. He is fully human and fully God. As the Son of Man, Jesus had God-given authority to do the Father's will on earth as it is in heaven. When you believe that Jesus is the Son of Man you acknowledge that He is the Messiah. The blind man came to Jesus and found sight. The Pharisees did not believe and remained spiritually blind.

JOHN 9 SUMMARY

Jesus is the light of the world. His light would shine as He made available to this world the power of this light. How many people saw a halo above Jesus's head? If the anointing were always visible then there would be no reason for Jesus to preach saying that it was there.

We know that for any problem there is a work of God, a solution to the problem.

In this chapter Jesus gives us insight into His work. We know that for any problem there is a work of God, a solution to the problem. Jesus first reveals to us how important it is that we know every difficulty can be solved. Also, it is God's will that every difficulty be solved. Because there are so many problems in the world, could we conclude that God is waiting on someone to move the answer into the open, where everyone can see?

Jesus seemed to indicate this as He spoke concerning the blind man, that the works of God should be manifested in his life. God certainly desires that no case of need be left unmet. However, those who recognized that they possessed the answers are used to set people like this man free.

In verses 3 and 4 there is much information given for those who desire to be used in the work of the Lord. Understanding the heart of the Father is paramount to exercising the anointing with boldness. Notice this simple, yet profound, revelation. God the Father desires to manifest His works in the lives of those you confront with His truth. You could say that God is definitely backing you up to produce a manifestation in someone's life. For that matter, God is backing you up to see a manifestation in your own life.

From God's perspective, these works are already done. There is no need that God hasn't already met. What if we knew that every problem from God's perspective was already solved? Wouldn't this encourage faith? As we look at Jesus in the midst of battle, He never flinched or acted unsure of the outcome. If the problems

were not just solvable but solved, and you were confident that you possessed the power to reveal the answer, wouldn't you be confident as Jesus was when confronted with life's difficulties? Could this be the reason why the apostle Paul prayed for the church to have revelation concerning insight into our calling and the power to make it profitable? If the church needed revelation then, we certainly need it now.

Jesus released the anointing through His words.

The skill that Jesus exhibited in using the anointing is part of the revelation that the church must understand. Jesus released the anointing through His words. The command of faith that Jesus gave the blind man was the catalyst that made possible the working of the works of God. Since the man was making no effort to believe, Jesus gave him something simple to do that connected the man to the power of God. If the man followed the words of Jesus, he would receive the blessing that Jesus possessed.

We must become confident in the anointing of God just as Jesus was. The skill of using the anointing is activated by believing in its possibilities and undeniable ability to produce results. Jesus worked the works of God and brought forth the miraculous. We can do the same, and are instructed to do so by the Lord in John 14:12: "The works that I do [you] will do also; and greater works than these [you] will do, because I go to My Father."

We must become confident in the anointing of God just as Jesus was.

MEDITATIONS FOR SUCCESS

- God's works are available for every problem.
- Understand His heart; He desires every problem solved.
- His power is always ready to accommodate faith.
- You must move toward every uncertainty with complete confidence in the power of God.
- Work the works; release the anointing where it will produce results.
- God is light. His influence will be visable as we reveal his power.

CHAPTER 10

[1]"Most assuredly, I say to you, he who does not enter the sheepfold by the door, but climbs up some other way, the same is a thief and a robber. [2]But he who enters by the door is the shepherd of the sheep. [3]To him the doorkeeper opens, and the sheep hear his voice; and he calls his own sheep by name and leads them out. [4]And when he brings out his own sheep, he goes before them; and

10:1-6 Speaking to the Pharisees, Jesus reminded them what a true shepherd is. With their false doctrine and judgment the Pharisees actually harmed the sheep more than liberated and cared for the flock. Jesus showed us the true heart of God—to lovingly protect and nurture each member of His family.
10:3-5 Jesus is the door through which all sheep must pass. When we come to

the sheep follow him, for they know his voice. ⁵Yet they will by no means follow a stranger, but will flee from him, for they do not know the voice of strangers." ⁶Jesus used this illustration, but they did not understand the things which He spoke to them.

⁷Then Jesus said to them again, "Most assuredly, I say to you, I am the door of the sheep. ⁸All who *ever* came before Me are thieves and robbers, but the sheep did not hear them. ⁹I am the door. If anyone enters by Me, he will be saved, and will go in and out and find pasture. ¹⁰The thief does not come except to steal, and to kill, and to destroy. I have come that they may have life, and that they may have *it* more abundantly.

Jesus, He will forever know our name. Salvation is a personal experience in which God calls and approaches us individually. Every aspect is for the benefit of our leading a godly, Christ-centered life.

Jesus remarked that each sheep hears His voice and follows Him because they know Him. However, the voice of a stranger they will not follow. If you hardly know God at all but know all too well the voice of a stranger, then you will have to receive these words of our Lord by faith. God actually knows the truth about you—truth that you, in your renewed mind, are just finding out. To accept the words of Jesus and openly acknowledge them as your own will release unto you the experience of this truth. For example, give God praise that you hear His voice and follow Him always because you know Him so well. Don't worry if it doesn't register in your flesh; do it by faith, convincingly believe that it's true because Jesus said it is. This is an important part of your relationship with God which will last a lifetime.

10:7-9 Because Jesus is the door to the things of God, notice the freedom of coming in and out to find provision. Salvation includes all the wonders of a godly life as God created life to be in Genesis 1 and 2. Every conceivable need and desire are met. Having such a Good Shepherd is the security that the sheep need to remain content.

10:10 Jesus revealed to us the areas in which the enemy comes. He would like to steal, kill, and destroy us if he could. What weaponry does the enemy have? If Jesus spoiled and stripped the enemy of power and ability to harm us, then we certainly have nothing to worry about. The only avenue that the devil has for tempting us is the power of suggestion, which works well on unlearned and ignorant minds. To the mind that is renewed to God's blessings and the enemy's defeat, the works of the enemy are useless.

Jesus said that the key to our victory is the life of God. This is the cure for anything that the devil will try to do to us. Jesus came that we might have life *(zoe)* and have an abundance of it. You can be sure that you are not short in supply of the necessary life to conquer and maintain

¹¹"I am the good shepherd. The good shepherd gives His life for the sheep. ¹²But a hireling, *he who is* not the shepherd, one who does not own the sheep, sees the wolf coming and leaves the sheep and flees; and the wolf catches the sheep and scatters them. ¹³The hireling flees because he is a hireling and does not care about the sheep. ¹⁴I am the good shepherd; and I know My *sheep*, and am known by My own. ¹⁵As the Father knows Me, even so I know the Father; and I lay down My life for the sheep. ¹⁶And other sheep I have which are not of this fold; them also I must bring, and they will hear My voice; and there will be one flock *and* one shepherd.

¹⁷"Therefore My Father loves Me, because I lay down My life that I may take it again. ¹⁸No one takes it from Me, but I lay it

---

your victory through life. The greatest work accomplished was the death, burial, and resurrection of our Lord. This is where the life of Christ that conquered death comes from. Our responsibility is to become exceedingly confident that we possess it and are skilled at using it.

10:11-14 Jesus is the Good Shepherd. A good shepherd will care for His own sheep. Ezekiel prophesied against the shepherds who feed themselves and leave their sheep hungry, naked, beaten, and bruised (Ezekiel 34). He said that they were to have fed and clothed their flock, healed and brought back what was driven away. These characteristics you will find exceedingly in our Lord. He gave His life that we might live in His abundance.

10:15 In the same way that the Father knows the Son, even so the Son knows the Father. If it is true that I know the Father as well as He knows me, what impact would that have on my life? Getting to know the heart of the Father would help you to identify with people. Laying down your life for the desires of God is a privilege and honor.

10:16 The whole world was to experience the joy of being a part of God's heavenly family. The plan of God through Christ is toward anyone who would believe.

10:17-18 When you effectively learn to accept and love the heart of God, you will begin to really live. Living life to the fullest is seeing life through the eyes of the One who created all things. There is such protection in the will of God. As Jesus said, no one could take His life unless He willingly, of His own accord, laid it down. Many times crowds of people desired to kill Jesus and even tried. Yet, Jesus went unharmed because it was not the will of God that someone would have the power to take His life until He had accomplished His mission. Even then, no one took Jesus's life, He willingly gave it. Do you desire to live in God's will to the fullest, where you finish the will of God without the fear of failure? Then lay aside your rights to direct your own life and experience the hand of God and His direction.

down of Myself. I have power to lay it down, and I have power to take it again. This command I have received from My Father."

¹⁹Therefore there was a division again among the Jews because of these sayings. ²⁰And many of them said, "He has a demon and is mad. Why do you listen to Him?"

²¹Others said, "These are not the words of one who has a demon. Can a demon open the eyes of the blind?"

²²Now it was the Feast of Dedication in Jerusalem, and it was winter. ²³And Jesus walked in the temple, in Solomon's porch. ²⁴Then the Jews surrounded Him and said to Him, "How long do You keep us in doubt? If You are the Christ, tell us plainly."

²⁵Jesus answered them, "I told you, and you do not believe. The works that I do in My Father's name, they bear witness of Me. ²⁶But you do not believe, because you are not of My sheep, as I said to you. ²⁷My sheep hear My voice, and I know them, and they follow Me. ²⁸And I give them eternal life, and they shall never perish; neither shall anyone snatch them out of My hand. ²⁹My Father, who has given *them* to Me, is greater than all; and no one is able to snatch *them* out of My Father's hand. ³⁰I and *My* Father are one."

10:27 Hearing the voice of God and knowing Him are synonymous with being a sheep. Regardless of how well you have followed God in the past, go ahead and act like you never miss it and the voice of God is clear as a bell. Paul said to put on the new man who is made in the image of Christ. By faith, act like you hear and you will.

10:28-29 If God is for me, who can be against me (Romans 8:31). My surety and confidence are in the Lord. We ought to be bold about what we believe. Many religions of the world are quick to tell about their philosophy, yet they have no security in eternal matters. How forthright should we as believers be to a lost and dying world, when we have the answer in God?

10:30 Union produces results. Jesus spoke of His complete union or oneness with God. There is no mistake. Jesus declared that He and the Father are one. In a similar manner, we (the church) are to declare that we are one with the Father through Jesus Christ our Lord. This does not make us God as Jesus is God the Son, but it does declare our inheritance as adopted sons of Almighty God. One of the worst things you can do after you become born again is to consider yourself to be only human ever again. Once God's Spirit comes to live in you and Jesus is your Lord, you become a new creature. You are nothing at all like you were.

³¹Then the Jews took up stones again to stone Him. ³²Jesus answered them, "Many good works I have shown you from My Father. For which of those works do you stone Me?"

³³The Jews answered Him, saying, "For a good work we do not stone You, but for blasphemy, and because You, being a Man, make Yourself God."

³⁴Jesus answered them, "Is it not written in your law, '*I said, "You are gods"*'? ³⁵If He called them gods, to whom the word of God came (and the Scripture cannot be broken), ³⁶do you say of Him whom the Father sanctified and sent into the world, 'You are blaspheming,' because I said, 'I am the Son of God'? ³⁷If I do not do the works of My Father, do not

---

Once God's Spirit comes to live in you and Jesus is your Lord, you become a new creature.

10:31 If the work of the Pharisees represented the work of the devil to stop Jesus, then we can learn something from this passage. Is it possible that knowing the significance of our oneness with the Lord is so important that the devil will do anything he can to keep us ignorant? If the Jews wanted to kill Jesus over this revelation, then Satan will deceive you into considering yourself only as human and unworthy of spiritual victories.

10:32 This text shows us that the power of being one with God will produce notable signs and wonders. Jesus verified His claim that He was God by the works He accomplished. The greater our belief and understanding that we are one with God, the more lasting results we will produce.

10:33 The Jews said that Jesus made Himself God. Actually it was God who came to dwell in a human body called

Jesus and made Him deity and humanity at the same time. God has the master design to all things. If He created man on a level to fellowship and co-labor with Him in running things on earth, then who are we to complain? Just as much as God was responsible for making Jesus God and man at the same time, so God through Christ has made us new Spirit-filled beings ready to take dominion on this earth. We have the same earthly advantages that Jesus had on the earth. We also share His origin of existence because Jesus has personally come to live in us.

Jesus has personally come to live in us.

10:34-36 Jesus quoted Psalm 82. Here leaders and rulers are mentioned as corepresentatives of God. David said that God (Elohim) stands in the congregation of elohim *(gods)*. God is the One who sees us as His sons in the earth. Very simply, God created a race of beings who so

believe Me; ³⁸but if I do, though you do not believe Me, believe the works, that you may know and believe that the Father *is* in Me, and I in Him." ³⁹Therefore they sought again to seize Him, but He escaped out of their hand.

⁴⁰And He went away again beyond the Jordan to the place where John was baptizing at first, and there He stayed. ⁴¹Then many came to Him and said, "John performed no sign, but all the things that John spoke about this Man were true." ⁴²And many believed in Him there.

---

closely resembled Himself that He could turn over the responsibility of running the earth to them. Man is that being. Our distorted view of humanity comes from a fallen race, headed up by a liar who desperately desires to keep all creation ignorant to our strength and authority—his ultimate defeat. The word "gods" here does not mean deity; it simply means "representatives acting like God." The word in the New Testament is "ambassadors."

10:37-38 This is one of the single most powerful statements of the Bible. If we all would see the power of our salvation as Jesus saw His place in God, then we too could declare and bring to pass results as He did. The whole ministry of Jesus was

placed on the line, with reference to whether or not He could produce what He said. If not, Jesus would willingly surrender as a phony and an imposter.

However, given the fact that He was right and He willfully fulfilled His promises with tangible results, then the fact remains; He is one with God. At this point, even if His doctrine was questioned, the results would speak for themselves. God is waiting on this kind of boldness to prove the power of the gospel message that all who come to Jesus are changed into His image and likeness for the good of all. No foe, tribulation, or trial will compete with a child of God who comprehends the power of being one with the Almighty God of the universe.

JOHN 10 KEY WORDS

Shepherd (*poimen* ποιμήν NT: 4166) Used figuratively here in John 10 to refer to Jesus as the shepherd of His sheep—those who follow Him. The shepherd nurtures, protects, and feeds His sheep, protecting them from predators like wolves, which represent the devil and his minions.

🖋 **Abundant** (*perissos* περισσός NT: 4053) A quantity surpassing what one might expect or imagine. For life to be abundant, it far exceeds anything known or experienced in existence. Grace and favor define abundant life. It's a gift from the Creator that the creature cannot earn or work for. Such life contains provision for every need, healing for any hurt, and overflowing supply.

🖋 **Have** (ἔχω *echo* NT: 2192) To possess or to be in a certain state. Having life is possessing or laying claim to life in such a way that what is possessed actually becomes the state of that person's being. Having life (*zoe*) means that a person is filled and overflowing with all the qualities of life from the Father.

🖋 **Good** (*kalos* καλός NT: 2570) When Jesus is called the good shepherd, He is defined by God's quality. Good is that which is superior, surpassing all else. There is no shepherd like Him. That which He is, He produces. So, all that He does for us is good and becomes a blessing in every way. Good speaks of being fruitful and productive.

Jesus as the good shepherd reproduces Himself in us and we become fruitful in our relationships with others.

🖋 **Life** or **Soul** (*psuche* ψυχή NT: 5590) Interestingly, Jesus refers to the laying down of His own life (*psuche*) in John 10:11 for the sheep and the surrender of His soul—the human seat of emotions, will, and thoughts. Jesus died as a natural being, man, in order to shed His physical body for a spiritual one. He gives up the breath of existence in the natural realm for the eternal life of God.

🖋 **Know** (*ginosko* γινώσκω NT: 1097) The shepherd's knowledge of His sheep and the sheep *knowing* the shepherd's voice arise out of an intimate relationship. Such intimacy is birthed out of listening, caring, and spending time together. The wolf has no care for the sheep and isn't interested in being with them. But, the Good Shepherd has given Himself to the sheep so that they might fellowship with one another for eternity.

JOHN 10 SUMMARY

Throughout the ministry of Jesus men marveled at the words that Jesus spoke. They were not as the words of others; they had the ring of mastery and authority that came from the absoluteness of truth. Much can be learned from chapter 10 and the way Jesus spoke to His followers. Concerning His ministry and the work of His Father, Jesus revealed secrets that would open our hearts to our relationship with Him.

Truly, Jesus is the Shepherd of the sheep, the body of Christ. As sheep, we would be lost without the leading of the Shepherd. Herein Jesus remarkably reveals a truth that connects the church with her Lord. Jesus further mentioned three ideas that are revolutionary to the body of Christ and her participation in the realm of the spirit. Jesus said that (1) His sheep know His voice; (2) the voice of a stranger they will not follow; (3) His sheep know Him and follow Him. These statements are true regardless of how we view them. This is the secret of faith.

When God speaks, His words are fact and truth.

When God speaks, His words are fact and truth. There is no reason to question Him or stubbornly resist His words just because they don't appear so. To the unregenerate mind, most of what God speaks about you will seem incorrect. God never looks at the natural to determine the real you. You are to God what God has made you. If through Christ, you are more than a conqueror, yet it seems like you're going under, you then have a choice to make. Your choice will determine how well you apply yourself to faith. You can choose to look at the natural or you can choose to see yourself as God does and act like it.

When your faith is active, the things you are acting on become the reality that supersedes the natural.

Regardless what your mind sees at the moment, when you choose to act as if what God says about you is true, you engage your faith. When your faith is active, the things you are acting on become the reality that supersedes the natural.

So, to the church, when Jesus says that you know Him, then you do. Don't wait until it seems like you do, accept it as fact now and begin to act as if you do. Your faith will cause you to actually know and experience God. Likewise, if Jesus says that we hear His voice and then follow Him, then we do. Either Jesus is lying about it, or we are incorrectly seeing through the eye of reason. Wonderful relationships can be established right here through your faith. Obviously, believing that you know Him without spending the necessary time to fellowship would be counterproductive. When we begin to vocalize that we hear His voice, we will hear it more clearly and with much less effort. God does want to speak to us and share His heart concerning our lives. What would give parents more joy than to see their child follow in the steps of right doing?

God receives great joy when His children follow Him and accurately recognize His leadings. Any man or woman who has done great things for God was God-inside-minded. They were sensitive to the Lord. With the words in John 10, Jesus is jump-starting our relationship with Him. We must take advantage of the Lord's insight and knowledge in our lives.

Jesus revealed that as the Shepherd of the sheep, He is interested in our well-being. There is a stranger who would like to kill, steal, and destroy us. The devil is that enemy who hates the very sight of believers who are the joy of God's life. Jesus is always triumphant in His perspective. He counteracts the work of Satan by saying that He came to give us life in abundance. This life, or the divine nature of God, is the answer for any one of the devil's schemes. The divine life of God is the great mystery of the church.

Christ in us, His very life, is the hope of glory. There is no need to look any further for answers when a believer knows that they contain the very substance and ability of God. With joy Jesus came to give us this renewal of life, so that His sheep would be fortified with divine ability for all of life's difficulties. Never again would the church cower to the enemy in shame or fear. Forever we, the body of Christ, will assume our divine rights and privileges to rule and reign in this lifetime as kings and priests for our God.

Finally, Jesus drew attention to the relationship that He shares with the Father. He said that He and the Father are one.

As we develop our relationship with the Lord by choosing to embrace the facts of our keen ability to understand and comprehend the voice of God, and we see the magnitude of God's love that would empower us with His divine ability and nature, we are ready to intertwine these truths with God's plan of the ages.

God's purpose is to make within Himself a nation of people who indeed are one with Him as Jesus was one with Him.

The ultimate grace for man is God reproducing Himself in humanity to make us children of God.

No longer would man hide in shame from God, but constant approval and unconditional love would provide man complete access to God's heart at all times.

Man unites with God when God's Spirit subdues and possesses man until all intentions of man's heart bring honor and glory to Him.

Man unites with God when God's Spirit subdues and possesses man until all intentions of man's heart bring honor and glory to Him. This is the work of salvation: man drawn into union with God in such oneness that man can and will accomplish the exercise of the divine will of God that began and was consummated in Christ.

Jesus explained that the reason that the works of God were so evident in His ministry was that as a man He was one with His Father. Jesus was willing to put His entire ministry on the line if anyone could prove that what He was saying was not backed up with the outward evidence to prove His claims.

This blatant boldness is not just the work of the Holy Spirit, but also a thorough understanding of His place and privilege as the Son of God and the Son of Man. United together there is no difference. Yet to finish His work on the earth, Jesus must, as the Son of Man, lift Himself in consciousness to see and yield to His divine right to work the works of God as God Incarnate.

MEDITATIONS FOR SUCCESS

- Believe that you hear the voice of God and that you actually know Him. Then following Him will be a joy, not a burden.
- Know that your relationship with the Father is far beyond anything you have experienced to this point.
- Faith and time with Him will catapult you into the experiences you have always desired.
- God's love has reproduced inside of you what is inside of Him.
- Life (*zoe*) is the supreme quality of being that any creature could attain. You have an abundance of it.
- Life made Jesus undeniably the greatest human being who ever lived on this planet. Now it's our turn. The baton has been passed.
- God couldn't make a Christian any more one with Himself if He tried all over again.
- Our union with Christ is the great secret to the works of God being worked all over the earth.
- When you know you are one with Christ, your actions of faith will cause the ability of God in you to flow unhindered. Remember, out of your heart shall flow rivers of living water. Therein is your answer to all of life's questions!

CHAPTER 11

¹Now a certain *man* was sick, Lazarus of Bethany, the town of Mary and her sister Martha. ²It was *that* Mary who anointed the Lord with fragrant oil and wiped His feet with her hair, whose brother Lazarus was sick. ³Therefore the sisters sent to Him, saying, "Lord, behold, he whom You love is sick."

⁴When Jesus heard *that,* He said, "This sickness is not unto death, but for the glory of God, that the Son of God may be glorified through it."

⁵Now Jesus loved Martha and her sister and Lazarus. ⁶So, when He heard that he was sick, He

---

11:1-3 Jesus was very close to Lazarus's family; He had developed a wonderful relationship with them. The sisters' inquiry for help from Jesus is an example for us to follow. Our faith should be in the power of God and His willingness to help in any situation before we consult the medical world around us. Remember, Jesus is now our doctor, our Great Physician. Anything that the world can offer, Jesus can do it better. This of course is the ultimate physical goal for the believer—living in the health of the Lord. While all believers should exercise faith and confidence in God for healing, if they need the use of medical science there should be no condemnation. However, our goal is to live completely in the hands of the Lord.

11:4 Jesus proclaimed with words of power that Lazarus would live. In verse 41 is His statement about being heard by the Father, and it was the reason why Lazarus would arise. It is important for you to release your faith with your words when crises come. Put the power of God in motion with your proclamation.

Does sickness glorify God? Very simply, if it did, then why did Jesus heal, which would have nullified this glory? Sickness and death are real enemies that exist in the world through the fall of man. Walking through the Gospels with Jesus gives us a foretaste of the ultimate event when Jesus would in His death, burial, and resurrection spoil every principality and power, including sickness and disease. Jesus's whole purpose was to glorify the Father which He did by destroying the works of the devil. The glory of God is the cure for every problem known to man. Jesus being glorified through this situation means that He would use the glory that was upon Him for the overall purpose of doing good to raise Lazarus. The glory of God that is upon us is for the same purpose: to destroy the works of the devil and magnify God.

11:5-6 I believe that these two verses contain significant revelation for us. Jesus loved this family. Knowing that He was only a very short distance, approximately two miles away from this home, then why stayed two more days in the place where He was. ⁷Then after this He said to *the* disciples, "Let us go to Judea again."

⁸The disciples said to Him, "Rabbi, lately the Jews sought to stone You, and are You going there again?"

⁹Jesus answered, "Are there not twelve hours in the day? If anyone walks in the day, he does not stumble, because he sees the light of this world. ¹⁰But if one walks in the night, he stumbles, because the light is not in him." ¹¹These things He said, and after that He said to them, "Our friend Lazarus sleeps, but I go that I may wake him up."

¹²Then His disciples said, "Lord, if he sleeps he will get well." ¹³However, Jesus spoke of his death, but they thought that He was speaking about taking rest in sleep.

¹⁴Then Jesus said to them

---

didn't He quickly heal Lazarus before He died? First, He must have had a leading from God the Father to handle the situation differently than would be expected in the natural. Certainly it would be to our advantage to have the mind of God concerning any situation that arises.

Second, it's obvious that Jesus never allowed any situation to become a crisis. He was in control of His surroundings. We see that He stayed two more days, and during this time He had, as verse 14 reveals, spiritual insight into what was going on. Jesus knew when Lazarus died. He waited until He died to go and raise Him. Is it possible that Jesus waited on purpose until Lazarus died so that He could exercise His power over death one more time?

I think it ironic that Jesus waited until Lazarus was four days in the tomb. As Jesus mentioned in John 10:18, He had been given power to lay His life down and power to take it up. If Jesus could raise someone dead and in the grave after four days, would this not give Him confidence in God's resurrection power? If we think of the progression of Jesus's dominion of soul-consciousness over death, then the first person He raised was dead only a few minutes. This was Jairus's daughter. The second person who was raised from the dead was dead for many hours. This was the widow's son, whom Jesus raised up during the funeral procession in Nain.

Now as we see in this chapter, Jesus completely conquers the power of death in His own heart by raising up Lazarus after four days. He stands ready now to conquer in three days His own death, burial, and resurrection. Read John 2:19-22.

11:9-10 Walking by revelation of the Word of God, which is the mind of God, is walking in the light. There are many obstacles that are in the world which need to be avoided. God orders your steps to succeed, not fail, so walk with purpose and insight into your spiritual advantages.

11:14-15 What were the disciples to believe by Jesus's insightful words? They

plainly, "Lazarus is dead. ¹⁵And I am glad for your sakes that I was not there, that you may believe. Nevertheless let us go to him."

¹⁶Then Thomas, who is called the Twin, said to his fellow disciples, "Let us also go, that we may die with Him."

¹⁷So when Jesus came, He found that he had already been in the tomb four days. ¹⁸Now Bethany was near Jerusalem, about two miles away. ¹⁹And many of the Jews had joined the women around Martha and Mary, to comfort them concerning their brother.

²⁰Then Martha, as soon as she heard that Jesus was coming, went and met Him, but Mary was sitting in the house. ²¹Now Martha said to Jesus, "Lord, if You had been here, my brother would not have died. ²²But even now I know that whatever You ask of God, God will give You."

²³Jesus said to her, "Your brother will rise again."

²⁴Martha said to Him, "I know that he will rise again in the resurrection at the last day."

²⁵Jesus said to her, "I am the resurrection and the life. He who believes in Me, though he may

---

would gain understanding into the will and purpose of God. Jesus's steps were orchestrated by the Father to produce the ultimate good and awareness of God's ability in the earth. This became an incredible training session for the disciples. They would learn how to see beyond the natural and appropriate the mind of God.

11:21-22 Jesus had already made enough of an impact into the life of Martha that she believed Jesus could have kept her brother from dying. Thank God for this revelation. The church needs to walk in this truth. Next, Martha revealed her faith in Jesus's relationship with God. Her words sounded so full of faith that anything is possible.

We must be careful that our words don't become religious, sounding good, yet denying the power of God.

11:23-24 Jesus revealed to Martha His intentions. With the words of faith that Martha had already spoken, you would have thought that she would be elated with Jesus's insight. However, now we see what Martha did and didn't believe. We must be careful that our words don't become religious, sounding good, yet denying the power of God. Why would Martha indicate that Jesus could receive anything that He asks the Father if it wasn't to change the outcome of her brother Lazarus? Religion is like the dog who barks but has no bite.

11:25-27 If Jesus had not conceptualized the bigness of His place in God the Father, He might not have obeyed or approached the situation with the confidence which is evident. It would be incorrect for you to assume that just because you hear God

die, he shall live. ²⁶And whoever lives and believes in Me shall never die. Do you believe this?"

²⁷She said to Him, "Yes, Lord, I believe that You are the Christ, the Son of God, who is to come into the world."

²⁸And when she had said these things, she went her way and secretly called Mary her sister, saying, "The Teacher has come and is calling for you." ²⁹As soon as she heard *that,* she arose quickly and came to Him. ³⁰Now Jesus had not yet come into the town, but was in the place where Martha met Him. ³¹Then the Jews who were with her in the house, and comforting her, when they saw that Mary rose up quickly and went out, followed her, saying, "She is going to the tomb to weep there."

³²Then, when Mary came where Jesus was, and saw Him, she fell down at His feet, saying to Him, "Lord, if You had been here, my brother would not have died."

³³Therefore, when Jesus saw her weeping, and the Jews who came with her weeping, He groaned in the spirit and was troubled. ³⁴And

---

speak to you concerning the miraculous that you will obey.

If you will not dare to go beyond where you have been, it is extremely possible that you will pass up opportunities to work in the miraculous.

If you will not dare to go beyond where you have been, it is extremely possible that you will pass up opportunities to work in the miraculous. Jesus believed Himself to be the answer before He was ever confronted with the need for what He could supply. Martha was definitely struggling with the depth of Jesus's revelation. We must see the place where we limit God by our lack of insight into God's plan and purpose for our lives. Like Martha, we too can hinder God's ability by remaining childlike in our understanding.

Martha recognized and confessed that Jesus is both the Christ and the Son of God. This confession arose out of a relationship with Him and seeing the signs and wonders He had done. Her confession came by faith even before Christ is raised from the dead.

11:28-37 The general consensus as we see in Mary and those who stood around is that if Jesus had been there earlier, He could have kept Lazarus from dying. No one seems to portray the attitude of faith which believes that Jesus is never late, but stands as the answer to any problem at any time. I hardly believe that Jesus would shed tears over a man whom He is about to raise up. Yet it is highly possible that Jesus shed tears over the general unbelief of the people to see His place in the earth. We certainly cannot trust the judgment of

He said, "Where have you laid him?" They said to Him, "Lord, come and see."

³⁵Jesus wept. ³⁶Then the Jews said, "See how He loved him!"

³⁷And some of them said, "Could not this Man, who opened the eyes of the blind, also have kept this man from dying?"

³⁸Then Jesus, again groaning in Himself, came to the tomb. It was a cave, and a stone lay against it. ³⁹Jesus said, "Take away the stone." Martha, the sister of him who was dead, said to Him, "Lord, by this time there is a stench, for he has been *dead* four days."

⁴⁰Jesus said to her, "Did I not say to you that if you would believe you would see the glory of God?" ⁴¹Then they took away the stone *from the place* where the dead man was lying. And Jesus lifted up *His* eyes and said, "Father, I thank You that You have heard Me. ⁴²And I know that You always hear Me, but because of the people who are standing by I said *this,* that they may believe that You sent Me."

⁴³Now when He had said these things, He cried with a loud voice, "Lazarus, come forth!" ⁴⁴And he who had died came out bound hand and foot with graveclothes, and his face was wrapped with a cloth. Jesus said to them, "Loose him, and let him go."

---

the unbelievers who stood by.

11:39 Martha again revealed her struggle with seeing beyond the natural. Anytime the natural becomes too real to you, you run the risk of forfeiting the power of the supernatural.

11:40 Here is the simple key to the supernatural, believing in the possibility of the result. No one could see the miracle about to happen except Jesus. No one except Jesus believed in the possibility. The glory of God is not hiding from you. Yet it is possible that your unbelief is like a cloud, blocking your view to the world where all things are possible to them who believe. When you believe, the probability of the miracle you need becomes 100 percent fact that it will happen.

11:41-42 The words that Jesus spoke were not superficial but powerful in their results. The Father heard Jesus in verse 4 when Jesus revealed the outcome of the miracle that would happen. Supernatural things always happen for Jesus because He is so confident that His Father always hears Him. These things He said so that people would believe in Him and also for the purpose of training the disciples how to work the miraculous.

11:44 Once the work was done, Jesus gave the responsibility of loosing Lazarus and letting him go to the people. Likewise, through our redemption, Jesus has already finished the work of raising up the body of Christ to a place of authority in the earth. It's up to us to loose and let people

⁴⁵Then many of the Jews who had come to Mary, and had seen the things Jesus did, believed in Him. ⁴⁶But some of them went away to the Pharisees and told them the things Jesus did. ⁴⁷Then the chief priests and the Pharisees gathered a council and said, "What shall we do? For this Man works many signs. ⁴⁸If we let Him alone like this, everyone will believe in Him, and the Romans will come and take away both our place and nation."

⁴⁹And one of them, Caiaphas, being high priest that year, said to them, "You know nothing at all, ⁵⁰nor do you consider that it is expedient for us that one man should die for the people, and not that the whole nation should perish." ⁵¹Now this he did not say on his own *authority;* but being high priest that year he prophesied that Jesus would die for the nation, ⁵²and not for that nation only, but also that He would gather together in one the children of God who were scattered abroad.

⁵³Then, from that day on, they plotted to put Him to death. ⁵⁴Therefore Jesus no longer walked openly among the Jews, but went from there into the country near the wilderness, to a city called Ephraim, and there remained with His disciples.

⁵⁵And the Passover of the Jews was near, and many went from the country up to Jerusalem before the Passover, to purify themselves. ⁵⁶Then they sought Jesus, and spoke among themselves as they stood in the temple, "What do you think—that He will not come to the feast?" ⁵⁷Now both the chief priests and the Pharisees had given a command, that if anyone knew where He was, he should report *it,* that they might seize Him.

---

go from the bondages that have been destroyed by Jesus's finished work.

11:47-48 When you do the works of our Lord, you will be ostracized by the religious. The light and power of the Lord revealed through signs and wonders will expose the unbelief in those who pretend to know something.

JOHN 11 KEY WORDS

✍ **Light** (*phos* φῶς NT: 5457) Quantum physics has discovered what Scripture has revealed since the beginning. The basic building block of the universe is light. All matter is energy and all energy derives from light. The source of all light is God (1 John 1:5) and His light dispels all darkness, sin, and death. Light and darkness cannot occupy the same space at the same time. Hence, whenever *phos* appears, darkness must flee. Jesus as the light of the world overcomes all darkness and sin and gives us direction and power to live abundantly (John 10:10). Jesus teaches in John 11 that God's light indwells a believer. That indwelling light which He gives keeps the believer from stumbling in sin.

✍ **Life** (*zoe* ζωὴ NT: 2222) Life is more than physical existence. After physical birth, we must be born of the Spirit (John 3) through faith in Christ so that we have life both abundantly (John 10:10) and forever (John 6:51, 58). The only source of *zoe* is Jesus (see John 14:6). Life is the very nature and power given

by the living God through faith in His Son, Jesus, to experience the supernatural and the miraculous every day.

In John 11, Jesus identified Himself as the source of eternal life. Martha acknowledged that life comes from Him. Jesus makes us alive. Death is overcome in us by His life.

✍ **Resurrection** or **Rise Again** (*anastasis* ἀνάστασις NT: 386) Literally to stand up again or rise up from the dead. The Pharisees believed in the resurrection of the righteous but the Sadducees denied it. Jesus not only affirmed the resurrection of the dead, He declared that He is the source of life that will enter the dead and raise them up to new life (*zoe*) through Him. Without Christ and His resurrection, there is no hope of our resurrection (1 Corinthians 15).

✍ **Comfort** (*paramutheomai* παραμυθέομαι NT: 3888) To cause someone to be consoled; to encourage those who are losing heart. Jesus was filled with compassion for those who are sick, bound by sin, poor, oppressed, and grieving. Compassion moved Him to go beyond comfort to the miraculous in raising Lazarus from the dead.

JOHN 11 SUMMARY

The attention of chapter 11 is focused upon Jesus raising Lazarus from the dead. This alone is a tremendous thought: the raising of a human being from the dead. Jesus was so confident about His ability to conquer death that He commissioned the disciples to also raise the dead. The renewing of our minds to the thoughts of Jesus is the purpose of these commentaries. If you would never consider the thought that God would use you to work the miraculous in this area then you can be sure that you won't.

> *The renewing of our minds to the thoughts of Jesus is the purpose of these commentaries.*

On the other hand, when Jesus heard that Lazarus was sick, He declared that this sickness was not unto death, but that the Son of God would be glorified through it. The word "glorified" is past tense, so Jesus must be planning on working with the glory in order to be glorified through this situation.

The first miracle that Jesus publicly worked at the wedding feast of Cana was done so that His glory would be manifested, so His disciples would believe. When glory touches even the dead, they will rise. This must be true, for our existence in heaven is indebted to the glory of God raising the church to heaven.

Many things Jesus did were way beyond where the people were. It was difficult for them to understand the significance of the miracles, yet they certainly enjoyed the benefits. When Martha met Jesus, she spoke words of honor to Jesus whom she believed to be the answer to her brother's death. As close as she was to Jesus, Martha still had trouble seeing her brother rise again. We may, like Martha, believe that indeed Jesus is the Christ, the Son of God, yet what does this mean to our present circumstances?

When it comes right down to

it, is Jesus our comfort blanket who makes us feel a little better about the struggle we are going through? Or is Jesus the Christ actually the remedy to every problem and the solution to all the riddles in our lives?

When Jesus was about to raise Lazarus, He told Martha that if she would believe she would see the glory. Jesus wasn't talking about seeing a cloud or a bright light. He was saying that when the glory is working, we will see physical evidence to the power of God. Believing God is only difficult to our minds that live by the senses. Believing God is the most sensible thing we could do once our minds have been renewed by the Word of God. If heaven and earth could pass away, yet the Word of God will never pass away, then it would be ridiculous to consider anything but the words of God.

Notice that Jesus prayed a prayer before raising Lazarus. This may seem uncustomary, because this wasn't Jesus's practice. When it came time to deliver, Jesus just worked with the anointing to produce results. Why did He pray this time? Jesus told us that it was for those standing around, that they might believe that He was indeed the Son of God. The words that Jesus

used are wonderful: "Father, I thank You that You have heard Me." In 1 John 5:14-15, John recorded that it is extremely significant that we know that God hears us when we pray: "Now this is the confidence that we have in Him, that if we ask anything according to His will, He hears us. And if we know that He hears us, whatever we ask, we know that we have the petitions that we have asked of Him."

When we pray according to the will of God, God hears us.

Our confidence is in the power of a Christian to pray according to the will of God. Of course we will receive if our prayers are already God's will. God's will is the written Word of God that was given to us to establish us in the thoughts of God. When we pray according to the will of God, God hears us. Notice that we need to know that God hears us. Many pray prayers that God hears and answers; yet because they don't know that God hears them when they pray, they look to the natural to see if anything is happening. We must first know that God hears us when we pray. Jesus spoke this very revelation to the hearing of those present. He obviously was certain that the Father was attentive to His prayers.

Knowing that He hears you is the same thing as knowing that you have the answer.

The certainty of knowing that God hears you is praying in line with His Word. Knowing that He hears you is the same thing as knowing that you have the answer. Believing is responding as though the thing you desire is already in your possession.

Faith brings heaven's realities into view. Nothing in the world can stop the invisible from becoming visible when a person believes God. Jesus raised Lazarus from the dead to prove this fact. Answers are waiting on us. Knowing that we possess the answer is why our faith is so excited to respond to the supernatural.

MEDITATIONS FOR SUCCESS

- When problems arise, release your words toward the end result. The power of life and death is in the tongue.
- Know in your heart that God's power is enough for your contest.
- The glory is all around us; believe that you can touch it by faith.
- Pray the will of God.
- God will hear you.
- Knowing that God hears you is the confidence to know that you have the answer.
- Faith always rejoices in the result even if it temporarily remains unseen.
- We must conquer these lessons of faith; there is a whole world that needs to be loosed and released into the life and resurrection power of God through Christ.

CHAPTER 12

¹Then, six days before the Passover, Jesus came to Bethany, where Lazarus was who had been dead, whom He had raised from the dead. ²There they made Him a supper; and Martha served, but Lazarus was one of those who sat at the table with Him. ³Then Mary took a pound of very costly oil of spikenard, anointed the feet of Jesus, and wiped His feet with her hair. And the house was filled with the fragrance of the oil.

⁴But one of His disciples, Judas Iscariot, Simon's *son,* who would betray Him, said, ⁵"Why was this fragrant oil not sold for three hundred denarii and given to the poor?" ⁶This he said, not that he cared for the poor, but because he was a thief, and had the money box; and he used to take what was put in it.

⁷But Jesus said, "Let her alone; she has kept this for the day of My burial. ⁸For the poor you have with you always, but Me you do not have always."

⁹Now a great many of the Jews knew that He was there; and they came, not for Jesus' sake only, but that they might also see Lazarus, whom He had raised from the dead. ¹⁰But the chief priests plotted to put Lazarus to death also, ¹¹because on account of him many of the Jews went away and believed in Jesus.

¹²The next day a great multitude that had come to the feast, when

---

12:1-8 This pound of spikenard was one year's wages worth of oil. Mary's act not only showed the value she placed on the Lord, but it also became a prophetic symbol of the death and burial of the Lord. Jesus was not devaluing the necessity of reaching out to the poor; He was however emphasizing the importance of His time and purpose. Our relationship with Jesus is worth all that life can offer. There is no price too great for our commitment to serve the Lord.

12:9-11 Notice that a great many people were interested in Jesus because of the miracle performed on Lazarus. Never forget the importance of signs and wonders. Jesus said that these all-important signs would follow the believer. As you can see, great crowds will follow the signs.

12:12-19 When Jesus rode into Jerusalem on the donkey, He was fulfilling Scripture concerning His place as the Messiah. There was great excitement because the Jews desired greatly to

they heard that Jesus was coming to Jerusalem, [13]took branches of palm trees and went out to meet Him, and cried out:

"Hosanna!

'Blessed is *He who comes in the name of the LORD!*'

The King of Israel!"

[14]Then Jesus, when He had found a young donkey, sat on it; as it is written:

[15] *"Fear not, daughter of Zion; Behold, your King is coming, Sitting on a donkey's colt."*

[16]His disciples did not understand these things at first; but when Jesus was glorified, then they remembered that these things were written about Him and *that* they had done these things to Him.

[17]Therefore the people, who were with Him when He called Lazarus out of his tomb and raised him from the dead, bore witness. [18]For this reason the people also met Him, because they heard that He had done this sign. [19]The Pharisees therefore said among themselves, "You see that you are accomplishing nothing. Look, the world has gone after Him!"

[20]Now there were certain Greeks among those who came up to worship at the feast. [21]Then they came to Philip, who was from Bethsaida of Galilee, and asked him, saying, "Sir, we wish to see Jesus."

[22]Philip came and told Andrew, and in turn Andrew and Philip told Jesus.

[23]But Jesus answered them, saying, "The hour has come that the Son of Man should be glorified. [24]Most assuredly, I say to you, unless a grain of wheat falls into the ground and dies, it remains alone; but if it dies, it

---

experience freedom from the Roman rule. They mistakenly viewed this entry as the possible earthly kingdom reserved for Christ's second coming. God has always known the sequence to the events of your life that will last forever.

Receive now your liberty in Christ and begin by faith to walk in the supernatural.

12:23 Notice that Jesus didn't say the Son of God should be glorified, but the Son of Man. A man would redeem mankind from their horrible plight of sin. This was only possible because Jesus was a spotless Lamb, free from the nature of sin.

12:24 Jesus was alluding to Himself as the grain that must die in order for that grain to multiply. Paul said in 1 Corinthians 2:8 that if the devil knew what he was

produces much grain. ²⁵He who loves his life will lose it, and he who hates his life in this world will keep it for eternal life. ²⁶If anyone serves Me, let him follow Me; and where I am, there My servant will be also. If anyone serves Me, him *My* Father will honor.

²⁷"Now My soul is troubled, and what shall I say? 'Father, save Me from this hour'? But for this purpose I came to this hour. ²⁸Father, glorify Your name." Then a voice came from heaven, *saying,* "I have both glorified *it* and will glorify *it* again."

²⁹Therefore the people who stood by and heard *it* said that it had thundered. Others said, "An angel has spoken to Him."

³⁰Jesus answered and said, "This voice did not come because of Me, but for your sake. ³¹Now is the judgment of this world; now the ruler of this world will be cast out. ³²And I, if I am lifted up from the earth, will draw all *peoples* to Myself." ³³This He said, signifying by what death He would die.

³⁴The people answered Him, "We have heard from the law that the Christ remains forever; and how *can* You say, 'The Son of Man must be lifted up'? Who is this Son of Man?"

³⁵Then Jesus said to them, "A little while longer the light is with you. Walk while you have the light, lest darkness overtake you; he who walks in darkness does

---

doing when he influenced the Jewish and Roman leaders to crucify the Lord of glory, he never would have done it. The reason is extremely wonderful: out of death God would raise up a whole nation of those just like Jesus, called Christians. God's plan all along was to produce children like you who would walk in the light of His life.

12:25-26 You don't have to die in order to follow Jesus. However, you must lose sight of yourself in light of His glory. Our foremost thoughts must be to serve Him wholeheartedly without reservation.

12:27 There may be times when your flesh speaks loudly to resist the will of God

for your life. Keep yourself focused on your purpose. God's will satisfies even the most perplexed soul. The rewards of honoring God will be seen in this lifetime and in the one to come.

12:30 God will do supernatural things through you for the benefit of others. Always highly respect and magnify God for the supernatural in your life, He desires to use you greatly for the good of others.

12:32 Jesus revealed how He must die—through crucifixion. Without this single most important sacrificial act, the whole earth would be without a salvation that they so desperately need.

12:35-36 Believer, take advantage of the

not know where he is going.
³⁶While you have the light,
believe in the light, that you may
become sons of light." These
things Jesus spoke, and departed,
and was hidden from them.

³⁷But although He had done so
many signs before them, they did
not believe in Him, ³⁸that the
word of Isaiah the prophet might
be fulfilled, which he spoke:

*"Lord, who has believed our
report?*
*And to whom has the arm of the
Lord been revealed?"*

³⁹Therefore they could not
believe, because Isaiah said again:

⁴⁰*"He has blinded their eyes and
hardened their hearts,*
Lest they should see with their eyes,
*Lest they should understand with
their hearts and turn,*
So that I should heal them."

⁴¹These things Isaiah said when
he saw His glory and spoke of Him.

⁴²Nevertheless even among the
rulers many believed in Him, but
because of the Pharisees they did
not confess *Him,* lest they should
be put out of the synagogue; ⁴³for
they loved the praise of men more
than the praise of God.

⁴⁴Then Jesus cried out and said,
"He who believes in Me, believes
not in Me but in Him who sent
Me. ⁴⁵And he who sees Me sees
Him who sent Me. ⁴⁶I have come
as a light into the world, that
whoever believes in Me should
not abide in darkness. ⁴⁷And if

---

times in your life when your heart is tender towards the Lord. The light is shining; walk in the light while you have opportunity. Don't put off until tomorrow what must be done today.

The light is shining; walk in the light while you have opportunity.

12:37-41 Isaiah foresaw the Lord in His glory lifted up where the world should have believed in Him, and yet there were so many who refused to believe. Thankfully our eyes have been opened,

our ears do hear and our hearts are receptive to all that the Lord has in store. The devil will use religion to harden the hearts of those who would naturally accept the Lord. It is the Word of God preached that enlightens the world to the truth

12:42-43 It is possible to believe in a truth and yet remain immovable. Faith without works or corresponding actions is unprofitable. A great key to spiritual success is to immediately respond to the light. When He speaks truth to you, then you must act. Don't delay lest that truth be stolen from you.

12:45 To behold Jesus is to behold the Father. Our responsibility is to imitate Jesus exactly as He portrayed the Father. If anyone hears My words and does not believe, I do not judge him; for I did not come to judge the world but to save the world. [48]He who rejects Me, and does not receive My words, has that which judges him—the word that I have spoken will judge him in the last day. [49]For I have not spoken on My own *authority;* but the Father who sent Me gave Me a command, what I should say and what I should speak. [50]And I know that His command is everlasting life. Therefore, whatever I speak, just as the Father has told Me, so I speak."

Jesus is alive, and He is, then the world is entitled to see the results of a risen Savior. **12:48** Paul said in Hebrews 4:12 that the Word of God is living and powerful. Jesus reveals the same thought when He says that the Word is the tool of judgment. To receive it is to escape judgment; rejecting it will cause the power of its truth to eventually judge you. If God places this much weight on the power of the Word, then we would be wise to value each nugget of truth worth its weight in gold.

12:49-50 Jesus showed the ultimate commitment to His Father's principles. Without adding to or taking away from, Jesus relied on every word that proceeded from His Father's lips as eternal and authoritative. To stray from the words of God would be to stray from Him. He is one and the same with His Word. The Word of God is for you personally and it is up to date with society. To act on it and value it as your source of success is to live continually in the anointing of God.

JOHN 12 KEY WORDS

✒ **Very Precious** or **Very Costly** (*polus* πολύς NT: 4183) Abundant; of great cost or price. Mary uses a very pricey ointment to anoint Jesus. The odor of her offering filled the house so that all knew what she had given. Read Song of Solomon 1:12.

The composition of this ointment (spikenard) is given by Dioscorides in 1, 77, Περὶ ναρδίνου μύρου, where it is described as being made with nut oil, and having as ingredients malabathrum, schoenus, costus, amomum, nardus, myrrha, and balsamum— almost all the most valued perfumes of antiquity. It was also a valuable article in ancient pharmacy.

✏️ **King** (*basileus* βασιλεύς NT: 935) The crowd praised Jesus as king of the Jews. They were looking for an earthly king who would drive out the hated Roman rule. However, Jesus came as a heavenly king who would reign in the hearts of men. This spiritual kingdom was difficult for the Jews and Jesus's disciples to understand until after God raised Christ from the dead thus demonstrating in power that Jesus was the King of kings.

✏️ **Lose Life** (*psuche*=soul) (*apollumi* ἀπόλλυμαι NT: 622) To lose, to cease to exist or perish in a spiritual sense. In other words, Jesus taught that to lose one's self, self-centeredness, and soulish pride was to die to self and gain true life (*zoe*). Holding on to earthly existence dooms one to destruction. Giving up earthly gain opens one up to receive the life of the Spirit which lasts forever.

✏️ **Love Life** (*phileo* φιλέω NT: 5368) Jesus uses the Greek word for love (*phileo*) which means brotherly love or friendship-based love. Love based on relationships of affection but not unconditional love which is *agape*. Life in this text (John 12:25) refers to soulish existence (*psuche*) not eternal life from God. If we hold onto physical affections instead of loving God fully, we will not enter into the fullness of life (*zoe*) that God has for us in Christ Jesus.

✏️ **Serve** (*diakoneo* διακονέω NT: 1247) To serve or minister is the same word used for *deacon*. When we serve or minister to Christ, we make His will and desires our own instead of serving out of selfish motives. All ministry is done in service to Him not out of our own agendas and needs.

JOHN 12 SUMMARY

Jesus said in verse 23 that the hour had come for His glorification. He was talking about His death, burial, and resurrection. An interesting truth concerning the resurrection is that Jesus died and rose again as our substitute. Therefore, we are identified in His death, burial, and resurrection. Positionally in Christ, we have been glorified with Him and raised up to sit together with Him in heavenly places (Ephesians 2:4-10).

The same glory that raised Jesus is upon us at this moment to work the works of God and magnify His name. This is what Paul meant in the book of Ephesians when he revealed to the Ephesians that he was praying that they might have their eyes open to understand the magnitude of the power that raised Jesus from the dead. It is this power that is toward us, available to enforce the victory of the Lord.

We must not forget that what Jesus did and obtained, was for us to walk in as though we were the ones who purchased it. Identification simply means one

and the same. What He did for us has been appropriated to us. His victory is our victory. Glory to God!

Jesus revealed that the heart attitude and the priorities of one's life will dictate the success that he or she will experience.

There is no need to seek riches and fame when knowing God is paramount to fulfillment in life.

There is no need to seek riches and fame when knowing God is paramount to fulfillment in life. Jeremiah 9:23-24 declares,

> *Thus says the LORD:*
> *"Let not the wise man glory in*
> *his wisdom,*
> *Let not the mighty man glory*
> *in his might,*
> *Nor let the rich man glory in*
> *his riches;*
> *But let him who glories glory in*
> *this,*
> *That he understands and*
> *knows Me,*
> *That I am the LORD, exercising*
> *lovingkindness, judgment,*
> *and righteousness in the earth.*

For in these I delight," says the LORD.

Let me encourage you again; there is nothing so important as your relationship with the Lord. Many times the Lord spoke of Himself as the light of the world. With darkness all around us, there is no question as to the seriousness of knowing and following the light. Every step out of the light is a step in rejection of the goodness of God. Some follow the darkness out of ignorance, but others do so willingly. Walking in the light is how you fellowship with the anointing. The Holy Spirit is always light! If you want spiritual aid, then get in the light and stay there. Walking in the power of the Word of God and staying in communion with the Lord is walking in the light. Proper priorities will keep you in the light. Even Jesus said that He only spoke the words that He heard

His Father speak. No other words have eternal life. This is our passion—to understand and know God. That He is the Lord, exercising lovingkindness, judgment, and righteousness in the earth.

MEDITATIONS FOR SUCCESS

• Your hour of glory is here. Act like the glory that Jesus used is available to you also.
• Are your priorities straight? Is the Lord first place in your life? The time you spend with Him will give you your answer.
• All the riches and blessings will overtake you as you gain dependence in God.
• Jesus is the light of the world. Through our union with Him we have become the lights in the world. Let your light shine, at home, on the job, with family, on the street, and in your personal relationship with the Master.

CHAPTER 13

¹Now before the Feast of the Passover, when Jesus knew that His hour had come that He should depart from this world to the Father, having loved His own who were in the world, He loved them to the end.

²And supper being ended, the devil having already put it into the heart of Judas Iscariot, Simon's *son,* to betray Him, ³Jesus, knowing that the Father had given all things into His hands, and that He had come from God and was going to God, ⁴rose from supper and laid aside

---

13:1-2 In John 13-17 we have recorded the last words of Jesus before His death. These words are very focused on relationship. Jesus had a thorough understanding of the Word and commission of His Father and still, He emphasized so strongly the development of relationship. Without the time that He spent in the presence of His Father, there would be no continuity to the purpose of His commission. Knowledge of the Father is revealed in the Word; but intimacy with the Father comes from much time in worship and prayer empowered by the Holy Spirit. Your knowledge of the Word of God lays the foundation for your relationship with the Father. In truth, the study of the Scriptures instructs and inspires your relationship with God.

> *Knowledge of the Father is revealed in the Word; but intimacy with the Father comes from much time in worship and prayer empowered by the Holy Spirit.*

13:3 This verse gives the believer backbone to do the will of God no matter what the circumstances. Jesus knew where He had come from; He was in the world, but not of the world. Jesus had a tremendous advantage for living on the earth since the supernatural realm He came from had greater laws and power than the natural realm He resided in. Jesus knew that all things had been given into His hands, which means that He was in control of the steps that He would willingly take. No one had any power to hinder the destined outcome except Jesus Himself. Jesus even stood before Pilate and said that he had no power unless it had been given from above. This is a very secure platform. Jesus also knew where He was going. If those in Satan's kingdom believe that they are going to a wonderful afterlife and therefore willingly sacrifice their lives for their cause, then what about the Christian who knows the truth concerning eternal life? Shouldn't we above all be persistent concerning our cause to spread the gospel of the Lord Jesus Christ who willingly sacrificed His life for ours?

13:4-17 The apostle Paul said in Philippians 2:5-7 that Jesus, being in the

His garments, took a towel and girded Himself. ⁵After that, He poured water into a basin and began to wash the disciples' feet, and to wipe *them* with the towel with which He was girded. ⁶Then He came to Simon Peter. And *Peter* said to Him, "Lord, are You washing my feet?"

⁷Jesus answered and said to him, "What I am doing you do not understand now, but you will know after this."

⁸Peter said to Him, "You shall never wash my feet!" Jesus answered him, "If I do not wash you, you have no part with Me."

⁹Simon Peter said to Him, "Lord, not my feet only, but also *my* hands and *my* head!"

¹⁰Jesus said to him, "He who is bathed needs only to wash *his* feet, but is completely clean; and you are clean, but not all of you."

¹¹For He knew who would betray Him; therefore He said, "You are not all clean."

¹²So when He had washed their feet, taken His garments, and sat down again, He said to them, "Do you know what I have done to you? ¹³You call Me Teacher and Lord, and you say well, for *so* I am. ¹⁴If I then, *your* Lord and Teacher, have washed your feet, you also ought to wash one another's feet. ¹⁵For I have given you an example, that you should do as I have done to you. ¹⁶Most assuredly, I say to you, a servant is not greater than his master; nor is he who is sent greater than he who sent him. ¹⁷If you know these things, blessed are you if you do them.

¹⁸"I do not speak concerning all of you. I know whom I have chosen; but that the Scripture may be fulfilled, *'He who eats bread with Me has lifted up his*

---

form of God, humbled Himself and came in the form of a servant by coming in the likeness of men. The ultimate lesson being displayed by our Lord to His disciples was that servanthood is godly leadership. To possess great ability, authority, and power comes with the price of stewardship. Learning to value others above yourself is a primary principle of love. God loved the world and gave the best He had. We must also see our place in this world as a privilege to honor God by serving those we have contact with.

So much of our Christian world is wrapped up in selfishness and greed. The longing to be the best and have the most has taken a toll on God's people. We should be aware that it was Satan who desired to have what was not given and be what he was not. One of the greatest needs in the pulpits today is for ministers to understand their identity in Christ. So

heel against Me.' ¹⁹Now I tell you before it comes, that when it does come to pass, you may believe that I am *He.* ²⁰Most assuredly, I say to you, he who receives whomever I send receives Me; and he who receives Me receives Him who sent Me."

²¹When Jesus had said these things, He was troubled in spirit, and testified and said, "Most assuredly, I say to you, one of you will betray Me." ²²Then the disciples looked at one another, perplexed about whom He spoke.

²³Now there was leaning on Jesus' bosom one of His disciples, whom Jesus loved. ²⁴Simon Peter therefore motioned to him to ask who it was of whom He spoke.

²⁵Then, leaning back on Jesus' breast, he said to Him, "Lord, who is it?"

²⁶Jesus answered, "It is he to whom I shall give a piece of bread when I have dipped *it.*" And having dipped the bread, He gave *it* to Judas Iscariot, *the son* of Simon. ²⁷Now after the piece of bread, Satan entered him. Then Jesus said to him, "What you do, do quickly." ²⁸But no one at the table knew for what reason He said this to him. ²⁹For some thought, because Judas had the money box, that Jesus had said to him, "Buy *those things* we need for the feast," or that he should give something to the poor.

³⁰Having received the piece of bread, he then went out immediately. And it was night.

³¹So, when he had gone out, Jesus said, "Now the Son of Man is glorified, and God is glorified in Him. ³²If God is glorified in

---

much insecurity exists in those who have been suppressed and belittled. We as leaders must learn the value of those with whom we are surrounded. Instead of judging one another, we must empower people to become all that they can be. Our service is to minister confidence and support to them so they can excel.

13:27 Satan didn't suddenly barge into Judas's life and enter him without permission. This ultimate betrayal was in motion for many months if not years. The strength of Jesus's commitment to follow the course of God began many years before

He ever confronted His ultimate destiny. Beware that certain practices that may seem small at the moment can ultimately set you up for a great fall later. It is important to live each day pleasing God each step of the way.

13:31-38 Isn't it interesting to see the insight of the Lord in the lives of those who traveled with Him? He knew ahead of time their shortcomings and yet loved them regardless. Paul said in Romans 5:8 that while we were yet sinners, Christ died for us. God desires for us to understand His unconditional love. There are no

Him, God will also glorify Him in Himself, and glorify Him immediately. ³³Little children, I shall be with you a little while longer. You will seek Me; and as I said to the Jews, 'Where I am going, you cannot come,' so now I say to you. ³⁴A new commandment I give to you, that you love one another; as I have loved you, that you also love one another. ³⁵By this all will know that you are My disciples, if you have love for one another."

³⁶Simon Peter said to Him, "Lord, where are You going?" Jesus answered him, "Where I am going you cannot follow Me now, but you shall follow Me afterward."

³⁷Peter said to Him, "Lord, why can I not follow You now? I will lay down my life for Your sake."

³⁸Jesus answered him, "Will you lay down your life for My sake? Most assuredly, I say to you, the rooster shall not crow till you have denied Me three times."

---

strings attached; God's love goes beyond your sin, straight to your heart.

God desires for us to understand His unconditional love.

You will be able to see yourself through the eyes of God's love and not through the condemning eyes of judgment.

13:31-32 Jesus was glorified as a man. It was the Son of Man who glorified the Father that in turn allows the Father to glorify the Son of Man in Himself. This revelation is the central focus of the ministry of our Lord. To create in Himself a new nation of people who would be glorified in Him. God took two, Jesus and you, and made one single being. This new creation exists fully and completely in God. This is the great mystery of the church, Christ in you, the hope of glory.

The last statements in life which a person makes are usually very important. Endeavoring to prepare the disciples for His departure, Jesus revealed to His disciples the secret of the kingdom as Jesus Himself had demonstrated: to love one another as you love yourself.

Even when Jesus in the flesh is not present, it will be possible to follow Him wholly through the guidance of the Holy Spirit.

13:36 With such great wisdom revealed in the new commandment, Peter got hung up with the place Jesus was going where we cannot come. Jesus's response foretold the disciples of the work of the Holy Spirit who would come in Jesus's place to make a home in their hearts. Even when Jesus in the flesh is not present, it will be possible to follow Him wholly through guidance of the Holy Spirit.

JOHN 13 KEY WORDS

Clean (*katharos* καθαρός NT: 2513) To be pure. This cleanness goes beyond physical hygiene. It refers to clean or pure in the eyes of God. Paul said in Romans 1:4 that Jesus was the Son of God with power according to the Spirit of holiness. His shed blood cleanses us from all sin. In John 15:3, Jesus teaches that His Word cleanses. God desires for us to have clean and pure hearts and consciences (1 Timothy 1:5; 2 Timothy 2:22).

Servant (*doulos* δοῦλος NT: 1401) *Doulos* literally means "slave." Paul uses this word to describe His calling and relationship with Christ. A servant willingly submits himself to another so that the needs of that person can be met. We are set free from bondage to sin and death to become the willing servants of Christ. We serve others as He has served us. (Read Philippians 2.) Jesus sets the example of servanthood in John 13 by washing feet—a dirty, humbling task usually reserved for menial servants without social status.

Blessed (*makarios* μακάριος NT: 3107) "Blessed" is the same word that Jesus used in the Beatitudes to describe the qualities of the Christian life. Literally referring to being happy or enjoying favor, *makarios* refers to a state of being or an attitude or orientation toward life which recognizes that intimacy with the Father is the source of all joy and happiness. Being blessed isn't an emotion or feeling; rather, it's an inner work of the indwelling Spirit of God. Every blessing of the Lord is joyful and full of victory.

Receive (*lambano* λαμβάνω NT: 2983) *Lambano* is not to passively get something. Rather, receiving is "to grasp, to take hold of" something with assertiveness. When one receives from God, that person has literally grabbed that which God offers and refuses to relinquish it. Receiving those who come in the name of the Lord is also receiving Christ.

Glory (*doxa* δόξα NT: 1391) It is appropriate to first mention the Old Testament use of the word glory (*kabod* כָּבוֹד OT: 3519) which refers to the outer garment, weight, or covering of splendor and light. God's iridescent light and the profound weight of His presence is His glory. God's glory is resident in Jesus (John 1:14) and once we trust Him, His glory is transforming us (2 Corinthians 3:18).

Doxa refers to the supernatural power of God that deserves one's respect and honor. *Doxa* is the excellence and majesty of God that demands our praise. So when Jesus does a miracle, it's a sign pointing to the majesty, honor, and excellence of God that has been revealed so that persons might give Him praise. Glory brings to light God's presence and power which dispel all darkness—sin, sickness, and bondage. In the presence of His glory, all that is not of His glorious nature must flee (Psalm 104:31-35). Jesus spoke of being glorified with the glory of the Father for the sacrifice He is making.

As the Son of Man, Jesus was glorified because He did the will of the Father. In the same way, God is glorified in our lives when we do His will.

Love (*agapao* ἀγαπάω NT: 25) God's unconditional love in giving His Son, Jesus, could not be merited or earned. Rather, God's nature is love (1 John 4:7-8). God initiated a loving relationship for us to enter into by faith or trust in Jesus. His love neither judges nor condemns. *Apape* accepts the believer as he is and begins to transform the believer into who Christ is. Jesus commands us to love (*agapao*) others with the Father's love. When the world sees such love in us, they will know that we follow Jesus and will be attracted to the Father's love as well.

JOHN 13 SUMMARY

Jesus displayed the heart of a servant prior to His departure. We are commanded to love God with all our heart, soul, and mind and to love one another. The only debt that we have to pay in the New Testament is to love one another. Whether or not we want to do this does not lessen the demand of this command. We must love one another and seek to serve one another as Jesus demonstrated in chapter 13.

It was difficult for the disciples to allow Jesus to wash their feet. It is very humbling to be served in such a way by someone you highly respect and honor. Jesus clearly paved the way for all to see the heart of the Father.

> **Jesus clearly paved the way for all to see the heart of the Father.**

There is a real need in the body of Christ for its followers to exhibit the true love of God. For so many, the emphasis of Christian living has been solely placed on the power of God. However, the fruit of the Spirit is just as necessary an ingredient for complete service for the Lord as is the power of God. The balance would be split down the middle. While we concern ourselves with service toward one another and the love of God for the world, we are actively stirring up the gifts within us that display the power of God.

From this point on in the gospel of John, Jesus, through His teaching, was preparing His disciples for His departure. He continued to point out the new commandment, which is to love one another. Even though the disciples didn't understand, Jesus alluded to the time when He would be gone and they will have to follow Him through a different means. Jesus was referring to being led by the Holy Spirit as all of us as believers experience in the new covenant.

MEDITATIONS FOR SUCCESS

- The commandment of the New Testament is a pleasure to fulfill. We must love God with all our hearts and love one another.
- The Old Testament law was a bondage to all followers. The New Testament law of love is liberating.
- Every believer must enforce his or her duty to serve and honor one another.
- God is love. Our faith works through love. Our highest call is to love the world with the life-changing message of Jesus Christ.

CHAPTER 14

¹"Let not your heart be troubled; you believe in God, believe also in Me. ²In My Father's house are many mansions; if *it were* not *so,* I would have told you. I go to prepare a place for you. ³And if I go and prepare a place for you, I will come again and receive you to Myself; that where I am, *there* you may be also. ⁴And where I go you know, and the way you know."

⁵Thomas said to Him, "Lord, we do not know where You are going, and how can we know the way?"

⁶Jesus said to him, "I am the way, the truth, and the life. No one comes to the Father except through Me.

14:1 God is always interested in your heart. Here Jesus encouraged His disciples to believe in Him even though their hearts may be filled with anxiety and concern. It is a benefit for God as well as for you if your heart is trusting and confident versus full of anxiety and fear. Faith is a by-product of the heart.

Faith is a by-product of the heart.

14:2-3 God has made great preparation for His people in heaven. For Jesus, we the church are His bride. If resources are available, what husband would not provide the best of accommodations for his bride? God has been planning this great homecoming for a long time. We should be extremely secure in our glorious future.

14:4-6 When the Bible speaks emphatically to us about truth that we already know, we ought to embrace it instead of question it. Maybe God knows something about us that we need to know ourselves. Thomas did know the way, because Jesus was and is the way. There are things that our hearts know which become clouded by traditionalism and need to be revealed.

14:6 Jesus is the only way to God. Some secularists will fight to maintain the idea that every religion has a place in the world with God being the center of every thought. The fact remains that Jesus is God's answer to the need of the world. Think of the chaos if there were multiple ways to approach God. It is God's love to make salvation so simple through one and only one name, Jesus.

Also, Jesus is heaven's reality alert to the natural world. Everything that Jesus did and said is the absolute truth. Jesus brought heaven's truth to demons and they responded by coming out; He

7"If you had known Me, you would have known My Father also; and from now on you know Him and have seen Him."

8Philip said to Him, "Lord, show us the Father, and it is sufficient for us."

9Jesus said to him, "Have I been with you so long, and yet you have not known Me, Philip? He who has seen Me has seen the Father; so how can you say, 'Show us the Father'? 10Do you not believe that I am in the Father, and the Father in Me? The words that I speak to you I do not speak on My own *authority;* but the Father who dwells in Me does the works. 11Believe Me that I *am* in the Father and the Father in Me, or else believe Me for the sake of the works themselves.

12"Most assuredly, I say to you, he who believes in Me, the works that I do he will do also; and greater *works* than these he will

---

brought heaven's truth to sickness and disease and they responded by being healed. In every arena, Jesus proved that things that are seen are subject to the truth of the unseen world.

Lastly, Jesus is life personified. The cure for every ill is eternal life. Without life being the highest authority in the earth and heaven, death would continue to destroy the human heart. Thank God for the answer, life (*zoe*).

14:7-11 Jesus revealed a powerful truth that explains why He as a man was able to manifest the works of God.

> ***If union with God is a key to manifestations, then the church should be working with God regularly.***

The works display the presence and ability of God. The revelation of being made one with God is the key to working the works. Now, every believer has the potential of declaring that the Lord Jesus is one with them. If union with God is a key to manifestations, then the church should be working with God regularly.

14:12 What happens when you believe in Jesus? You become one with Him, flesh of His flesh and bone of His bone. Your spirit becomes one with Jesus, capable of duplicating everything that Jesus did and more. You fulfill your original design, "Be fruitful and multiply." Jesus starts this thought with covenant strength by saying, "Most assuredly." These words simply mean that it would be impossible for this saying to fail. From God's point of view, we are fully equipped to do the works of Jesus.

Notice that the word "believe" is mentioned only once, while the word "do" is mentioned three times. This would seem to suggest that the emphasis is on being a doer not just believing something. If our

do, because I go to My Father. ¹³And whatever you ask in My name, that I will do, that the Father may be glorified in the Son. ¹⁴If you ask anything in My name, I will do *it*.
¹⁵"If you love Me, keep My commandments. ¹⁶And I will pray the Father, and He will give you another Helper, that He may abide with you forever— ¹⁷the Spirit of truth, whom the world cannot receive, because it neither sees Him nor knows Him; but you know Him, for He dwells with you and will be in you.

---

belief means anything, then there would be actions to back it up. For Jesus to say this and it not be possible, would be lying. The lack of results that the church has produced thus far is no indication that the church is unable or ill-equipped to do the job. The ability, power, and wisdom are here; we need to do what we say we believe.

14:13-14 Immediately Jesus capitalized on telling the believers to do the works of God by revealing a sure way to initiate the work. The power of the name of Jesus in conjunction with prayer makes tremendous results possible. Using His name and the authority in that name, we can demand that demon forces, sickness, and anything else that would hinder, leave, and Jesus said He would personally make sure it happens. The original language suggests that Jesus was saying that if you ask for anything that He doesn't have, He will make it for you. The focus of Jesus's statement, which is in context from the last few verses, is to prepare your faith to believe that when you use His name (authority) you invite the Resurrected One in you to perform as He always has, this time through your physical body.

14:15-18 To make all this possible, the Father will give the Holy Spirit who will be everything that Jesus was and is to abide with us forever. He is called the Spirit of truth who will aid us in knowing and revealing the truths of heaven just as Jesus did.

The natural world will know that Jesus is alive through the work of the Holy Spirit in our lives.

In every situation of life, we have a Helper who will reveal the truth or reality of God that will benefit us. Some of the areas in which the Holy Spirit helps us come from the definition of the name, *Paraclete*: helper, guide, counselor, standby, strengthener, intercessor, and advocate. The days of not knowing what to do are over. The natural world will know that Jesus is alive through the work of the Holy Spirit in our lives.

14:17 Jesus said that we know the Spirit of truth. The Amplified Bible says that we "know and recognize Him." Regardless what your mind thinks at this moment, you do know and recognize the Holy Spirit. The more you talk about and meditate on

¹⁸I will not leave you orphans; I will come to you. ¹⁹"A little while longer and the world will see Me no more, but you will see Me. Because I live, you will live also. ²⁰At that day you will know that I *am* in My Father, and you in Me, and I in you. ²¹He who has My commandments and keeps them, it is he who loves Me. And he who loves Me will be loved by My Father, and I will love him and manifest Myself to him."

²²Judas (not Iscariot) said to Him, "Lord, how is it that You will manifest Yourself to us, and not to the world?" ²³Jesus answered and said to him, "If anyone loves Me, he will keep My word; and My Father will love him, and We will come to him and make Our home with him. ²⁴He who does not love Me does not keep My words; and the word which you hear is not Mine but the Father's who sent Me. ²⁵"These things I have spoken to

---

this truth, the bigger it becomes to your conscience. Then you will find the experiences with the Holy Spirit that will last for a lifetime.

14:18 Orphans have no parents to care for them. Everyone deserves to have good, loving parents who will care and nurture them. Jesus as the way to God the Father will provide access to a brand-new family. Our Father God has always desired a family as much as we desire to be loved as a child. This great love brought Jesus to the earth to purchase with His blood the title to a heavenly family.

14:19-21 Again, Jesus reveals that He will be going where the disciples cannot see Him, at least physically. Jesus does assure His disciples that though the world may not see Him, they will. Seeing Jesus is learning how to respond to the inner promptings of the Holy Spirit. We see Jesus in the Word of God, and we see

Him as we work with the Holy Spirit. Great deposits of God's attributes have been given at the new birth. Yielding to these benefits of God will show the Lord's presence. Our faith is the reason why Jesus is able to manifest Himself to us.

14:20 Think of the implications of being in Jesus and Jesus being in us. Through the new birth, we have become inseparable as one single spirit being. As much as Jesus is in us, we are in Him. If Jesus never failed, then this is our expectation for life. As victorious as it is to be in Christ we are also in the Father. Paul said in Colossians 3:3 that we are hidden in the very being of God. This would seem to indicate that if we were applying our faith, then everything that we do from the moment we are born again, would be influenced by God's supernatural presence and power. Wow!

14:22-24 Jesus explained how it is that

you while being present with you. ²⁶But the Helper, the Holy Spirit, whom the Father will send in My name, He will teach you all things, and bring to your remembrance all things that I said to you. ²⁷Peace I leave with you, My peace I give to you; not as the world gives do I give to you. Let not your heart be troubled, neither let it be afraid. ²⁸You have heard Me say to you, 'I am going away and coming *back* to you.' If you loved Me, you would rejoice because I said, 'I am going to the Father,' for My Father is greater than I. ²⁹"And now I have told you before it comes, that when it does come to pass, you may believe. ³⁰I will no longer talk much with you, for the ruler of this world is coming, and he has nothing in Me. ³¹But that the world may know that I love the Father, and as the Father gave Me commandment, so I do. Arise, let us go from here.

He will be manifest to them. Acting on God's Word will always bring the manifest presence of God into view.

Acting on God's Word will always bring the manifest presence of God into view.

14:26 The knowledge of the work of the Holy Spirit will cause our faith to produce the work. The disciples were eyewitnesses of the life and ministry of Jesus. When Jesus commanded the disciples to carry on His ministry, it was the promise of the Holy Spirit's work which gave them confidence. Relying on the Spirit's inspiration and presence will always produce revelation and great vision for our future. Even as the disciples experienced—we also should expect the Holy Spirit to work with us in the supernatural.

14:27-29 When God is present there will always be peace. When you walk without peace you have just missed God's provision of peace for you. Back up to where the peace of God was ruling and follow your heart at that point. Jesus never entered an environment without changing it and bringing peace. This is what God's peace will do for you.

14:29 Jesus shared with the disciples the reason why He spoke so thoroughly. He knew it would take faith for them to walk with the Holy Spirit and thereby bring the same lasting results to the earth. If for any reason someone imagines that their experiences will be difficult, faith will almost certainly be absent. The way we see a situation will determine how we use our faith.

14:30 Even in death Jesus triumphed. Satan never had anything on Jesus and for this reason, through our redemptive rights, Satan has nothing on us either. When Jesus said that all power and authority had been given to Him, He meant *all*.

JOHN 14 KEY WORDS

Troubled (*tarasso* ταράσσω NT: 5015) To be distressed both emotionally and mentally. Being troubled means that we lack inner calm and peace that only Jesus brings. Just as He calmed the storm on the Sea of Galilee, Jesus also calms inner storms. When we lack direction or destination in life, we feel confused, lost, anxious, and troubled. But when we have His peace, all the emotional storms of doubt and fear melt away.

Believe (*pisteuo* πιστεύω NT: 4100) To believe or have faith (*pisteuo*) involves complete trust in Jesus. Trust surrenders self-reliance and has total faith in His ability to work in and through us as He desires. Trusting Jesus is active faith that lays ultimate claim to eternal life through Him.

Way (*hodos* ὁδός NT: 3598) Figuratively, *hodos* means a way of life; a lifestyle; a direction, path, or course that one walks. It also implies the purpose of life. Jesus affirms that He is "the" way. No other way exists for entering the kingdom of God and to be saved (Acts 16:17).

Truth (*aletheia* ἀλήθεια NT: 225) That which really is and really happens in time and eternity is true. The Old Testament word for truth (*'amet*) literally speaks of absolute consistency between the inner and outward man. Truth refers to complete integrity, openness, and transparency. Through Christ all truth about ourselves is revealed. Through Jesus, every truth we need for living life abundantly is available.

Life (*zoe* ζωὴ NT: 2222) Life is more than physical existence. After physical birth, we must be born of the Spirit (John 3) through faith in Christ so that we have life both abundantly (John 10:10) and forever (John 6:51, 58). The only source of *zoe* is Jesus (John 14:6). Life is the very nature and power given by the living God through faith in His Son, Jesus, to experience the supernatural and the miraculous every day. The only way to know or experience true life is through Jesus.

Spirit (wind) (*pneuma* πνεῦμα NT: 4151) The Hebrew word (*ruach*) for Spirit as well as the Greek word *pneuma* means "breath, wind." The effect of the Spirit entering our beings is to create within us new life as we are "born of the Spirit." The Holy Spirit that Jesus gives comes to indwell our lives and empower us to do the works of the Father. His indwelling us gives us wisdom, truth, guidance, and direction. He is as close and intimate to us as breath itself!

𝟘⸍ **Helper** or **Counselor** (*parakletos* παράκλητος NT: 3875) Jesus names the Holy Spirit as the *paraclete.* He gives counsel and consoles. The Holy Spirit as *paraclete* ministers to us through encouragement and help. The Louw and Nida Greek-English Lexicon says, "A term such as 'Helper' is highly generic and can be particularly useful in some languages. In certain instances, for example, the concept of 'Helper' is expressed idiomatically. For example, 'the one who mothers us' or, as in one language in Central Africa, 'the one who falls down beside us,' that is to say, an individual who upon finding a person collapsed along the road, kneels down beside the victim, cares for his needs, and carries him to safety." What a powerful insight

into the person of the Holy Spirit! He is also our advocate with the Father continually making a case for our needs.

𝟘⸍ **Teach** (*didasko* διδάσκω NT: 1321) To teach or instruct means to impart knowledge in such a way that it is not only learned but also lived. Simple head knowledge doesn't mean that one has received or really "knows" the subject taught. When the Holy Spirit teaches, He deposits truth into our inner beings so that we can think, feel, and act righteously, like the Father.

𝟘⸍ **Peace** (*eirene* εἰρήνη NT: 1515) Freedom from anxiety and inner turmoil. John 14 begins with Jesus exhorting His disciples not to be troubled. The chapter ends with His promise of peace from such turmoil. Freedom from worry deep within you is a gift from the Lord that comes through His indwelling Holy Spirit. Even though we are tempted with outer conflict, war, struggle, trials, tribulations, or battles, God's peace has the power to calm the storms and catapult us through the circumstance to the other side.

JOHN 14 SUMMARY

Chapter 14 informs the disciples of their wonderful awaited home in glory and the Father's care to provide for them. Jesus assured them that *He* is the way into the loving care of God. As Jesus mentioned the Father with such intimacy, the disciples were moved to know more about Him. Jesus told them that they know the Father, a statement that seems to be in error. As Philip questioned Jesus, Jesus revealed that seeing the Father is the same as seeing Himself. Jesus revealed that He is one with the Father in the same way that the Father is one with Him. Jesus understood that these words may be hard for the disciples to accept, so He mentioned that the works of God He continually performed are verification that He and the Father are working together.

This passage is extremely informative for the believer.

> **We have been given the responsibility to manifest the works of Jesus on the earth.**

We have been given the responsibility to manifest the works of Jesus on the earth. When we manifest the works of Jesus, we are revealing to the world that Jesus is not only living, but that He lives in us. Even as Jesus mentioned that the Father does the works, so we understand that it is Jesus who does the works through us.

The ability for the supernatural comes from God. The greater our comprehension of our life being one with the life of Christ, the greater our works will be. We should be an expression, an exact duplicate, of the living Christ. What does our mind do with these intense thoughts? Can we really expect to duplicate the ministry of Jesus? Is this too far-fetched?

Jesus answered this question emphatically. In verse 12 He said that we the believers shall do the exact works that He Himself did and even greater because He was going to His Father. The fact that Jesus was talking about being with the Father shows that He was talking about our day. Remember, from chapter 13 forward in John, Jesus prepared His followers for the day when He would be taken up into glory to reign with His Father. The work that Jesus began must be finished through His body. We, the body of Christ, are the only Jesus that the present world will ever see. If we are duplicating His results, then this will serve as proof to the fact that Jesus is alive. Signs and wonders are the dinner bell to salvation. Every believer must come to grips with the fact that the church can and must do the works of Jesus.

We have a very explicit Great Commission (Matthew 28 and Mark 16) that tells us why to believe and what to expect. The message that Jesus is Lord and Savior of all will save the lost. Using the name of Jesus as our authorization to manifest His power will cast out demons, heal the sick, and provide for the infilling of the Spirit of God with the outward evidence of speaking in other tongues. And if there are deadly things around us, we are exempt from their harm.

Next, Jesus revealed to His disciples the great secret of the ages. All this and more is pos-

sible because it is the plan of God to fill every believer with the same Spirit that Jesus Himself possesses. There is no need to fret that Jesus is gone to the Father, for He will more than adequately supply us with ability and authority to continue His work. Granted, the work at Calvary is complete. Redemption is settled, and the devil is defeated, yet the believer must enforce this victory in order for the tangible results to be visible to the world. In the power of the Holy Spirit, we as believers are the offensive force on the earth.

In the power of the Holy Spirit, we as believers are the offensive force on the earth.

The Holy Spirit shall equip all believers with supernatural insight into their own lives and the necessary steps to avoid and overcome danger and opposition. The Spirit of God is the great witness of the power and majesty of God. He is the key to producing evidence to the resurrection. After all, He is the glory and power that raised Jesus from the dead. He is acquainted with the forces of hell and their defeat. His glory was the defining factor in the resurrection. He then becomes for the believer the defining factor for our continued success and dominion. What Jesus did shall, through the Spirit of Christ, become evident and irrefutable to the world.

We will never sit and wait for the enemy to reveal himself through pain and affliction. Quite the contrary, we will take this overcoming dominion and glory to the world and manifest God in every area that challenges God's authority.

How wonderful is the work of God! While we were yet sinners, Jesus died for us, that we might be filled with His victory and presence. With the blink of an eye we were transformed into the glory of the resurrected Christ. This is the army that will reveal God!

MEDITATIONS FOR SUCCESS

- Jesus is the way, the truth, and the life. You cannot afford to live without Him.
- Jesus is my hero! He paved the way for all who dare to believe, that we might live in His power and labor with Him in this victorious fight.
- We reveal Jesus exactly as Jesus revealed and expressed Himself to the Father.
- This task is not based on natural strength or wisdom; we are empowered with God's presence and ability to more than adequately do the work.
- Believe it! It is possible to do the work of Christ.
- God's peace is simply the supremacy of the victorious work of Christ living in your heart, assuring you of complete and absolute dominion in the earth.

CHAPTER 15

¹"I am the true vine, and My Father is the vinedresser. ²Every branch in Me that does not bear fruit He takes away; and every *branch* that bears fruit He prunes, that it may bear more fruit. ³You are already clean because of the word which I have spoken to you. ⁴Abide in Me, and I in you. As the branch cannot bear fruit of itself, unless it abides in the vine, neither can you, unless you abide in Me.

⁵"I am the vine, you *are* the branches. He who abides in Me, and I in him, bears much fruit; for without Me you can do nothing. ⁶If anyone does not abide in Me, he is cast out as a branch and is withered; and they gather them and throw *them* into the fire, and they are burned. ⁷If you abide in Me, and My words abide in you, you will ask what

---

15:1 Rank is very important when it comes to falling in line with submission. God is the gardener and Jesus is the vine. The Father lovingly cares for each branch that proceeds from the vine. Throughout Israel's history, the vine and the grapes that are produced symbolize fruitfulness in doing God's work on the earth.

15:2 Immediately Jesus gives the purpose for each branch—to produce fruit. The church, those who believe in Christ, are the branches through whom fruit shall be produced on the earth. Those who through a living union with Christ produce much fruit will be cut back or pruned for further growth. Yet those who fail to maintain vital contact with God will fail to produce fruit and in turn will be lifted up. The literal Greek here (αἴρω *airo* NT:142) can mean to lift up and clean a soiled, muddy branch that cannot bear fruit. In other words, the vinedresser will take those

branches too close to the soil or dirt and lift them up, cleaning them with water, so that they may bear fruit. After cleaning, if they still are fruitless, they are cut off.

15:4-5 Jesus explains just how vital it is to remain in fellowship with Him. A branch cannot sustain itself; it is dependent upon the life that flows through the vine. Jesus says that to remain constantly in union with Him is to continually develop one's relationship with God. Without our strength being drawn from the Lord, there is no power to accomplish any task.

15:7-8 Jesus demonstrated that there is a twofold need in a believer's life. One is that we have an ongoing relationship with the Father.

Just as Jesus regularly pulled away from the crowd and His disciples to commune with His Father so must we.

you desire, and it shall be done for you. [8]By this My Father is glorified, that you bear much fruit; so you will be My disciples.

[9]"As the Father loved Me, I also have loved you; abide in My love. [10]If you keep My commandments, you will abide in My love, just as I have kept My Father's commandments and abide in His love.

[11]"These things I have spoken to you, that My joy may remain in you, and *that* your joy may be full.

[12]This is My commandment, that you love one another as I have loved you. [13]Greater love has no one than this, than to lay down one's life for his friends. [14]You are My friends if you do whatever I command you. [15]No longer do I call you servants, for a servant does not know what his master is doing; but I have called you friends, for all things that I heard from My Father I have made known to you. [16]You did not choose Me, but I chose you and appointed you that you

---

Time is a necessary ingredient for your prayer life. Praying the Word and singing psalms, hymns, and spiritual songs and praying in the Holy Spirit are ways to commune with God. Just as Jesus regularly pulled away from the crowd and His disciples to commune with His Father so must we. Second, our time spent in the written Word of God is crucial to our development as believers. If David could hide the Word in his heart and not sin, then the Word of God richly stored in your heart from personal study will secure every blessing that God has provided. These times of meditation through prayer and the written Word make fruit producing a natural and regular experience.

15:9-12 Acting on the Word of God is as Jesus put it, abiding in His love. If we receive this as a legal right and not a privilege, we'll miss the blessing that comes from fellowshiping with God. There is a supernatural joy that accompanies the believer who walks uprightly before God. When we see the benefits of following the Lord, we approach our duty as one who joyfully responds to a relationship which we adore.

15:12-13 This commandment must be woven throughout the New Testament, because God is Love. God loved us so much that He sent Jesus. Our love for one another is also a sacrificial giving. We must give up our rights and privileges so that we might honor and esteem one another.

15:14-16 We are co-laborers with Christ Jesus. We are working together with God to accomplish His will on the earth. He honors us by calling us friends. Now we begin to see God's perspective toward us; He esteems what we can do as much as we esteem what He can do. Any revelation that provides you with more confidence to do the works of Jesus becomes necessary for the church. Jesus reminds us that with this wonderful privilege of working

should go and bear fruit, and *that* your fruit should remain, that whatever you ask the Father in My name He may give you. [17]These things I command you, that you love one another.

[18]"If the world hates you, you know that it hated Me before *it hated* you. [19]If you were of the world, the world would love its own. Yet because you are not of the world, but I chose you out of the world, therefore the world hates you. [20]Remember the word that I said to you, 'A servant is not greater than his master.' If they persecuted Me, they will also persecute you. If they kept My word, they will keep yours also. [21]But all these things they will do to you for My name's sake, because they do not know Him who sent Me. [22]If I had not come and spoken to them, they would have no sin, but now they have no excuse for their sin. [23]He who hates Me hates My Father also. [24]If I had not done among them the works which no one else did, they would have no sin; but now they have seen and also hated both Me and My Father. [25]But *this happened* that the word might be fulfilled which is written in their law, '*They hated Me without a cause.*'

[26]"But when the Helper comes, whom I shall send to you from the Father, the Spirit of truth who proceeds from the Father, He will testify of Me. [27]And you also will bear witness, because you have been with Me from the beginning."

---

with Him, we are always just a prayer away from supernatural assistance from God the Father.

15:18-25 "They hated me without a cause." These words spoken by David in Psalm 35:19 describe what happens when light exposes darkness. The words that Jesus spoke and the works that He did exposed the sin and error in the world. Therefore people will naturally retaliate against those whose good works reveal their bad works.

Recognize that this world is not your home. As Jesus was aware of His heavenly home, so are we.

We talk and live differently from those in the world; we are to produce supernatural wonders which cause the world to admit their need. Recognize that this world is not your home. As Jesus was aware of His heavenly home, so are we.

15:26 Thank God for the work of the Holy Spirit. We are not left alone to do the works of Jesus without help. The same assistance that Jesus had, we have in the person of the Holy Spirit. He will testify or produce evidence of the Lord Jesus and His resurrection. Dare to believe that His help is trustworthy and reliable.

JOHN 15 KEY WORDS

𝄢 **Bear Fruit** (*phero* φέρω NT: 5342 *karpos* καρπός NT: 2590) To bear (*phero*) fruit is to be in the constant state of fruitfulness. That fruitfulness isn't just maintaining a certain level but increasing to abundance, that is, bearing more fruit and much fruit. Our original purpose to "be fruitful and multiply" (Genesis 1:28) isn't simply speaking of natural children but also having spiritual children. Who are you witnessing to or discipling in the kingdom?

𝄢 **Remain** or **Abide** (*meno* μένω NT: 3306) To continue, remain in, keep on and stay. Abiding refers to dwelling in a place without leaving. Abiding is a willing continuing on in a relationship. Nothing is forced or required. Abiding in Christ is a constantly joyful friendship.

𝄢 **Commandment** (*entole* ἐντολή NT: 1785) An authoritative order; a word that must be imperatively obeyed. What Jesus has commanded goes beyond a single act of obedience. Jesus commands a lifestyle of selfless love that is evidenced in every relationship between and among His disciples.

𝄢 **Choose** (*eklegomai* ἐκλέγο 1586) To make a significant choice based on special significance. Jesus chose His disciples not based on what they deserved or who they were; rather His choice of them imparted significance and importance to the calling on their lives.

𝄢 **Appointed** or **Ordained** (*tithemi* τίθημι NT: 5087) To decide that someone has a particular position or status; to make a deposit with the intent of earning interest. Jesus has appointed and ordained His disciples not to simply set them apart for a position but to deposit into them His Spirit so that they will reproduce His call and purpose in others. Disciples beget disciples. God's children are to be fruitful and to multiply having more spiritual children.

𝄢 **Friend** (*philos* φίλος NT: 5384) A peer relationship in which intimacy is shared. The friend that Jesus spoke of is loyal, close, and intimate, loving sacrificially, being willing to die for others. Jesus elevated His disciples from being simply servants to being friends.

Truth (*aletheia* ἀλήθεια NT: 225) That which really is and really happens in time and eternity is true. The Old Testament word for truth (*'amet*) literally speaks of absolute consistency between the inner and outward man. Truth refers to complete integrity, openness, and transparency. God is truth; Jesus is truth. Anyone who disagrees with the Father or the Son is a liar. The Holy Spirit is the teacher of truth as He imparts or deposits truth in us.

Testify (*martureo* μαρτυρέω NT: 3140) To testify is to bear witness and give truthful evidence concerning that of which the witness has firsthand knowledge. Jesus walked in the truth so His life testified or gave witness to the truth that He knew the Father. The Holy Spirit testifies to us of the truth which we then become witnesses of to the world.

JOHN 15 SUMMARY

Our relationship with the Lord sometimes needs defining. Jesus declared that He is the vine, we are the branches, and the Father is the vinedresser. Every ounce of life that the branch draws must come from its source. Jesus is the source or author of Life. Anyone who understands this analogy can see that without the vine there would be no branch.

Every ounce of life that the branch draws must come from its source. Jesus is the source or author of Life.

Divine union is the greatest privilege in the earth. We who were once sinners have been drawn into union with deity through our acceptance of Christ as Lord. We are no longer beings who just exist. We are human beings fully alive (*zoe*) as God created and intended us to be! God in His lovingkindness has come to live within our hearts. This wonderful experience is the message of the Gospels and the Epistles.

Paul spoke often of our position in Christ. Through this position we are indwelt with the presence of Almighty God. What do you call a man who becomes possessed with God? Paul called him a Christian, one who is just like Christ. God calls him a son.

The position of a son has all the benefits of family. Receiving those benefits is set in motion by simply abiding in the vine. When we consider the prescription for results which represents fruit, it is extremely simple. Jesus instructs us to abide in Him, which speaks of our relationship: spending time in prayer and abiding in the Word of God. Abiding in Him and the Word is not difficult, yet it does demand the reprioritizing of our time. Faith is always present when the Word of God is the only thing that makes sense. There is one thing for sure; this prescription is sure to work.

Abiding in Him and the Word is not difficult, yet it does demand the reprioritizing of our time.

There is a side to producing fruit that most Christians have not been as diligent to do. It is easy to enter into our relationship with God and produce results for ourselves if we are in need. When we are hurting, it doesn't take much for us to get inspired to stop the hurting. However, the fruit that pleases the Father is not just personal. We are instructed that it is our responsibility to produce fruit in others as well. As we do, the world will respond to us the same way that they responded to Jesus.

Thank God that Jesus has given us the peace that surpasses the realm of reason. Throughout our lives, our peace of mind and our knowledge that even though we are in this world we are not of it will hold us steady to the work of producing fruit that pleases the Father.

MEDITATIONS OF SUCCESS

- Jesus is the source of all our strength.
- Without spending time with the Lord we lack insight and inspiration to do the works of Jesus.
- How do you spell "success"? Read your Bible with the intention of acting on it and pray. Spend time in the presence of the Lord.
- Producing fruit pleases God.
- If we are continually reminded of heavenly things by abiding in Him, then it will be fairly easy to respond accordingly.
- We are in the world; however, we are not "of" it. What you are "of" defines your ability to succeed. So, when your source is the Vine, you can do all things!

CHAPTER 16

¹"These things I have spoken to you, that you should not be made to stumble. ²They will put you out of the synagogues; yes, the time is coming that whoever kills you will think that he offers God service. ³And these things they will do to you because they have not known the Father nor Me. ⁴But these things I have told you, that when the time comes, you may remember that I told you of them. And these things I did not say to you at the beginning, because I was with you.

⁵"But now I go away to Him who sent Me, and none of you asks Me, 'Where are You going?' ⁶But because I have said these things to you, sorrow has filled your heart. ⁷Nevertheless I tell you the truth. It is to your advantage that I go away; for if I do not go away, the Helper will not come to you; but if I depart, I will send Him to you. ⁸And when He has come, He will convict the world of sin, and of righteousness, and of judgment: ⁹of sin, because they do not believe in

---

16:1 Let me reiterate that Jesus revealed everything that helps us to consciously brave the impossible with complete confidence in God. Within the context of chapters 13-17, Jesus prepared the disciples for a transition. Everything He spoke empowered them with ability and confidence to do the work after He left.

16:2-4 Persecution is part of the gospel. To preach with conviction the wonderful gospel message is to provide access for some to receive Jesus as Savior. However, for others, it becomes the fuel that ignites animosity.

16:5-7 The disciples had not questioned the meaning of Jesus's words about going away; their only concern was what was going to happen to them when He was gone. It's easy to think only of yourself when you are in the process of transition.

Many today would be elated if Jesus would show up in the flesh to deliver them from their peril. We associate so much with the natural that we think that things are not as good today as they were when Jesus walked on the earth. However, Jesus said that the Holy Spirit is an advantage to us in this life. Obviously, man in the natural can be limited by natural sight. Our privilege is to use our faith to receive all the advantage that the Holy Spirit is for us today.

It's easy to think only of yourself when you are in the process of transition.

16:8-11 The Holy Spirit performs three distinctive tasks on earth. First, He convicts the world of their sin. Conviction is not the

Me; ¹⁰of righteousness, because I go to My Father and you see Me no more; ¹¹of judgment, because the ruler of this world is judged.

¹²"I still have many things to say to you, but you cannot bear *them* now. ¹³However, when He, the Spirit of truth, has come, He will guide you into all truth; for He will not speak on His own *authority,* but whatever He hears He will speak; and He will tell you things to come. ¹⁴He will glorify Me, for He will take of what

is Mine and declare *it* to you. ¹⁵All things that the Father has are Mine. Therefore I said that He will take of Mine and declare *it* to you.

¹⁶"A little while, and you will not see Me; and again a little while, and you will see Me, because I go to the Father."

¹⁷Then *some* of His disciples said among themselves, "What is this that He says to us, 'A little while, and you will not see Me; and again a little while, and you will

---

end result, but leads those convicted to repentance. Second, He delivers revelation of righteousness to those who believe. One of the greatest topics that the church needs to be immersed in is the righteousness of Christ. Without this understanding, the church is almost certain to revert back to works and legalism. Third, He demonstrates Christ's judgment over Satan. Jesus came with the purpose of destroying the works of the devil. The Holy Spirit through the believer will continue to emphasize the victory of Christ over the devil. All these tasks of the Holy Spirit are visible to the world to keep Jesus visible to the world.

16:12-15 The Holy Spirit would share many things the Lord wanted the apostles to know. Jesus referred to the Holy Spirit as the Spirit of truth. There is no falsehood or deceit in Him. He is a faithful guide you can trust with your life. Jesus remarked that the Holy Spirit would speak only what

He hears. Therefore, there is no difference in Jesus receiving "word" from His Father and us receiving "word" from our Father.

16:13 Our supernatural guide will reveal only those things that are truthful or real. If we could look into the realm of the spirit and see the many advantages that we have through our victory in Christ, we would certainly act differently about what we think is a problem. Part of the job description of the Holy Spirit is to show and tell us things that exist in the realm of God, which will more than adequately provide victory after victory. Jesus became an expert in the things of the Spirit.

Part of the job description of the Holy Spirit is to show and tell us things that exist in the realm of God.

Fine-tuning our conscience to the voice of the Lord will definitely increase our sensitivity to heaven's solutions.

see Me'; and, 'because I go to the Father'?" 18They said therefore, "What is this that He says, 'A little while'? We do not know what He is saying."

19Now Jesus knew that they desired to ask Him, and He said to them, "Are you inquiring among yourselves about what I said, 'A little while, and you will not see Me; and again a little while, and you will see Me'? 20Most assuredly, I say to you that you will weep and lament, but the world will rejoice; and you will be sorrowful, but your sorrow will be turned into joy. 21A woman, when she is in labor, has sorrow because her hour has come; but as soon as she has given

birth to the child, she no longer remembers the anguish, for joy that a human being has been born into the world. 22Therefore you now have sorrow; but I will see you again and your heart will rejoice, and your joy no one will take from you.

23"And in that day you will ask Me nothing. Most assuredly, I say to you, whatever you ask the Father in My name He will give you. 24Until now you have asked nothing in My name. Ask, and you will receive, that your joy may be full.

25"These things I have spoken to you in figurative language; but the time is coming when I will no longer speak to you in figurative

16:18-22 Jesus revealed the path He must take to redeem humanity from sin. He would leave them in His death, yet He would visit them again in His resurrection. The disciples would understand these prophetic occurrences after the Lord has risen. The joy the disciples experienced was the supernatural pleasure of seeing the Lord exalted and glorified. No worldly experience can rob you of this joy. Likewise, when we see the Lord through the power of His written Word we also experience an insatiable joy which cannot be explained. Nehemiah 8:10 declares that the joy of the Lord is our strength. Paul said that joy is a part of the fruit of the Spirit that comes from God.

16:23-24 "In that day" is referring to the day of this present dispensation. Jesus has ascended to the Father, making possible the work of righteousness in the heart of every life that accepts Him as Lord. Now, all believers have direct access to the Father for their every need exactly like Jesus. This thought is the central theme of the family of God. We are fathered by God just like our elder brother, Jesus. This is our seat of authority and place of inheritance. Anything we ask the Father in the name of Jesus is immediately given. There is no greater joy for a believer than being useful in the plan and purpose of God for the earth. Thank God, prayer works!

language, but I will tell you plainly about the Father. ²⁶In that day you will ask in My name, and I do not say to you that I shall pray the Father for you; ²⁷for the Father Himself loves you, because you have loved Me, and have believed that I came forth from God. ²⁸I came forth from the Father and have come into the world. Again, I leave the world and go to the Father."

²⁹His disciples said to Him, "See, now You are speaking plainly, and using no figure of speech! ³⁰Now we are sure that You know all things, and have no need that anyone should question You. By this we believe that You came forth from God."

³¹Jesus answered them, "Do you now believe? ³²Indeed the hour is coming, yes, has now come, that you will be scattered, each to his own, and will leave Me alone. And yet I am not alone, because the Father is with Me. ³³These things I have spoken to you, that in Me you may have peace. In the world you will have tribulation; but be of good cheer, I have overcome the world."

16:32 In Acts 10:38 Peter said that God anointed Jesus with the Holy Spirit and power to do good and heal all who were oppressed by the devil, *for God was with Him*. The same confidence and determination to do the will of God that Jesus displayed as He worked the works of God also inspired Him to finish His work at the cross of Calvary. This work was flawless because Jesus relied on the Father's presence at all times. If the whole world forsook Him, He knew that the Father would be with Him. Jesus declared that He would always be with us, even to the end of the age. What great inspiration and confidence we should express to the world knowing that Jesus has won every battle and finished as a champion, paving the way for each of us to succeed in living in the miraculous.

16:33 Jesus released His disciples to believe in Him by providing such absolute assurance in His promises that they were able to boldly venture out on their own. The world will continually provide plenty of tribulation to believer and nonbeliever alike. We, however, are fortified in the finished work of Jesus to handle any trial that comes knowing that the victory is already sure. As long as every situation always works to our advantage, where then is there room for fear and anxiety? This is the peace of the Lord, the solid confidence that regardless of how things look we shall prevail if we stand steadfast in the faith of God.

JOHN 16 KEY WORDS

⚷ **Advantage** or **Expedient** (*sumphero* συμφέρει NT: 4851) To bear or bring together at the same time. To profit. When we are brought together with the Holy Spirit, we profit or have an advantage beyond anything the world can bring to us. Together with the Spirit, we have the advantage of being able to overcome any trial, obstacle, or tribulation.

⚷ **Convict** (*elegcho* ἐλέγχω NT: 1651) To rebuke, reproach, convince someone of something done wrong. The conviction of the Holy Spirit is not for the purpose of condemning the world (John 16:8) but to confront them with sin so they will turn away from their iniquity. Concerning the believer, we are convicted by our own conscience. Because God lives in us, our Spirit immediately knows when we have sinned. Live true to your conscience and your heart will stay pure before God.

⚷ **Righteousness** (*dikaiosune* δικαιοσύνη NT: 1343) Righteousness is imputed to us through Christ—He is our righteousness (1 Corinthians 1:30). As such, we have access to the Father through the Spirit just as Christ did. That access empowers us to hear His words to us and to live in the miraculous. Righteousness is a virtue, the position of being purified by God.

⚷ **Judgment** (*krisis* κρίσις NT: 2920) Judgment implies a process of making decisions. The Holy Spirit evaluates the decisions of this world according to the decisions of God. Everything we say and do is evaluated by the Spirit who compares everything to the character of a holy and righteous God. The Spirit helps us to conform to the mind of Christ.

⚷ **Joy** (*chara* χαρά NT: 5479) Joy is a state of continually being glad or happy. Such a state of joy isn't controlled by outside circumstances. Rather, joy springs from the indwelling Holy Spirit who fills us with His ability to rejoice and experience great contentment.

🔑 **Peace** (*eirene* εἰρήνη NT: 1515) Freedom from anxiety and inner turmoil. Freedom from worry deep within you is a gift from the Lord that comes through His indwelling Holy Spirit. Even though we are tempted with outer conflict, war, struggle, trials, tribulations, or battles, God's peace has the power to calm the storms and catapult us through the circumstance to the other side.

JOHN 16 SUMMARY

Jesus's message was encouraging and prophetic; He continued to prepare the disciples for the day when He would no longer be with them in the flesh. Chapter 16 leaves no room for the disciples to question the preparation that the Father has made for them to be well taken care of.

Jesus tells the apostles it is more to their advantage for the Holy Spirit to come than for Him to remain on the earth. The word "advantage" is even in our day one of the great words used in our relationship with the Holy Spirit that fuels our expectancy for success. There are few words to describe how important it is to know that as we abide in God, we will continually display the power of our advantage in our constant victory over the works of darkness in the world.

We are well fortified by spiritual power and ability.

I love how Jesus portrayed His relationship with the Father as both Word based and prayer based. Not only is the Word of God revelation that both informs us and inspires us, but as Jesus mentions, the Holy Spirit will also reveal to us things to come. We are well fortified by spiritual power and ability.

Just how important is it that the Holy Spirit declares, transmits, reveals, and manifests to us the things of Jesus and the

Father? Just one word from God is worth more than all the riches in the world. Just one word from God in the midst of adversity, whether it be a promise in the Word of God or the spoken Word from the Holy Spirit, will still any storm. With all the complexities in the world and with the cares of life eating away at the peace and stability of men, what a tremendous privilege to have such an overcoming guide and helper in the Holy Spirit.

A very trustworthy work of the Holy Spirit is that His guidance will always be in line with truth. The devil is a liar and endeavors to lead us through our senses and the circumstances of life into works of darkness and destruction. The Holy Spirit, on the contrary, leads us in the truth. The word "truth" is *reality*.

Paul instructed us to look not at the things that are seen, but at the things that are not seen (1 Corinthians 4:18). These unseen things are the benefits and power of our redemption. It is the Holy Spirit who reveals and manifests these things in our lives. For ultimate success, if we are to see these wonders manifest, we must act in faith according to the guidance of the Word and the Holy Spirit.

How wonderful it is then that the Holy Spirit guides us into these realities. Unless spiritual insight comes to the heart of man, he will remain ignorant of the blessing of God and therefore, remain as he is. However, we are promised the help of a greater one, the Holy Spirit, who will give us the advantage over the works of the devil. God has never been in a tough spot. If a man were to acknowledge the Holy Spirit in his life on a regular basis, he would develop himself in the ways of the Spirit and take full advantage of his presence.

All this revelation concerning the power of the Holy Spirit and His advantage in our lives means that the works of Jesus are within the reach of every believer. How about you? Since the victory is already ours, the works of God are already established in heaven as complete, and you have the overcoming help of the Holy Spirit, what is stopping you from stepping out to set someone free?

How could we keep from witnessing with great excitement if hearing God's voice and acting in accordance with the Spirit's power would grant us a promised result? The words of Jesus in these last few chapters are not the kind of words that simply comfort us; they challenge us.

Jesus was being extreme in presenting success and confidence. He was preparing His disciples and the church with challenging truths that would liberate the most depressed soul with optimism beyond the need.

We are a highly blessed people who have every reason to tell the world about Jesus because He is the only way, the Savior of the world. With all the advantages that God has given the church to overcome and succeed in life with strength beyond our own, the message should be preached with greater zeal and might than ever before.

MEDITATIONS FOR SUCCESS

- Preparation is never wasted time.
- Knowing your advantages in battle brings understanding of your strengths and sharpens your resolve.
- The Holy Spirit is the Spirit of truth. He will always show you what is real and trustworthy about any situation.
- You can trust the Holy Spirit with your life. He will always produce the evidence of what you believe and act on.
- Get acquainted with the Holy Spirit. Include Him in every area of your life. Just His presence alone will drive away all fears.

CHAPTER 17

¹Jesus spoke these words, lifted up His eyes to heaven, and said: "Father, the hour has come. Glorify Your Son, that Your Son also may glorify You, ²as You have given Him authority over all flesh, that He should give eternal life to as many as You have given Him. ³And this is eternal life, that they may know You, the only true God, and Jesus Christ whom You have sent. ⁴I have glorified You on the earth. I have finished the work which You have given Me to do. ⁵And now, O Father, glorify Me together with Yourself, with the glory which I had with You before the world was.

17:1 Jesus knew that what was about to happen would include the fulfillment of His mission on the earth. The glory of God was the necessary element to the ministry of Jesus to unveil the miraculous. Without the glory of God at work, there would be no resurrection and ascension for our Lord. Every work of glory that the Son of Man involved Himself with on the earth always resulted in heavenly fruit. This brought great honor to the Father.

17:3 The plan of salvation is rather simple—coming to the Father through the Lord Jesus Christ. This great plan of God is about family. The same Elohim, the one and only God of Genesis, is the one, true God mentioned here. God started a race of people by creating Adam. His plan was that through Adam and Eve a nation of people would be birthed, each after their own kind. It was God's design that humanity stay sinless and holy. In this verse, we see that Jesus is God's man who stands to correct what the first Adam failed at. God's plan would succeed, and through Christ a new race of people will be birthed, sinless and holy.

17:4 This prayer in which we see the Lord petitioning the Father must be prophetic in nature. The work of the Father included Jesus dying on the cross, rising again, and taking His rightful place beside the Father in heaven. Jesus was talking about what would happen when all was done and everything was complete. Once Jesus had completed His mission, He petitioned the Father for the glory which He had before the world was. We know from the apostle Paul that Jesus laid aside His glory and privilege as God when He came to the earth (Philippians 2:7-8). We know that He walked as a man anointed by the Holy Spirit.

This verse seems to indicate that the anointing that Jesus walked in while on earth was not all that He originally had before He came. If Jesus came to take Adam's place, then it seems only right that Jesus walked in the anointing that God gave Adam. This obviously was unlimited power for what was required of Him as stated in John 3:34. Be assured that

6"I have manifested Your name to the men whom You have given Me out of the world. They were Yours, You gave them to Me, and they have kept Your word. 7Now they have known that all things which You have given Me are from You. 8For I have given to them the words which You have given Me; and they have received *them,* and have known surely that I came forth from You; and they have believed that You sent Me.

9"I pray for them. I do not pray for the world but for those whom You have given Me, for they are Yours. 10And all Mine are Yours, and Yours are Mine, and I am glorified in them. 11Now I am no longer in the world, but these are in the world, and I come to You. Holy Father, keep through Your name those whom You have given Me, that they may be one as We *are.* 12While I was with them in the world, I kept them in Your name. Those whom You gave Me I have kept; and none of them is lost except the son of perdition, that the Scripture might be fulfilled. 13But now I come to You, and these things I speak in the world, that they may have My joy fulfilled in themselves. 14I have

---

Jesus now stands complete in all the glory of God, and we have been raised up to sit with Him in heavenly places (Ephesians 2:6).

17:6-10 Jesus shared with His Father that all He had done will be fulfilled in the lives of those birthed after His resurrection. Jesus has great passion for His followers remaining true to the faith. The work that Jesus finished within Himself is only as good as its ability to reproduce itself in us. We are to be the glory of the Lord. Every ounce of glory that the Lord displayed in His work that revealed the Father should now be worked in the church to reveal a risen Savior.

The more you consider yourself to be of God and no longer in the world, as far as its hold on you, the easier it will be to acknowledge your oneness with God. This is salvation summed up in one simple phrase, *"that they may be one as We are one."*

17:14-17 The Word of God acted on is the truth that separates us from the world and its ways. The Word is truth, yet it will only separate us as we walk in its light. Keeping the Word before our eyes and in our heart will enable us to live free from the enemy. One of the worst things you can do once you become born again is to consider yourself to be human, as we know humanity. We are not of this world, because we are born of God. Becoming God-inside-minded is a great secret of success. This then becomes the reason why the world hates us. We are continual reminders of the difference between righteousness and lawlessness, light and darkness.

given them Your word; and the world has hated them because they are not of the world, just as I am not of the world. ¹⁵I do not pray that You should take them out of the world, but that You should keep them from the evil one. ¹⁶They are not of the world, just as I am not of the world. ¹⁷Sanctify them by Your truth. Your word is truth. ¹⁸As You sent Me into the world, I also have sent them into the world. ¹⁹And for their sakes I sanctify Myself, that they also may be sanctified by the truth.

²⁰"I do not pray for these alone, but also for those who will believe in Me through their word; ²¹that they all may be one, as You, Father, *are* in Me, and I in You; that they also may be one in Us, that the world may believe that You sent Me. ²²And the glory which You gave Me I have given them, that they may be one just

---

17:18 The same way the Lord was sent into the world to make a difference and bring light to those in darkness, so we have been sent on a mission as well. As children of light, we are to make plain the freedom that God brings to those bound in darkness.

17:20-21 Jesus revealed the heart of God for the entire world. The believers that Jesus talked about include the Gentiles as well. The purpose is the same for all, that we might all know and understand our place as sons of God. Jesus in His earth walk knew not only who He was, but that He was one with the Father in purpose, substance, and ability. His union with the Father was the central reason why He could produce results. Jesus prayed for us to comprehend as He did that we are not just a part of the family as separate beings.

We actually become one with Jesus, intertwined spiritually, until there is no separation. This means that we are one in the same measure and quality as Jesus is one with the Father. What Jesus is, we are. We

don't lose our individuality, we simply gain His. The heart of this teaching has been to loose you from the human walls that religion has erected, so that you can explore the depth of Christ as Jesus gave Himself to the world. The only way the world will believe is when they see the difference that Jesus makes in our lives. Whether it's the smile on our face or the miracle we produce, the world has a right to see that we serve a risen Savior who lives forevermore.

17:22

God's glory must be present in order to produce results.

When Jesus was anointed with the Holy Spirit and power at the river Jordan, He then began His miracle ministry. The first miracle He did in Cana of Galilee was to manifest His glory so that His disciples might believe. God's glory must be present in order to produce results. If we

as We are one: ²³I in them, and You in Me; that they may be made perfect in one, and that the world may know that You have sent Me, and have loved them as You have loved Me.

²⁴"Father, I desire that they also whom You gave Me may be with Me where I am, that they may behold My glory which You have given Me; for You loved Me before the foundation of the world. ²⁵O righteous Father! The world has not known You, but I have known You; and these have known that You sent Me. ²⁶And I have declared to them Your name, and will declare *it*, that the love with which You loved Me may be in them, and I in them."

---

have this glory, and this scripture declares that we do, why shouldn't we also be able to manifest it for the world to see?

17:23 If there is one thing that the world doesn't understand it's the love of God. Each step of Jesus's ministry was a declaration of God's love. His love had such control and strength and it was selfless and caring to the point of meeting the need instead of pacifying the problem. God demonstrated His love in Jesus; He longs to demonstrate His love in us.

17:25-26 The reason why we can know God the Father is because Jesus knew Him. Without Jesus being a revelation of His Father's love, we would be helpless. We have a duty to know God. The world will never know Him outside of what we represent. How do you represent Him?

Jesus revealed the Father to the disciples over and over again. Being saved and living in the joy of the Lord for a week is not good enough. We must mature in the Lord and learn to fellowship with Him as Jesus did.

We have a duty to know God.

Learning to manifest the power and grace of God is not for the clergy alone. This is the privilege of the body of Christ, to grow in grace and favor with God and powerfully bring His ability to the world. If you had the one thing that the world was missing which could revolutionize our planet, wouldn't you be compelled to give it away? Jesus is that answer!

JOHN 17 KEY WORDS

Manifest (*phaneroo* φανερόω NT: 5319) To manifest is to cause to appear and to make visible. In Jesus, the invisible becomes visible. The will, word and glory of the Father appear (*phaneroo*) in Christ. In the same manner, the glory of God's miraculous power is manifested in and through us when we walk and act by faith in Christ.

◊ **Glory** and **Glorify** (*doxa* δόξα NT: 1391 *doxazo* δοξάζω NT: 1392) It's appropriate to first mention the Old Testament use of the word "glory" (*kabod* כָּבוֹד OT: 3519) which refers to the outer garment, weight, or covering of splendor and light. God's iridescent light and the profound weight of His presence is His glory. God's glory is resident in Jesus (John 1:14) and once we trust Him, His glory is transforming us (2 Corinthians 3:18). *Doxa* refers to the supernatural power of God that deserves one's respect and honor. *Doxa* is the excellence and majesty of God that demands our praise. So when Jesus does a miracle, it's a sign pointing to the majesty, honor, and excellence of God that has been revealed so that persons might give Him praise. Glory brings to light God's presence and power which dispel all darkness—sin, sickness, and bondage. In the presence of His glory, all that is not of His glorious nature must flee (Psalm 104:31-35). When Jesus speaks of being glorified (*doxazo*), He

refers to His original state of glory in the presence of the Father. When He indwells us by His Spirit, His glory shines through us so that the world can see the Father's love in us.

◊ **Sanctify** (*hagiazo* ἁγιάζω NT: 37) To be set apart and made holy solely for God's use. What is sanctified belongs solely to Him. By giving us His Holy Spirit and cleansing us with His shed blood, Jesus sanctifies us for His use. So, what we do and say reflects holiness or the presence of the Father. Living in the miraculous is a holy, sanctified life surrendered to and serving God completely as one with Him.

◊ **Truth** (*aletheia* ἀλήθεια NT: 225) That which really is and really happens in time and eternity is true. The Old Testament word for truth (*'amet*) literally speaks of absolute consistency between the inner and outward man. Truth refers to complete integrity, openness, and transparency. God is truth; Jesus is truth. Anyone who disagrees with the Father or the Son is a liar.

◊ **One** (*heis* εἷς NT: 1520) United and undivided. The oneness of will and Spirit shared by the Father and Son is to exist with us and the Father. This also makes us one body as the church. Division is always the work of the enemy who attempts to separate and thereby weaken believers and the church. Operating as one with the Father, we will always say and do what the Father wills.

Perfected (*teleioo* τελειόω NT: 5048) Being perfected speaks of being completed or attaining the goal intended by the Father. As we are perfected in Christ, we will walk in the miraculous and continue to offer our bodies as a living sacrifice to Him. This results in His works being manifested through us so that others will give the Father glory (Read Matthew 5).

Love (*agapao* ἀγαπάω NT: 25) God's unconditional love in giving His Son, Jesus, could not be merited or earned. Rather, God's nature is love (1 John 4:7-8). God initiated a loving relationship for us to enter into by faith or trust in Jesus. His love neither judges nor condemns. *Apape* accepts the believer as he is and begins to transform the believer into who Christ is. The Father's love is expressed through Christ to us so that we might live in the confidence of being loved unconditionally and might also be empowered to love others as God loves them.

JOHN 17 SUMMARY

The seventeenth chapter is a masterpiece of prayer. We often say that Matthew 6:9-13 which begins with, "Our Father in heaven . . . " is the Lord's prayer. In truth, that's the prayer for the disciples, and John 17 is truly the Lord's prayer for us! The entire chapter is devoted to the church to live in the blessings of our rela-tionship that Jesus paid such a great price for. Jesus began His prayer in the spirit of prophecy. He spoke of events that were to come shortly. It is so important to understand the way Jesus saw His place in the plan of God.

Jesus was well aware of the work that must be accomplished in order to finish the will of

God. He knew that when all things were finalized, He would be restored to His rightful place with the Father—a place that encompasses all that He had before the world began.

It is interesting to see how Jesus viewed the glory of God. Many times we beg God for more power, for we feel so inadequate when confronted with adversity. Jesus knew that He walked on the earth with less of a measure of the glory than before He came to the earth. Yet we never see Him doubt or question the significance of the power of God to perform the miracles that brought Him such fame.

Without destroying the works of the devil, Jesus would not have fulfilled His purpose. This is an important point. Jesus must have known that the power He had was more than sufficient to accomplish anything that the Father sent Him to do. Since the Father commissioned Jesus, it was His responsibility to provide the anointing that would more than adequately complete the job. Take a moment and believe that you are anointed as the Word of God declares you are.

Consider the anointing that is upon your life to be more than sufficient to meet the need that you face. Begin to act, because

the anointing will work with your confident demeanor of faith that rejoices and laughs at destruction and famine. Don't wait for a feeling; create your own feelings.

There is a theme of oneness that embraces the rest of the chapter. Jesus reiterated this thought more than once, which shows us its importance. He prayed to the Father that the believers would comprehend their place in God. Since this was of vital importance in Jesus's ministry, He knew its significance for the church. For Jesus to pray that we might see this truth must mean that, (1)either the normal mind-set of a human being would not comprehend it on its own, or (2) the devil will try to distract us from this truth.

If the world is going to see the results of a risen Savior, they will have to see these results—signs, wonders, and good fruit—through the church. When Jesus approached all the miracles, signs, and wonders that He did, He never looked to God the Father to do something that He wasn't willing to do Himself. The profound truth that He believed He could do the miracle is head and shoulders above where the church is today. The result of knowing that you are one with someone is the right to produce what he or she would. Jesus knew that His oneness with the Father gave Him the ability to act in His stead because there was no difference between the Father and Jesus. Jesus prayed that in the same way as He and the Father were one, He desired for us to know that we are one with Him and the Father as well.

What if we were to consider that there is no difference between Jesus and us? The truth is that if you desire to find me, you will have to look into Jesus to do so; conversely, if you desire to find Jesus, you will have to look into me to do so. This is the extent to which we must believe: the Lord Jesus is one with our spirit as if only one spirit exists. If we are one, wouldn't that qualify us to do the works of Jesus in the same way as the Lord? Begin by renewing your mind to these truths. As you meditate on them, they will lift you into a consciousness of what you can do through Christ who strengthens you. God sees you ready to produce results right now. Do you see it?

MEDITATIONS FOR SUCCESS

- Jesus finished His assignment; so did the apostle Paul; now it's our turn.
- We must glorify the Father on the earth by finishing the work that He gave us to do.
- More than enough power and ability has been supplied to accomplish all tasks at hand.
- Believing that we are one with the Father is the backbone to our confidence that allows the anointing to work through us.
- When we stretch out our hand, Jesus is stretching out His.
- What a privilege to be in fellowship with the Father in the same degree and under the same conditions as Jesus.
- Union with the Father produces results.

CHAPTER 18

¹When Jesus had spoken these words, He went out with His disciples over the Brook Kidron, where there was a garden, which He and His disciples entered. ²And Judas, who betrayed Him, also knew the place; for Jesus often met there with His disciples. ³Then Judas, having received a detachment *of troops,* and offi-cers from the chief priests and Pharisees, came there with lanterns, torches, and weapons. ⁴Jesus therefore, knowing all things that would come upon Him, went forward and said to them, "Whom are you seeking?"

⁵They answered Him, "Jesus of Nazareth." Jesus said to them, "I am *He.*" And Judas, who betrayed

---

18:1-4 As the eighteenth chapter begins, we find Jesus in the Garden of Gethsemane about to be betrayed. We know from other Gospels that Jesus struggled even to the unusual physical manifestation of His sweat turning to blood—a phenomenon that would happen only through great soul travail. Jesus knew the great sacrifice that awaited Him in the death, burial, and res-urrection. Therefore, He struggled with the human will that draws back from difficulty.

I believe that Jesus conquered the cross in the garden as He willingly chose to lay His life down on our behalf. This is why there was such dominion in His posture and words as He was confronted by His betrayer. As verse 4 indicates, He knew what awaited Him and therefore, with great confidence, boldly faced it.

There will be many opportunities in life to face our gardens of Gethsemane. One thing that Jesus did that would prepare us for those tough decisions of life is that He committed His heart to God with complete surrender long before He arrived at Gethsemane.

If you continually take control of your life void of surrender to God, when the tough times come you will automatically revert to your pattern and retreat from your faith. Remaining steadfast is a part of daily com-munion, abiding in Him. When you do, you like Jesus will have insight into your future and what lies ahead.

18:5-8 These verses clearly show us the dominion in the soul of Jesus. Paul said in Hebrews 12 that Jesus despised the shame of the cross and endured it with supernatural joy that He had after consid-ering the victory on the other side.

When you look at your deliverance in God, you develop the heart of a champion.

When you look at your deliverance in God, you develop the heart of a champion.

Him, also stood with them. ⁶Now when He said to them, "I am *He*," they drew back and fell to the ground.

⁷Then He asked them again, "Whom are you seeking?" And they said, "Jesus of Nazareth."

⁸Jesus answered, "I have told you that I am *He*. Therefore, if you seek Me, let these go their way," ⁹that the saying might be fulfilled which He spoke, "Of those whom You gave Me I have lost none."

¹⁰Then Simon Peter, having a sword, drew it and struck the

When Jesus answered that He was Jesus of Nazareth, the one they sought, all the soldiers and those with them fell to the ground. This is a passage that reveals men being slain in the Spirit. They didn't trip, they fell to the ground. When the Holy Spirit is very tangible, His presence will cause people to fall as they are touched by God. Falling doesn't secure the blessing, however it is a valid experience in ministry.

In this passage, Jesus didn't touch anyone; it was the power of His words that caused the Holy Spirit to come upon those men. If I were the captain of that regiment I might have run at that point. Even the mighty Caesar and his army have no power in the presence of the Lord.

Jesus's power is real for those who look beyond their pain and sorrow and instead, rejoice in their victory. Let's stop struggling with the problems of life and begin to cheer and praise God for His excellence and power. He is the Almighty God. When

Jesus's power is real for those who look beyond their pain and sorrow and instead, rejoice in their victory.

He is for you, who can be against you?

18:9-11 I want to know what possessed Peter to pull out a sword in the presence of a troop of soldiers. This alone is suicide. Notice that Peter went after the servant of the high priest. What good would it do to kill him? I believe that Peter considered those with Jesus as invincible as Jesus. In other words, Peter had been there when crowds of people attempted to throw Jesus off a cliff to kill Him.

The Scriptures declare that Jesus just walked right past these people and avoided them as if they didn't exist. Jesus said Himself in the tenth chapter that no one could take His life; He must of His own volition lay it down. Peter was also eyewitness to the soldiers falling over as Jesus declared, "I am He."

Peter's association with Jesus produced in him an overcoming spirit. It is so important to walk closely to the Lord. When we follow someone closely we develop the same spiritual characteristics. You will definitely be affected by the demeanor of those you relate to. When someone has an overcoming spirit of faith in them, if you remain close to them, you will begin to see things with the same spirit of dominion. Peter was larger than life because he lived with the Master of all things.

18:10 Peter struck the ear of Malchus,

high priest's servant, and cut off his right ear. The servant's name was Malchus.

¹¹So Jesus said to Peter, "Put your sword into the sheath. Shall I not drink the cup which My Father has given Me?"

¹²Then the detachment *of troops* and the captain and the officers of the Jews arrested Jesus and bound Him. ¹³And they led Him away to Annas first, for he was the father-in-law of Caiaphas who was high priest that year. ¹⁴Now it was Caiaphas who advised the Jews that it was expedient that one man should die for the people.

¹⁵And Simon Peter followed Jesus, and so *did* another disciple. Now that disciple was known to the high priest, and went with Jesus into the courtyard of the high priest. ¹⁶But Peter stood at the door outside. Then the other disciple, who was known to the high priest, went out and spoke to her who kept the door, and brought Peter in. ¹⁷Then the ser-

vant girl who kept the door said to Peter, "You are not also *one* of this Man's disciples, are you?" He said, "I am not."

¹⁸Now the servants and officers who had made a fire of coals stood there, for it was cold, and they warmed themselves. And Peter stood with them and warmed himself.

¹⁹The high priest then asked Jesus about His disciples and His doctrine.

²⁰Jesus answered him, "I spoke openly to the world. I always taught in synagogues and in the temple, where the Jews always meet, and in secret I have said nothing. ²¹Why do you ask Me? Ask those who have heard Me what I said to them. Indeed they know what I said."

²²And when He had said these things, one of the officers who stood by struck Jesus with the palm of his hand, saying, "Do You answer the high priest like that?"

---

who was the servant of the high priest. Other Gospel writers mention that Jesus touched the ear and healed it. The spiritual spontaneity and dominion of Jesus is

If you will live in the miraculous inwardly, you will live in the miraculous outwardly.

amazing. Jesus didn't have an all night prayer meeting or start quoting Scripture to get ready to handle the situation. He simply touched the ear and created a miracle. The things that Jesus did, He already conquered in His soul. If you will live in the miraculous inwardly, you will live in the miraculous outwardly.

18:15-18, 25-27 At this point Jesus was

23Jesus answered him, "If I have spoken evil, bear witness of the evil; but if well, why do you strike Me?"

24Then Annas sent Him bound to Caiaphas the high priest.

25Now Simon Peter stood and warmed himself. Therefore they said to him, "You are not also *one* of His disciples, are you?" He denied *it* and said, "I am not!"

26One of the servants of the high priest, a relative *of him* whose ear Peter cut off, said, "Did I not see you in the garden with Him?" 27Peter then denied again; and immediately a rooster crowed.

28Then they led Jesus from Caiaphas to the Praetorium, and it was early morning. But they themselves did not go into the Praetorium, lest they should be defiled, but that they might eat the Passover. 29Pilate then went out to them and said, "What accusation do you bring against this Man?"

30They answered and said to him, "If He were not an evildoer, we would not have delivered Him up to you."

31Then Pilate said to them, "You take Him and judge Him according to your law." Therefore the Jews said to him, "It is not lawful for us to put anyone to death," 32that the saying of Jesus might be fulfilled which He spoke, signifying by what death He would die.

33Then Pilate entered the Praetorium again, called Jesus, and said to Him, "Are You the King of the Jews?"

34Jesus answered him, "Are you speaking for yourself about this,

---

already led away to be questioned. These verses represent the changed demeanor of Peter since Jesus's arrest. Notice the cowardice of Peter; he was unable to admit that he was one of Jesus's followers. As Jesus foretold in verse 27, the rooster crowed as Peter denied the Master three times.

Do you think that this had anything to do with Peter no longer being in close proximity with Jesus? Also, what hope does Peter have if his hero has submitted Himself to man? This speaks volumes to us as believers. When you live in the natural, you will be submitted to man. In this situation, hopelessness abounds. However, when you stay in the presence of God and learn to fellowship with Him, you gain such supernatural confidence that you feel invincible.

We were not meant to fend for ourselves in the world as though we are orphans. Jesus said that He wouldn't leave us comfortless. We belong to God. The more developed our consciousness becomes in God and His ability, the stronger and more assertive our actions become.

What Peter lacked at this point, was

or did others tell you this concerning Me?"

³⁵Pilate answered, "Am I a Jew? Your own nation and the chief priests have delivered You to me. What have You done?"

³⁶Jesus answered, "My kingdom is not of this world. If My kingdom were of this world, My servants would fight, so that I should not be delivered to the Jews; but now My kingdom is not from here."

³⁷Pilate therefore said to Him, "Are You a king then?" Jesus answered, "You say *rightly* that I am a king. For this cause I was born, and for this cause I have come into the world, that I should bear witness to the truth. Everyone who is of the truth hears My voice."

³⁸Pilate said to Him, "What is truth?" And when he had said this, he went out again to the Jews, and said to them, "I find no fault in Him at all.

³⁹"But you have a custom that I should release someone to you at the Passover. Do you therefore want me to release to you the King of the Jews?"

⁴⁰Then they all cried again, saying, "Not this Man, but Barabbas!" Now Barabbas was a robber.

---

supplied at Pentecost in Acts 2. When the Holy Spirit was poured out on that day, Peter was reintroduced to the Spirit of faith that was on Jesus. It is the wonderful, powerful presence of the Holy Spirit who gives us an overcoming demeanor that exudes confidence and bold actions of strength. We have been born out of God's triumphant divine nature. It's natural for a believer to overcome. It is our birthright to produce miracles, signs, and wonders. We are invincible in Christ!

18:37 Hope is written all over this verse. Jesus stands in the presence of a king and proclaims His divine purpose for living. He is the King of all kings. His kingdom is not of this world; therefore His divine right to govern is not given by humanity. His purpose is to produce evidence to the truth. The truth is available for all to hear.

It is truth that we have so gladly heard. We are flesh of His flesh and bone of His bone. We are brothers and sisters to the Lord and Master. We are His body on the earth. We also have received our strength and commission from above. Even as Jesus is not of this world, so we are not of this world. The authority that we use to produce results has been given from God. Give your life over to the commands of a King. By faith accept your divine right to govern. Enforce the victory of the kingdom of God. For this reason you have been born!

JOHN 18 KEY WORDS

🔑 **King** (*basileus* βασιλεύς NT: 935) The crowd praised Jesus as king of the Jews. They were looking for an earthly king who would drive out the hated Roman rule. However, Jesus came as a heavenly king who would reign in the hearts of men. This spiritual kingdom was difficult for the Jews and Jesus's disciples to understand until after God raised Christ from the dead thus demonstrating in power that Jesus was the King of kings.

Jesus clearly identified His kingdom as being spiritual; the Jews simply failed to understand what He meant.

🔑 **World** (κόσμος *kosmos* NT: 2889) Though world (*kosmos*) can refer to the total universe, in this context, Jesus is speaking of the visible world which is the only reality those without faith can see. But through the eyes of faith, those who follow Jesus can see the invisible and pray God's will in heaven to be made manifest or visible in the world.

🔑 **Testify** (*martureo* μαρτυρέω NT: 3140) To testify is to bear witness and give truthful evidence concerning that of which

the witness has firsthand knowledge. Those testifying against Jesus did not know the truth because they did not know Him personally. Jesus Himself is the best testimony of truth, but the Jewish authorities had no interest in knowing the truth. They simply wanted excuses for killing Jesus.

🔑 **Give** (*didomi* δίδωμι NT: 1325) God's giving is an act of grace prompted not by what we deserve but rather by His giving nature. God's gift provides us with the opportunity to receive or grasp something that is eternal, lasting, and invisible. Without His giving, we would be completely lacking and lost. Jesus explains in John 18 that God has given Him to His disciples so that He will *always* be with them, that they might see His glory, and that God's love from before the foundation of the world would be revealed.

🔑 **Love** (*agapao* ἀγαπάω NT: 25) God's unconditional love in giving His Son, Jesus, could not be merited or earned. Rather, God's nature is love (1 John 4:7-8). God initiated a loving relationship for us to enter into by faith or trust in Jesus. His love neither judges nor condemns. *Apape* accepts the believer as he is and begins to transform the believer into who Christ is. Jesus is the manifesta-tion and revelation of God's love. In love, the Father planned from before the world's foundation to give Jesus as His gift of love rec-onciling the world to Himself.

JOHN 18 SUMMARY

The eighteenth chapter has great revelation to strengthen the relationship and communion of the believer with our Lord. Even though John doesn't record much concerning the soul struggle of Jesus in the garden of Gethsemane, the other writers did. You can certainly see the importance of developing your relationship in peaceful times when the pressure is not on.

Jesus was constantly commit-ting Himself to the plan and will of the Father throughout His earth walk. He was ever con-scious of the battle between the heart and the flesh. If you remember, He was tempted in all points as we are, yet without sin. Are you ever tempted to act out of your emotions and fleshly desires? If you are, then He was.

Jesus displayed unwavering resolve and dedication to the principles of righteousness and truth. He would never disobey His heart.

In truth, the commitment and genuineness of soul to fulfill that commitment is a very signif-icant reason why Jesus was so in touch with the realm of heaven.

When you stay focused on spiritual things, they become very real to you.

Just because they seem to the flesh as fantasies, the power of spiritual things are more real than the natural world we live in. Does an angel struggle with a wavering consciousness of spiri-tual things? Of course not, he only knows spiritual things. We are just as much spiritual as he is—even more so when you consider that we are sons of God Himself. Commit to meditate about spiritual things starting with the Father and Jesus. When you stay focused on spiritual things, they become very real to you.

As the Word gives you insight into their characteristics and ability, begin to consider how you too have been given these qualities. Then begin to consider the work and presence of the Holy Spirit. Why not talk to Him as though He were really there. Address Him when confronted with your day and include Him in on everything you do. It is here as you walk in faith concerning your time of fellowship that you begin to grow in alertness to spiritual things.

When you look at Peter and his boldness, first respect it, and then endeavor to emulate it. When you consider where it came from, you could say it was a part of his personality. However, it becomes apparent through this chapter that there is more to his boldness than just personality. Again we must talk about relationship. Peter, as well as the other disciples, were fixed

in their hearts as long as Jesus was continuing His successful journey. They believed, yet they remained enough in natural thinking that they easily could stumble. Their source of strength was Jesus and His continued success.

The moment that Jesus gave Himself up to be crucified, fear gripped them all. Peter, whom we esteem as the strong one, was the first to deny the Lord. It must have been heart wrenching for Peter. Up until this time, their complete confidence was in Jesus and the dominion that went before Him. Without the security of Jesus, the disciples became very skeptical, wavering people.

It is very interesting to see the comparisons of the day of Jude and the church today. Jude said in the third verse that we, meaning the church, must contend earnestly for the faith that was once for all given to us. The faith was given correctly through the heart and life of Jesus. Through the centuries we have lost our understanding of Him.

To contend earnestly almost gives you the idea that we must fight for the right to believe God. Even the clergy very rarely believe God during the tough times. Most Christians always use the professions that exist in the world. You could say that we have almost lost the heart that accompanies the faith message.

Daniel helps us unravel this great contention for the faith. He said in the eleventh chapter, verse thirty-two that they who know their God shall be strong and do exploits. We are right back where we started, knowing God.

On the day of Pentecost, the fulfillment of the great words of Jesus (John 7:37-38) was birthed as the Holy Spirit came as a rushing mighty wind. This great power, the same that anointed Jesus, filled everyone who anticipated it in the upper room. With this endowment and fresh tangible experience, the disciples, namely Peter, were again conscious of the dominion of Christ. No sooner had he been filled with the Holy Spirit than he was preaching to a great crowd of Jews, leading thousands to the Lord.

Can you hear the cry of the heart of the Lord?

We must move past knowing about Jesus and really know Him.

What a tragedy to live a Christian life and not experience the presence of the Holy Spirit. Not the theological experience of religion, but the good old Pentecostal fire of the Holy Spirit. This is why it is so important to build into your consciousness the thoughts of Jesus. We must move past knowing about Jesus and really know Him. Meditating and communing in His truth will bring His presence ever closer to your heart.

MEDITATIONS FOR SUCCESS

- Make a fresh commitment to follow the Lord.
- It's normal for your flesh to scream in resistance; follow your heart.
- Spending time with the Lord will provide great confidence and boldness.
- Paul prayed in Acts 4 that the church would be bold to preach the Word. Bold faith gets the job done!

CHAPTER 19

¹So then Pilate took Jesus and scourged *Him*. ²And the soldiers twisted a crown of thorns and put *it* on His head, and they put on Him a purple robe. ³Then they said, "Hail, King of the Jews!" And they struck Him with their hands.

⁴Pilate then went out again, and said to them, "Behold, I am bringing Him out to you, that you may know that I find no fault in Him."

⁵Then Jesus came out, wearing the crown of thorns and the purple robe. And *Pilate* said to them, "Behold the Man!"

⁶Therefore, when the chief priests and officers saw Him, they cried out, saying, "Crucify *Him*, crucify *Him!*"

Pilate said to them, "You take Him and crucify *Him,* for I find no fault in Him."

⁷The Jews answered him, "We have a law, and according to our law He ought to die, because He made Himself the Son of God."

19:1-3 Our redemption is a spiritual work. It would be easy to overlook the physical aspects of the crucifixion in light of spiritual victory that Jesus secured in His triumph over death, hell, and the grave. However, the physical punishment that Jesus endured as He was flogged and beaten is extremely significant for our physical healing. Because Jesus suffered in the flesh, we have exemption from physical infirmity. Every sickness and disease has been defeated at the hand of our Lord. He assumed the position physically of taking upon Himself our sicknesses and diseases. As a result of the torture that He endured, we are now free.

19:7 Here we see the real reason why the Jewish leaders wanted Jesus put to death. Jesus was not leading a rebellion as they said. They were indignant because of His works that proved that He was in relation with the Father. To the Jewish leaders, Jesus calling God His "Father" was the same as Jesus saying He was equal with God. Indeed, Jesus was equal with God. This phrase means "able to represent." As a man, Jesus represented His Father with outward demonstrations of power. He didn't make Himself equal with God, God made Jesus equal with Him. When God made man, He did so in His own image and likeness. Jesus came representing the works of the Father showing man that the original pattern was still possible.

Man was given dominion over the works of God's hands. In other words, man with God's authority could run the planet like God.

Jesus came representing the works of the Father showing man that the original pattern was still possible.

⁸Therefore, when Pilate heard that saying, he was the more afraid, ⁹and went again into the Praetorium, and said to Jesus, "Where are You from?" But Jesus gave him no answer.

¹⁰Then Pilate said to Him, "Are You not speaking to me? Do You not know that I have power to crucify You, and power to release You?"

¹¹Jesus answered, "You could have no power at all against Me unless it had been given you from above. Therefore the one who delivered Me to you has the greater sin."

¹²From then on Pilate sought to release Him, but the Jews cried out, saying, "If you let this Man go, you are not Caesar's friend. Whoever makes himself a king speaks against Caesar."

¹³When Pilate therefore heard that saying, he brought Jesus out and sat down in the judgment seat in a place that is called *The* Pavement, but in Hebrew, Gabbatha. ¹⁴Now it was the Preparation Day of the Passover, and about the sixth hour. And he said to the Jews, "Behold your King!"

¹⁵But they cried out, "Away with *Him*, away with *Him!* Crucify Him!" Pilate said to them, "Shall

God's design is for every person to imitate His Son in all areas of life. It's interesting that the real reason why the Jewish leaders fought for the crucifixion of the Lord is over being a Son. This whole study is for the purpose of realigning the body of Christ with God's intentions. By raising Jesus from the dead, God made possible for a whole world of people to be called and equipped as children of God—a family of God empowered to work on the earth with results exactly like Jesus.

19:10-11 Pilate spoke very boldly to the King of kings. Of course, he didn't recognize the authority standing before him. Pilate had very little authority in relationship to Jesus. Jesus said in John 10:17-18 that He had power to lay His life down and power to take it back up again. Jesus said that this power or authority came from His Father. Unless Jesus voluntarily laid His life

down, no man could take it, even Pilate.

As we become more familiar with God's superabundant authority, we must always remember to be gracious and loving as we do the works of Jesus. Even Jesus with such great power and authority did not use it haughtily. There is no other power or authority that has any merit next to God. We are a blessed people to be entrusted with the authority of God. As we use it for God's purposes, great change will occur on the earth.

19:15 "We have no king but Caesar." These words are definitely not the words of God's covenant people especially spoken by the leading priests. It's interesting how twisted a situation can become when you seek your own and not the heart of God or the well-being of others. Never allow ill will or animosity to stand between you and God.

I crucify your King?" The chief priests answered, "We have no king but Caesar!"

¹⁶Then he delivered Him to them to be crucified. Then they took Jesus and led *Him* away.

¹⁷And He, bearing His cross, went out to a place called *the Place* of a Skull, which is called in Hebrew, Golgotha, ¹⁸where they crucified Him, and two others with Him, one on either side, and Jesus in the center. ¹⁹Now Pilate wrote a title and put *it* on the cross. And the writing was:
JESUS OF NAZARETH, THE KING OF THE JEWS.

²⁰Then many of the Jews read this title, for the place where Jesus was crucified was near the city; and it was written in Hebrew, Greek, *and* Latin.

²¹Therefore the chief priests of the Jews said to Pilate, "Do not write, 'The King of the Jews,' but, 'He said, "I am the King of the Jews." ' "

²²Pilate answered, "What I have written, I have written."

²³Then the soldiers, when they had crucified Jesus, took His garments and made four parts, to each soldier a part, and also the tunic. Now the tunic was without seam, woven from the top in one piece. ²⁴They said therefore among themselves, "Let us not tear it, but cast lots for it, whose it shall be," that the Scripture might be fulfilled which says:

"They divided My garments among them,
And for My clothing they cast lots."
Therefore the soldiers did these things.

One thing to always remember: Stay on God's side. God is for you not against you.

One thing to always remember: Stay on God's side. God is for you not against you. **19:20** The sign nailed to the cross over Jesus's head read, "Jesus of Nazareth, the king of the Jews." This was meant to be an embarrassment. To have a king stripped naked and hanging on the cross meant that He had lost His kingdom. What appeared humiliating to the natural eye was only the beginning of the greatest kingdom that will rule forever. Jesus was coming out of the grave in three days as the ultimate ruler of the universe. He would be Lord of the Jews, Gentiles, and the whole world. What the devil means for harm, God always turns around for good.

Don't get caught up looking at the exterior of a situation. There is a redemption that supersedes any and all calamity with the peace and solitude to bring rest. There is more to you than meets the eye. There is an abundance of power and love that the physical eye cannot see. Overcoming deliverance is available when all looks bleak. Just like Jesus, look past your problem and with joy see your victory as real as if it were naturally present. Faith

²⁵Now there stood by the cross of Jesus His mother, and His mother's sister, Mary the *wife* of Clopas, and Mary Magdalene. ²⁶When Jesus therefore saw His mother, and the disciple whom He loved standing by, He said to His mother, "Woman, behold your son!" ²⁷Then He said to the disciple, "Behold your mother!" And from that hour that disciple took her to his own *home*.

²⁸After this, Jesus, knowing that all things were now accomplished, that the Scripture might be fulfilled, said, "I thirst!" ²⁹Now a vessel full of sour wine was sitting there; and they filled a sponge with sour wine, put *it* on hyssop, and put *it* to His mouth. ³⁰So when Jesus had received the sour wine, He said, "It is finished!" And bowing His head, He gave up His spirit.

³¹Therefore, because it was the Preparation *Day*, that the bodies should not remain on the cross on the Sabbath (for that Sabbath was a high day), the Jews asked Pilate that their legs might be broken, and *that* they might be taken away. ³²Then the soldiers came and broke the legs of the first and of the other who was crucified with Him. ³³But when they came to Jesus and saw that He was already dead, they did not break His legs. ³⁴But one of the soldiers pierced His side with a spear, and immediately blood and water came out. ³⁵And he who has seen has testified, and his tes-

---

lays hold of the realities of God, secures your fate, and transforms an evil report into good.

19:25-27 Jesus reveals to us the selflessness needed to walk in love with your family. When He could have brought all attention unto Himself, He lovingly extended concern for the welfare of His family. We, too, should learn from this example and extend our love towards our family. Learning to respond, as God would have you, instead of relying on your flesh, will turn many situations in your family around. Love never fails.

19:30 The word "finished" means "paid in full." Under the old covenant the sacrifice for sins was necessary often because the blood of bulls and goats was not sufficient to redeem the life from the nature of sin. Therefore, the people would continue to bring the consciousness of sin upon themselves and live under condemnation. Jesus came to abolish the old system and create a new one. As the surety of the new covenant, Jesus died once for all. Never again would another sacrifice be needed. In the new covenant the penalty for sin has been met and the price for redemption has been paid. No longer will man have to live under the guilt and condemnation of sin.

When Jesus is received into a person's life by confessing Him as Lord, the judgment of sin is removed. We are no longer judged as sinners. Thank God the plan for

timony is true; and he knows that he is telling the truth, so that you may believe. ³⁶For these things were done that the Scripture should be fulfilled, "*Not one of His bones shall be broken.*" ³⁷And again another Scripture says, "*They shall look on Him whom they pierced.*"

³⁸After this, Joseph of Arimathea, being a disciple of Jesus, but secretly, for fear of the Jews, asked Pilate that he might take away the body of Jesus; and Pilate gave *him* permission. So he came and took the body of Jesus.

³⁹And Nicodemus, who at first came to Jesus by night, also came, bringing a mixture of myrrh and aloes, about a hundred pounds. ⁴⁰Then they took the body of Jesus, and bound it in strips of linen with the spices, as the custom of the Jews is to bury. ⁴¹Now in the place where He was crucified there was a garden, and in the garden a new tomb in which no one had yet been laid. ⁴²So there they laid Jesus, because of the Jews' Preparation *Day,* for the tomb was nearby.

---

salvation creates in us a brand-new nature (2 Corinthians 5:17). We are instantly transformed into Spirit-filled men or women, children of the Most High. It is this new birth that will solve the need of the world. Someone has to tell the story.

19:36-37 John the Baptist by the Spirit of God called to Jesus as he was at the Jordan River and said, "Behold! The Lamb of God who takes away the sin of the world!" This prophetic word became true on this day of crucifixion. The mere fact that the legs of Jesus were not broken symbolizes the truth that He was God's Son. The Passover lambs were spotless animals, used for the atonement of sin. Not a bone was broken. As God's Lamb, Jesus also had not a bone broken. He became the great sacrifice for the sin of the world.

Paul writes in 2 Corinthians 5:21 that God made Jesus to be sin on our behalf. Jesus endured all the pains and afflictions of sin, sickness, and defeat so that we could walk in the newness of life. We are filled with God's life, the liberty of the children of God.

19:38-40 Joseph of Arimathea and Nicodemus were men who held Jesus in high regard. They believed in His testimony. However, as you can see from this passage, they feared losing their position and status in the eyes of the world. They became secret followers of the Lord.

There are many secret followers of the Lord today. They are also afraid of losing their friends and worldly status because of Jesus. We must openly confess Jesus as Lord before men. Our testimony should be known among our family, friends, and co-workers. We are not commanded to argue our belief before men, but simply tell them the good news making available the way to God. Jesus is coming back soon. You will want to come out of hiding and become a voice for God.

JOHN 19 KEY WORDS

𝄢 Scourge (*mastigoo* μαστιγόω NT: 3146) The scourging of Jesus was horrific. To punish Him severely, the Romans had Jesus whipped to the point of death. Jesus's back would have been virtually stripped of all flesh. This scourging produced the stripes in the natural by which we were healed, saved, and delivered. Read Isaiah 53.

𝄢 Crucify (*stauroo* σταυρόω NT: 4717) To nail to a cross, tree or crossbar. Crucifixion was the cruelest of punishment that the Romans reserved for the vilest of criminals, particularly murderers and traitors. They crucified Jesus after condemning Him as an enemy of the state, a pretender to the throne of Caesar.

𝄢 Fault (*aitia* αἰτία NT: 156) Cause or accusation that convicts. Pilate had no real reason to find Jesus guilty of treason. Jesus was innocent in every way. He was put to death by guilty men not because He was guilty. The basis for accusation against Jesus was false testimony conspired by men who hoped to silence truth! The religious leaders wanted Jesus killed because they accused Him of blasphemy. To appease them, the Roman authorities crucified Him for sedition.

𝄢 Power (*exousia* ἐξουσία NT: 1849) *Exousia* can be translated as power or authority. Pilate claimed temporal power but Jesus insisted that His power and authority came from beyond the world's power.

JOHN 19 SUMMARY

All who understand the truth about the finished work of Christ are grateful to the Lord for His dedication and perseverance to complete His work. Jesus died on the cross as a man. He endured His suffering as a man. All spiritual privileges have been secured by the man Jesus. Now you know why Jesus is the hero of heroes.

Redemption, which is the purchasing of our freedom by the sacrifice of another, is the greatest act of love that God could give a lost world. God the Father Himself was in Christ reconciling the world as Jesus hung on the cross. Most of the world would view the crucifixion as a religious act, not regarding the power and majesty that abide.

It was this physical act of suffering that secures for the believer and the world the rights necessary to walk in health. Isaiah and Peter help us to see the significance of the stripes that He willingly took upon His body. They both record that by His stripes we are healed (Isaiah 53:5; 1 Peter 2:24).

If going to the cross and enduring affliction and pain was the payment for our physical liberty, then every one of us ought to walk free from sickness and disease.

We know that all sickness and disease are a work of the devil.

Jesus in His earth walk was anointed by the Holy Spirit and power so that He lived in the miraculous and destroyed the works of the devil. We know that

dealing with the woman bowed over with infirmity, Jesus said that she ought to be healed seeing that for eighteen years she was afflicted by the devil. If going to the cross and enduring affliction and pain was the payment for our physical liberty, then every one of us ought to walk free from sickness and disease. It is a right that ought not to be ignored.

The power of this wonderful act is seen in the selfless love that Jesus died. Even before the cross, Jesus humbly flexed His muscles as He stood next to Pilate. Before any man who stood in his presence, Pilate under Caesar had complete authority. Yet when he stood before Jesus, I believe he understood that Jesus was not like any man he had ever met. Even the response of Jesus to his authority was unexpected. Jesus said, "You could have no power at all against Me unless it had been given you from above." These were powerful words spoken to a high-ranking official. Jesus was a conqueror before He died and after. It is this dominion and authority in the soul of Jesus that are so wonderful.

The cross has always represented a place of death. The world would see it as a place of defeat and shame. Naturally speaking, this would be true; however, in the case of Jesus, His death meant ultimate victory. In Galatians, Paul identifies the world with the death of Jesus. There was much more happening than just a physical crucifixion. Galatians 2:20 reads, "I have been crucified with Christ; it is no longer I who live, but Christ lives in me; and the life which I now live in the flesh I live by faith in the Son of God, who loved me and gave Himself for me."

The revelation that Paul received from the Lord is that when Jesus died, we all died with Him. As the substitute, Jesus was taking our place. Legally, Jesus paid our ransom. So that qualifies us to have died with Him as though we were actually there. *Arthur S. Way Translation* says, "Yes, I have shared Messiah's crucifixion. I am living indeed, but it is not I that live, it is Messiah whose life is in me. . . ." This is one of the clearest statements that the apostle Paul made concerning our identification with the Lord Jesus Christ. We actually shared in His death, burial, resurrection, triumph, and seating. Notice how definitive Paul made this truth come alive in Romans 6:6, "Knowing this, that our old man was crucified with Him, that the body of sin might be done away with, that we should no longer be slaves of sin." What is the old man that Paul talks about here? *The Cressman Translation* says, "The old person I used to be was nailed to the cross with Christ. I have no further role to perform as an offender because I was judged and crucified and the old person is dead and gone." This old person has to do with the old nature of sin and its expressions.

If believers could understand that they are no longer connected with the person they once were, there would be radical behavioral changes made.

If believers could understand that they are no longer connected with the person they once were, there would be radical behavioral changes made.

I like what *Richert Translation* says, "Our former evil identities have been executed, so to speak. Our old rebel selves were exterminated and leave us no further role to perform as offenders. We were linked with the Divine Representative in death." Seeing yourself through the shed blood at the cross leaves you without the identity that you once knew.

Paul stresses the revelation that the old is out and the new has come in the redeemed life.

Everything associated with the devil—sin and all the bondages that come with the sinful nature—are completely gone. You cannot dig up the old man that you were and blame your lack of success on him. He has been annihilated; there is no longer a record in heaven that he even existed. The only person that God sees is your new self in Christ. This is why Paul wrote in verse 11 that we are to consider this whole process completed, present tense. Romans 6:11 reads, "Likewise you also, reckon yourselves to be dead indeed to sin, but alive to God in Christ Jesus our Lord."

The word "death" simply means "to cease to exist." Everything connected with the sinful nature that all men were born with ceases to exist the moment you accept the substitutionary work that Jesus provided as He died on the cross. Paul said that it was so complete that we are no longer under the dominion of sin (Romans 6:14). One of the important words that Paul used in the book of Hebrews to describe this is "once." Jesus shed His blood *once* for all (Hebrews 10:10).

The sacrifice through Christ was a one-time sacrifice. "All" indicates that the work Jesus did was so thorough and complete that it couldn't be improved upon.

There is nothing left of what you were to remove and there is nothing else that God can do to improve on what you have become in Christ. Nahum 1:8-9 puts it this way, "But with an overrunning flood he will make an utter end of the place thereof, and darkness shall pursue his enemies. What do ye imagine against the LORD? he will make an utter end: affliction shall not rise up the second time" (KJV). All the failures and insecurities that follow the sinful nature, sicknesses and diseases, the bondages and works of darkness have come to an utter end. They shall not rise up a second time.

Can you understand that what Jesus did by hanging on the cross was so significant that your whole world has been turned upside down and inside out? His death was to identify Himself with our sin. When death was conquered we were removed from the family of death and brought into the family of God. We are indeed new creatures in Christ.

The purpose of this project has been to find the words and

thoughts of Jesus that produce such dominion so we might know that we are empowered to live in the miraculous. This inability to fail and living with complete confidence at all times is the spirit of a champion. Power is not effective unless it is released with a knowing and absoluteness that makes it work.

There is no timidity in the words and actions of Jesus. Jesus showed us how to believe in God wholeheartedly. Even in the midst of death, He knew nothing other than triumph. The nuts and bolts concerning "faith" are not just knowing the Greek interpretation of the word.

Faith is "knowing God" and utterly throwing yourself in His hands. Any and all other methods fail in comparison to His unfailing love. The grandeur of this story is that Jesus defeated death, hell, and the grave, and because we identify with Him, so have we. He is alive.

He took the risk; we can unreservedly throw caution to the wind and believe God.

MEDITATIONS FOR SUCCESS

- Jesus took our infirmity and bore our sickness.
- His physical suffering proves our deliverance from all infirmity.
- Salvation is free. Remember, someone named Jesus paid the price.
- Even in the tough spot, maintain your composure and recognize your dominion.
- No one has power over your faith. Use it as you wish.

CHAPTER 20

¹Now the first *day* of the week Mary Magdalene went to the tomb early, while it was still dark, and saw *that* the stone had been taken away from the tomb. ²Then she ran and came to Simon Peter, and to the other disciple, whom Jesus loved, and said to them, "They have taken away the Lord out of the tomb, and we do not know where they have laid Him." ³Peter therefore went out, and the other disciple, and were going to the tomb. ⁴So they both ran together, and the other disciple outran Peter and came to the tomb first. ⁵And he, stooping down and looking in, saw the linen cloths lying *there;* yet he did not go in. ⁶Then Simon Peter came, following him, and went into the tomb; and he saw the linen cloths lying *there,* ⁷and the handkerchief that had been around His head, not lying with the linen cloths, but folded together in a place by itself. ⁸Then the other disciple, who came to the tomb first, went in also; and he saw and believed. ⁹For as yet they did not know the Scripture, that He must rise again from the dead. ¹⁰Then the disciples went away again to their own homes.

20:1-2 When Mary saw the empty tomb, her first response wasn't to believe that Jesus had risen. The resurrection of Christ for many people at first glance is very difficult to believe. Reason will cloud the thinking and make the supernatural unbelievable.
20:3-7 Next we see Peter and John running to the tomb. While John stopped at the entrance, Peter ran inside. He beheld the empty linens that once occupied the Lord. Special notice is made concerning the linen cloth that was laid over Jesus's face, folded together in a place by itself. The text doesn't say that Peter immediately believed. He may have been pondering on the facts and possibilities of just what did happen. Who placed the linen cloth that covered the face of Jesus on the shelf all folded neatly?

For us who see the whole picture through the four Gospels, it is easy to conclude that Jesus upon coming alive and supernaturally leaving the cocoon that covered His body must have taken the cloth, folded it and placed it neatly on the shelf. Even here with Jesus's closest followers there is speculation concerning His whereabouts.
20:8 John was the first to believe in the resurrection. You too are required to believe in the resurrection if the Word of

¹¹But Mary stood outside by the tomb weeping, and as she wept she stooped down *and looked* into the tomb. ¹²And she saw two angels in white sitting, one at the head and the other at the feet, where the body of Jesus had lain. ¹³Then they said to her, "Woman, why are you weeping?" She said to them, "Because they have taken away my Lord, and I do not know where they have laid Him." ¹⁴Now when she had said this, she turned around and saw Jesus standing *there,* and did not know that it was Jesus. ¹⁵Jesus said to her, "Woman, why are you weeping? Whom are you seeking?" She, supposing Him to be the gardener, said to Him, "Sir, if You have carried Him away, tell me where You have laid Him, and I will take Him away." ¹⁶Jesus said to her, "Mary!" She turned and said to Him, "Rabboni!" (which is to say, Teacher).

¹⁷Jesus said to her, "Do not cling to Me, for I have not yet ascended to My Father; but go to My brethren and say to them, 'I am ascending to My Father and your Father, and *to* My God

---

God is to make sense and change your life.

20:11-18 It's interesting to see the significance of a personal encounter with Jesus. When Jesus spoke Mary's name, she was released from spiritual blindness and recognized Jesus immediately. God knows you by name and desires for your eyes to be open to His wonderful provision of redemption. Whenever someone hears the gospel message, a revelation that God loves him or her personally is made available.

> *God knows you by name and desires for your eyes to be open to His wonderful provision of redemption.*

People have to see Jesus as their answer to life. They must recognize in the face of Jesus their need of a Savior for redemption to work.

The progression in this passage is extremely relevant to our day. To move people past the skepticism of redemptive truth, past the questions that hinder our action even when confronted with facts to where people are able to encounter Jesus personally for themselves, is the goal of every soul winner.

20:17 As this verse reveals, Jesus had to complete His mission by ascending to the Father. Paul told us in Hebrews 10:10 that Jesus presented His blood as a one-time sacrifice for sins as our great high priest. It looks as though Jesus was on His way to complete this assignment when He encountered Mary. The Son of God paid for full redemption with something so holy as His own blood. Jesus's blood was the

and your God.' "

¹⁸Mary Magdalene came and told the disciples that she had seen the Lord, and *that* He had spoken these things to her.

¹⁹Then, the same day at evening, being the first *day* of the week, when the doors were shut where the disciples were assembled, for fear of the Jews, Jesus came and stood in the midst, and said to them, "Peace *be* with you." ²⁰When He had said this, He showed them *His* hands and His side. Then the disciples were glad when they saw the Lord.

²¹So Jesus said to them again, "Peace to you! As the Father has sent Me, I also send you." ²²And when He had said this, He breathed on *them,* and said to them, "Receive the Holy Spirit.

---

only blood that could make such a ransom for our sins. We are blood-washed and blood-bought children of God, created just as holy as God Himself, thoroughly cleansed by the blood of Jesus as though we never ever sinned. Redemption is the greatest miracle that a human being could experience.

20:19-20 Isn't it great that fresh from His victory over death, hell, and the grave, that Jesus desires to show Himself to the ones He loves? God has always been available for our experience. He doesn't hide Himself from us; on the contrary, He is looking for ways to reveal Himself to us continually. Why, even the beauty of nature reveals His handiwork of creation. We are living in a great day, where more than ever with time winding down, God desires to manifest Himself to the world. As you can see here, those who will be responsible for carrying His message to the world must themselves have a personal touch of the Lord for the message to be convincing and full of power.

20:21 I love how the Lord always brings peace into whatever situation He walks into. Peace is the supernatural wholeness that causes everything to yield to God. Fear isn't present when the peace of God is released. Jesus also gave the disciples orders to fulfill His work on the earth, by sending them as the Father sent Him. The word "as" means "in the same degree and under the same conditions."

Jesus is sending us with the same degree of ability, power, and wisdom to complete His assignment and under the same conditions of God's supernatural assistance to more than adequately finish. If Jesus delivered people and set them free from the devil's works, then we, as the church, have the same testimony as He.

20:22-23 When Jesus breathed upon the disciples the Holy Spirit confirmed their salvation. They were already followers of Jesus. However, until Jesus arose from the grave, the new birth was not available. Jesus made very plain the instructions for His followers to receive the power of the Spirit as fulfilled in Acts 2. There is no reason to expect the same results that

²³If you forgive the sins of any, they are forgiven them; if you retain the *sins* of any, they are retained."

²⁴Now Thomas, called the Twin, one of the twelve, was not with them when Jesus came. ²⁵The other disciples therefore said to him, "We have seen the Lord." So he said to them, "Unless I see in

His hands the print of the nails, and put my finger into the print of the nails, and put my hand into His side, I will not believe."

²⁶And after eight days His disciples were again inside, and Thomas with them. Jesus came, the doors being shut, and stood in the midst, and said, "Peace to you!" ²⁷Then He said to Thomas,

---

Jesus had if we, the church, lack equipment that Jesus had.

Jesus continues to reveal to His disciples that sin and all the powers of its working in the lives of men are under the dominion of the power of God. Our job is clear: Set men free from the bondages of sin. We are to release them with the power of God's Word and Spirit. If Jesus never had a difficulty in helping those who desired to be helped, then we, sent in the same fashion as Jesus, can expect the same results.

20:24-29 This passage portrays the idealism of the world. If I can see it or touch it then I will believe. The only problem is that there is more on this planet than the material world. The spirit world must be factored in if man ever hopes to find the answers that solve life's problems. Even in the midst of Thomas's unbelief, Jesus was still very accommodating by showing the scars of the crucifixion.

If you struggle with using your faith for the supernatural, then you need to be encouraged that it is God's desire to lift you up and move you onward. Jesus

didn't leave Thomas in this state of unbelief, but through the physical touch, encouraged Thomas to be believing and not unbelieving. Notice that the only difference in the two words is the "un." Even the world exercises the power of a human being made in the image of God to believe. They however, believe in themselves to solve life's problems with human invention. In many cases the world does well. However, they cannot solve with natural methods the problem that exists in the human soul.

Man must believe, that is, use the faith given by the receiving of the message to ignite the new birth experience. The things that you desire to see in your life are all a direct result of the spiritual principles that you learn to apply. Seeing is only believing when it's natural, but believing is seeing the supernatural blessings that come from God. All things that pertain to life and godliness have been given to every believer (2 Peter 1:3).

These blessings are the answers to all of life's problems and the great solutions that the world craves. When faith in the

"Reach your finger here, and look at My hands; and reach your hand *here,* and put *it* into My side. Do not be unbelieving, but believing."

²⁸And Thomas answered and said to Him, "My Lord and my God!"

²⁹Jesus said to him, "Thomas, because you have seen Me, you have believed. Blessed *are* those who have not seen and *yet* have believed."

³⁰And truly Jesus did many other signs in the presence of His disciples, which are not written in this book; ³¹but these are written that you may believe that Jesus is the Christ, the Son of God, and that believing you may have life in His name.

---

heart of every believer is released by a conscious trust in God for the change that is needed, everyone can behold the results in the natural. This is our responsibility—to change the results in our own lives and bring these same changes to the world.

20:30-31 I have read that the ministry of Jesus, if compressed chronologically from the Gospels, which reveal many identical stories, would consist only of about twenty-six days. If you took a day off for His birth and two or three for His death and resurrection, then you would be left with only twenty-two or twenty-three days for Jesus's public life and ministry. Considering this, then think of the implications concerning the miracle ministry that Jesus had. It certainly makes sense that John would write and reveal that the miracle ministry of Jesus could not be written down in completion for its vastness in numbers. If what we read happened all in the course of twenty-two days, then what did He do for the other three-and-a-half years?

He continued to do the same thing: teach, preach, and heal the sick. The work before us is never ending; there will always be someone who needs the ministry of the Lord. We must change our thinking. We cannot afford to think small anymore. We must see everyone able to receive the blessings of God. We must challenge our believing so that all things can be possible. God is waiting on us to rise to the occasion.

For good reason, Jesus passed His ministry on to others to help Him reach the people. That work has been entrusted to us, children of God with the mind of Christ, to duplicate His results as if He were still on the earth. The good news is that He is still on the earth using His body, the church, to reach the world with power and ability to set it free. If we were all doing the work as Jesus did with as many results as He produced, wouldn't it be amazing to behold the huge number of salvations, healings and miracles? Think of it!

JOHN 20 KEY WORDS

🔑 **Rise from the dead (Resurrected)** *(anistemi* ἀνίσταμαι NT: 450) To stand up; rise up again; to appear. Resurrection of the dead appears first in Job 19; Psalms 16-17; Isaiah 26; Ezekiel 37; and Daniel 12 in the Old Testament. In Jesus's day, the Sadducees refused to believe that the dead would rise at the end of time for judgment, but the Pharisees believed in the resurrection.

However, that the Messiah would die and rise again was a radical intrusion into the Jewish mind-set. No one had anticipated that the Messiah would first die for sins and then be raised by God to become King of kings and Lord of lords.

Jesus astounded and confounded His disciples by promising to rise again. Resurrection was so foreign to their thinking that they didn't even remember His prophetic promise until after His resurrection.

Resurrection is the firstfruits of our new life in Christ. His *life* is ours through vital union and identification with His life. Because He lives, we live abundantly and forever (John 10:10;

1 Corinthians 15). In the resurrection of the dead, the believer receives a spiritual body; in being born again, the believer becomes a new creation empowered by the Holy Spirit to overcome sin, disease, bondage, and ultimately death itself. Though the physical body may die even as Jesus's body was crucified, the *life* of God within us can never die!

🔑 **Rabboni** *(from Heb. rabbi, rhabboni* see NT: 4462) Literally, Mary spoke a term of endearment and recognition to the risen Jesus. "My rabbi" identified completely the Jesus whom Mary knew as her Master and earthy teacher, the Son of man from Nazareth, as the risen Lord, the Christ. Christ the risen Lord is the same person as Jesus, the rabbi and teacher from Nazareth whom the Jews and Romans crucified. Mary wasn't seeing a vision or having an illusion. The historical Jesus is the Risen Christ!

🔑 **Ascend** *(anabaino* ἀναβαίνω NT: 305) To go up, rise up, or move upward. Jesus promised to ascend into heaven, that is, to return to the Father to reign at the right hand of God ever making intercession for us (Hebrews 7; Romans 8). Jesus will also return again (John 14; 1 Thessalonians 4-5). Jesus gave final instructions to His disciples and ascended to heaven in Acts 1.

JOHN 20 SUMMARY

The tomb is empty! This phrase is what separates Christianity from every other religion. Every other religious leader, after giving the highest form of spiritual enlightenment possible, lies in a tomb somewhere. The idea that someone could be raised from the dead is completely possible if you have followed the message of the Bible. However, with all the resurrections that occurred, every one of the individuals eventually died as they entered into old age. Jesus, on the other hand, is still alive! He died once for all and He lives forevermore.

Never has another religion produced such a radical concept for the human race. The idea of eternal life has been sought throughout the centuries as the greatest possession man could attain. Is it possible that man could live forever? Jesus proved that it is. What are the implications for those who would follow Jesus as leader and Lord?

Before Jesus died for the sin of the world, He made it very clear that His purpose was to impart eternal life into the human race. He came that we might have life (*zoe*) and have an abundance of it.

Eternal life is not duration of time.

Most who have ever sought for the springs of eternal life have done so that they might continue living forever as they were. Eternal life is not duration of time. Eternal life is a drastic, radical change of being, so that what you were ceases to exist. Eternal life is taking on the very nature and being of God. You don't replace God, but you are filled with and created with the very *life* of God. Your potential in life is now fully empowered by God for solving the crises of life.

God placed the burden of life on His Son Jesus so that as our substitute, Jesus would pay the price for our sins and through His suffering, free the world from their debt of corruption. Jesus made possible an eternal transfusion of life like an IV to our veins. When He hung on the cross, the sin of the world was drained out of us and placed on Him. When God the Father raised Jesus from the dead by His glory and life, that life was supernaturally poured into as many as would receive Him.

The wonder of the resurrection of Christ is not just the coming to life of Jesus Himself, but the coming to life of the whole human race. We were in Christ as He reconciled the world unto Himself. We now have the potential of reaping the benefits of His victory. While we were encouraged in chapter 19 to consider ourselves dead to sin through His death, we are also to consider ourselves to be alive unto God through His resurrection. Every spiritual benefit that Jesus has provided must be acted on in order to visibly see and experience the result.

Redemption is awe-inspiring as we ponder its grandeur, but it is much better to experience its power in life. Just think; you are alive in Christ. The glory that raised Him is quickening your mortal body and mind as you fellowship with Him. There is no longer a need to fear the trials of life. If God's life is in us and we have come alive through Christ, then the truth that "greater is He who is in you than he who is in the world" is real (1 John 4:4). Even as the world had nothing on the Lord before He died, so it has nothing on us.

We truly are pilgrims walking through a foreign land. Our citizenship is from another world, called heaven or the kingdom of God. The laws that govern that kingdom are spiritual and supreme to the laws that govern the defeated kingdom of this world. Where sin and death seem to reign here, it is the law of the Spirit of life in Christ that governs our lives everywhere we go. Now we have the upper hand in the face of every trial, problem, temptation, or attack. If God be for us, then who can be against us?

The devil has lost; his reign is over.

Now it's time for the children of God to assume their rightful place in the authority of Jesus

Christ and rule this planet in righteousness. Christ's resurrection power makes eternal life possible for all who would have faith in Jesus. The devil has lost; his reign is over. What a future God has given us. What a hope, what an expectancy.

Maybe now we can appreciate the importance of Jesus's attitude toward faith. We are serving a risen Lord; He's not dead, but alive. Every other religion is dead and powerless. For the believer, there is nothing but optimism for our lives. Jesus being raised from the grave is the strength of the Gospel. Faith is a by-product of this knowledge. Our old unrenewed minds may struggle with the new law of faith that every believer is privileged to abide by. But for the spirit of man, faith in Christ transforms mere existence (with death as its expected end) into life with its expected future as eternity. How exciting!

Resist believing because you see; rather, honor the risen Lord by trusting Him with your life because He conquered the grave and lives forevermore as the surety of this great covenant from God. No man shall pluck us from our Father's hand, and no trial regardless how big it may seem shall lessen our faith to succeed and conquer.

Your faith will prevail today because Jesus is alive! Faith is transforming. Love is our language, and the hope of seeing Jesus is the motivation that inspires greatness. Thank God for the Resurrection of the Lord Jesus Christ.

MEDITATIONS FOR SUCCESS

- Identification means to be identical or one and the same. When Jesus died He identified with your sin by becoming sin. Therefore, you died with Him.

- When Jesus arose victorious over death, hell, and the grave with all authority, so did you.

- The apostle Paul wanted us to understand God's resurrection power that raised Jesus and also infused His overcoming power into our lives.

- When Jesus rose again, He paved the way for all who trust in Him to enter into eternal life. Speak it, shout about it, and give God thanks continually that you are filled with eternal life. Life has conquered death; you are now a conqueror.

- Dare to believe whether you see an answer immediately or not. It's worth the answer you'll receive.

CHAPTER 21

¹After these things Jesus showed Himself again to the disciples at the Sea of Tiberias, and in this way He showed *Himself:* Simon Peter, Thomas called the Twin, Nathanael of Cana in Galilee, the *sons* of Zebedee, and two others of His disciples were together. ³Simon Peter said to them, "I am going fishing." They said to him, "We are going with you also." They went out and immediately got into the boat, and that night they caught nothing. ⁴But when the morning had now come, Jesus stood on the shore; yet the disciples did not know that it was Jesus. ⁵Then Jesus said to them,

---

21:1 After His resurrection it is clear that Jesus desired to be seen by His followers and others. He showed Himself to His disciples again. In the beginning when God had finished creating, He revealed Himself as Jehovah. This name means "the self-existent One who reveals Himself." God's introduction to the world and man was as one who would always reveal Himself.

It's important that we understand and see God this way. He is not hiding from you. He actually desires for you to see Him and fellowship with Him. Jesus fulfills this wonderful characteristic of God by showing Himself after His resurrection. For the world to consider Jesus to be an unseen mystical thought in the minds of His followers is completely false. Jesus sent us the Holy Spirit to reveal to us the life and love of God the Father and Son. We know Him as one who is real and shows up for us in any situation of life.

In this verse it was important that Jesus establish with His disciples that He was indeed alive and that He would continue to be involved in their lives through the work of the Holy Spirit. Make sure that you see Jesus this way. He is real and certainly desires to be involved in every area of your life.

21:2-4 Notice that the disciples were unaware that the One standing on the shore was Jesus. You could say that the disciples were needful of recognizing Jesus in every situation. This is extremely needful for the church as well. As we grow in the knowledge of the Lord, we become more sensitive to the leadings and promptings of the Lord. Wouldn't it be wonderful to always recognize the Lord in everything that we do?

Jesus wouldn't have appeared if it were not for His disciples' benefit. The presence of the Lord by the power of the Holy Spirit is also for our benefit. The more proficient we become at hearing His voice and fellowshiping with His presence, the greater will be the results of the miraculous in our lives.

21:5-11 As the disciples were obedient to the suggestion of the One on the shore, even though they didn't know that it was

"Children, have you any food?" They answered Him, "No."

⁶And He said to them, "Cast the net on the right side of the boat, and you will find *some*." So they cast, and now they were not able to draw it in because of the multitude of fish.

⁷Therefore that disciple whom Jesus loved said to Peter, "It is the Lord!" Now when Simon Peter heard that it was the Lord, he put on *his* outer garment (for he had removed it), and plunged into the sea. ⁸But the other disciples came in the little boat (for they were not far from land, but about two hundred cubits), dragging the net with fish. ⁹Then, as soon as they had come to land, they saw a fire of coals there, and fish laid on it, and bread. ¹⁰Jesus said to them,

"Bring some of the fish which you have just caught."

¹¹Simon Peter went up and dragged the net to land, full of large fish, one hundred and fifty-three; and although there were so many, the net was not broken. ¹²Jesus said to them, "Come *and* eat breakfast." Yet none of the disciples dared ask Him, "Who are You?"—knowing that it was the Lord. ¹³Jesus then came and took the bread and gave it to them, and likewise the fish.

¹⁴This *is* now the third time Jesus showed Himself to His disciples after He was raised from the dead.

¹⁵So when they had eaten breakfast, Jesus said to Simon Peter, "Simon, *son* of Jonah, do you love Me more than these?" He said to

---

Jesus, a great load of fish was caught. Because of the similarity of an earlier miracle, John said to Peter, "It is the Lord."

When you experience the miraculous, you will begin to not only appreciate the power and love of God, you will learn to expect similar events.

Every step in the miraculous will endear your heart to the supernatural. When you experience the miraculous, you will begin to not only appreciate the power and love of God, you will learn to expect similar

events. You will begin to hunger for the power of God. The early church gained a healthy respect for the supernatural. Those early believers realized that they needed to walk in the power of the Holy Spirit so the works of Jesus could be accomplished.

21:15-17 As the disciples were eating their breakfast, Jesus used this opportunity to teach them concerning the love of God. The law of the New Testament is love. We have the responsibility and privilege of loving one another, even as Christ loved us. Even our faith works by love. When we were born again, the love of God was shed abroad in our hearts. We are well

Him, "Yes, Lord; You know that I love You." He said to him, "Feed My lambs."

¹⁶He said to him again a second time, "Simon, *son* of Jonah, do you love Me?" He said to Him, "Yes, Lord; You know that I love You." He said to him, "Tend My sheep."

¹⁷He said to him the third time, "Simon, *son* of Jonah, do you love Me?" Peter was grieved because He said to him the third time, "Do you love Me?" And he said to Him, "Lord, You know all things; You know that I love You." Jesus said to him, "Feed My sheep. ¹⁸Most assuredly, I say to you, when you were younger, you girded yourself and walked where you wished; but when you are old, you will stretch out your hands, and another will gird you and carry *you* where you do not wish." ¹⁹This He spoke, signifying by what death he would glorify God. And when He had spoken this, He said to him, "Follow Me."

²⁰Then Peter, turning around,

---

equipped to meet the needs of the world through the love of God.

Notice that Jesus questioned Peter concerning the love of God called in the Greek, *agape*. This is the love that has come to the human heart from God through salvation. Unless we are taught to respect and understand the benefits of our new birth, we will continue as did Peter to respond in life through old methods. Peter answered the Lord with the Greek term, *phileo*, which signified affection and brotherly love. This was all Peter knew, until now. Jesus taught about the love of God and the need to experience it through service to others.

If there is one thing at which we should excel, it is using the love of God effectively to change our lives and the world around us. Paul said in 1 Corinthians 13 that love (*agape*) never fails or comes to an end. When Jesus walked in an outward showing of compassion, which is simply the love of God displayed, He never failed to produce the works of the kingdom of God. You will be as successful as He if you will dare to defy the hatred and greed in the world and walk bravely in the love of God.

Walking in love is a great test to our faith. The love of God is a divine substance which must be exercised in order to take effect. You will have to make a choice to use the love of God. It's still way too easy for most to yield to their flesh when considering the choices of our actions. Whether we are confronted with issues in our marriage, home, job, or everyday interactions with people, we choose how we will respond.

Most likely you will have more opportunities to walk in love in the course of your day than to exercise your faith for the benefits of redemption. If there is one thing that we should focus on more than any other, it would be loving others as Christ

saw the disciple whom Jesus loved following, who also had leaned on His breast at the supper, and said, "Lord, who is the one who betrays You?" ²¹Peter, seeing him, said to Jesus, "But Lord, what *about* this man?"

²²Jesus said to him, "If I will that he remain till I come, what *is that* to you? You follow Me."

²³Then this saying went out among the brethren that this disciple would not die. Yet Jesus did not say to him that he would not die, but, "If I will that he remain till I come, what *is that* to you?"

²⁴This is the disciple who testifies of these things, and wrote these things; and we know that his testimony is true.

²⁵And there are also many other things that Jesus did, which if they were written one by one, I suppose that even the world itself could not contain the books that would be written. Amen.

---

loves us. As Jesus pointed out in this passage, the way we love others will be a clear sign of how we love Him.

21:22 Jesus's comment to Peter speaks volumes to us today. We ought not to be concerned with how God deals with someone else in life as a comparison to our faith and our relationship with God. We are responsible for how our hearts follow God. Comparison spreads insecurity. Become secure in your own relationship with God. You will answer to God for how well you followed His plan for your life, not someone else's.

21:25 John ended his gospel message telling us that he revealed only a small percentage of the things that Jesus did while on the earth. He stretches our imagination by stating that all the books of the known world could not contain all the things that Jesus did. John leaves etched in our minds the reality that we must produce results to authenticate the ministry of Jesus. The abundance of works Jesus did that are not recorded serve to challenge us to come up in thought, believe bigger, and definitely go beyond our comfort zone with God. If Jesus produced to His world the signs, wonders, and miracles with such quality and quantity as proof of the Father's love, then our world today deserves the same opportunity to believe.

JOHN 21 KEY WORDS

Love (*agapao* ἀγαπάω NT: 25) God's unconditional love in giving His Son, Jesus, could not be merited or earned. Rather, God's nature is love (1 John 4:7-8). God initiated a loving relationship for us to enter into by faith or trust in Jesus. His love neither judges nor condemns. *Apape* accepts the believer as he is and begins to transform the believer into who Christ is.

𝕍 **Love** (*phileo* φιλέω NT: 5368) This kind of love is brotherly love; natural affection that family members would have for one another; the kind of love that bonds people together when they have a common vision or task.

Jesus asked Peter in John 21 if he loves Him. Jesus was asking for the God kind of love, unconditional and fully surrendered (*agapao*). Peter could only respond with a brotherly or familial affection (*phileo*). After two tries, Jesus finally approached Peter where he was, not where he needed to be. Jesus asked Peter, "Do you love (*phileo*) Me?" And Peter responded with loving (*phileo*) Jesus on his own terms, not Christ's.

Jesus will accept you where you are, but He will stretch you to where He is. John's gospel continually challenges you to become more and more like Jesus and not to be comfortable where you are.

Now you may see the visible;

in Christ see the invisible.
Now you may trust what you know;
in Christ trust what He knows.
Now you may pray what you want;
in Christ pray what He wants.
Now you may do what's possible;
in Christ do the impossible.
Now you may exist in the world;
in Christ you *live* in His world.
Now you may focus on your needs;
in Christ focus on the needs of others.
Now you may do good works;
in Christ do His signs and wonders.
Now you may experience miracles sometimes;
in Christ live in the miraculous!

𝕍 **Tend** or **Feed** (*bosko* βόσκω NT: 1006) To pasture, feed, care for, and nurture. Such feeding implies that the shepherd finds good pastures and fresh, flowing waters for sheep. Christ wants His disciples to care for one another the way He cares for us as the Good Shepherd (read

John 10 and Psalm 23). Jesus uses this verb to speak of nurturing those young in the faith, lambs.

🔑 **Feed** (*poimaino* ποιμαίνω NT: 4165) To lead, guide, help, and care for. What mature sheep need is guidance, counsel, and direction. They can feed themselves on the milk and meat of the Word, but they still need the wise, godly counsel of others for direction. There are times when even mature sheep face crises and lose their way and need tending (*bosko*) as Jesus indicates the third time He instructs Peter.

JOHN 21 SUMMARY

We see a glimpse of the persistence of God after the resurrection of our Lord to reveal Himself to His disciples so that they would confidently get to work for Him. There is so much that must be done for the gospel message to be preached around the world. We must be confident in the message and the power of God to back it up. The disciples were confronted by the Lord many times after His resurrection for the benefit of convincing them of their rights and privileges of continuing in the service of the Lord.

Our relationship with Jesus through the Holy Spirit is just as life-empowering as Jesus's relationship with the Father.

We will only be as committed to life as our understanding of His commitment to us. Remember, we love Him because He first loved us. It is the unconditional love of God—that while we were yet sinners, Christ died for us—that has the power to melt the hardest heart.

Never forget the character of God displayed throughout the gospel of John. John and the other Gospel writers made plain the truth that God the Father is committed to showing us His love. John clearly showed us that Jesus is the Son of God and the Son of Man. Therefore, Jesus was and is the divine expression of God on the earth. His continual demonstrations of power are to convince us that God loves us and reveals to us our future expectations.

Our relationship with Jesus through the Holy Spirit is just as life-empowering as Jesus's relationship with the Father. Seeing the consistencies of overcoming power in the heart of our Lord should cause us to long for the same.

Jesus certainly reiterates the need for the church to operate in the love of God. His dialogue with Peter should convince us to take seriously the subject of God's love. *Agape* is the ability to manifest to others the heart of God. God's love is definitely His benevolent blessing and care for His children. His warm embrace that calms our fears and secures our future is experienced through our relationship with Him.

[God's love] gives us every reason to reach out to others with His same compassion.

God's love is the action that supplies every need. It gives us every reason to reach out to others with His same compassion. What a privilege to possess this love and what a joy to express it.

"Behold, what manner of love the Father has bestowed upon us that we should be called the sons of God" (1 John 3:1 KJV). God's love is also the knowledge that we have become sons of God just like Jesus. When God sent Jesus to the earth, it was with great purpose. God through Christ reconciled the world unto Himself, where all who call upon the name of the Lord, will be saved.

Being saved is far more than an entrance into heaven when we die. This salvation is the new creation at work within us, uniting us with God Himself. The sin problem is solved; man united with God is restored to His original dominion, power, and authority. The earth must recognize our words and actions as they did the actions of Jesus. John told us in his epistle that as Jesus is right now, so are we in this world. First John 4:17 reads, "Love has been perfected among us in this: that we may have boldness in the day of judgment; because as He is, so are we in this world."

Just as Jesus is raised up, seated, and enthroned over all, so are we to this world. The environment in which we dwell must surrender to the greater one on the inside. The regular occurrences that come upon the world will submit themselves to a Spirit-filled and alive child of

God. This is why we have boldness in the day of crisis.

We are fortified with the authority and power of the ages. Not since the day of Adam has the world seen such a man like the Christ, the Son of God. In the same manner the world must see the potential of man united with and filled with God. Every hindrance known to the devil's demise crumbled at the feet of Jesus. This is the message of the love of God: that man has become a new creature from heaven, made in the exact similitude of Jesus our Lord. He is positioned in right standing, empowered with strength and dominion to work the works of Jesus and destroy the hindrances of the enemy without fear of failure.

The love of God is so awesome that in His generosity we would be included in His family, to rule and reign on the earth as kings and priests unto God. Awesome love, isn't it?

MEDITATIONS FOR SUCCESS

- God is in the business of showing up.
- God delights in the confidence you have in His faithfulness.
- If you love Him, you will serve Him.
- God's love is His benevolent heart that insists on blessing you.
- The knowledge of God's love is revealed in sonship.
- As He is, so are we.
- There is no fear in God's love.
- When you understand your place in Christ and His great care for you, you will express yourself with great boldness. You cannot fail!

CONCLUSION

LIVE IN THE MIRACULOUS!

The gospel of John has been a fascinating look into the mind of our Lord. If a man's thoughts become at some point the sum total of his actions, then we can confirm this in the life and ministry of Jesus. He definitely developed His mind to see past the seen and behold the unlimited world of the unseen. Jesus firmly grasped the significance of the power of heavenly assistance. He recognized how important it is for man to rely on the ability of God the Father for absolute success in life.

Jesus showed us by example the necessity of walking in fellowship with the Father. Apart from the wisdom and comfort of the Father, Jesus considered Himself unable to complete His mission. Even as a young boy, at the tender age of twelve, Jesus sought the approval of His heavenly Father over the temporary ways of man. If the Father could do all things, then Jesus could do all things. He came to the earth completely united with the Father, one in spirit and purpose. Only this relationship and the knowledge of His empowerment would make possible all things.

Jesus showed us by example the necessity of walking in fellowship with the Father.

Jesus knew this to be true as He believed all things. Producing results are for those who are one with Christ in heart and mind. Even as Jesus taught us that we as branches, if apart from the vine, which represents Him, can do nothing, so He realized that apart from the Father He could do nothing.

The extreme need for Jesus to walk in all the will of God the Father seems to be a defining characteristic for His success. He knew that He was one with the Father and desired to walk and talk only as the Father would do. This then is the reason why a man from Nazareth would turn the world upside down in only three-and-a-half years of ministry. Why also this man would continue to astound the world with His teaching and provide heavenly access for His followers to multiply His efforts in the exact same degree.

Only a demonstration of the works that Jesus accomplished in His earth walk will serve to satisfy the claim that He is alive. Even though we know this to be true, the world will never accept His resurrection unless there is proof that through His followers His works are still being done. Jesus was very diligent in work to produce in a large but still limited number of people the surety that He was the Son of God. Every miracle revealed that the unseen God, the Father of our Lord, was indeed working through Jesus to demonstrate His love and plan for the entire world.

As a priority to the believer, Jesus taught the significance of a God-centered life. To have the mind of Christ while understanding the power of our place in Him would be sufficient for the Christian to reproduce the works of God. Zeal for the care of God's house, which is the believer's heart, consumed the Lord. As important as this subject is in our lives, Jesus desired

greatly to demonstrate it in His time on the earth. With such compassion in His voice, He prayed to the Father that we would ultimately understand and walk in the power of our union with God. John 17:21-25, *Riggs Translation,* reads:

"Such is my prayer for these beloved disciples, but my heart's desire reaches out beyond them to all believers in all times and places who shall by means of their preaching come to faith in me. May they all, O Father, be one! Let nothing imperil the unity of those who accept me as their savior . . . as thou are in me and I in thee . . . one in spirit and life . . . may they be one in us in order that by such a spiritual unity the world may be compelled to believe in the divine origin of my mission.

"I have given them what thou gave me, the glory of revealing the divine in human life, of knowing and showing forth the Father's love in order that they, as we, may live in and for each other, I in them, and thou in me, that in this absolute harmony of life a complete and final unity may be attained. The result will be that the world shall come to know, through evidence which cannot be gainsaid, that my mission is from thee and that the church is the church of God!"

Can you hear God's heart in this prayer? Do you understand your mission clearly? In order to effectively evangelize the world we must share with them the Good News that God in His great love sent us a Savior to destroy sin and its effect and bring us eternal life. We must then give them the proof of God's goodness. To preach this message without demonstrating through signs and wonders the power of God would be to preach another gospel than what Jesus preached.

THE CHURCH CAN PRODUCE CONFIRMING RESULTS!

In Luke 8:1 Jesus went throughout the surrounding villages teaching, preaching, and passing out samples. Only as Jesus considered Himself capable of producing miracles were miracles displayed. Without believing in the authority that came from the Father, there would be no initiative to produce results. Clearly Jesus believed that everything that He did was well within His power and authority to do so. Amazingly enough, His belief was so convincing that even the disciples caught on and when

authorized by Jesus, went around doing good and healing all who were oppressed by the devil.

If Jesus's Gospel and the ability to produce confirming results can be passed on to the servants of the Lord, who were not under the covenant of salvation through grace, how much more should the New Testament sons of God operate freely as Jesus did on the earth.

Jesus prayed that the church might comprehend the fact that we are one with Him, even as He and the Father are one. The word "as" means in the same conditions and in the same degree. As we see Jesus unlimited in His earthly ministry, so then we the church are also unlimited. The same mighty power that Jesus used as the Father backed Him up, is the same power that the church operates in today. The same favor and love that the Father bestowed on Jesus, is in the same degree for us. Jesus actually believed it to be true. This is what gave Him such command. For the church to walk in this love and power, we must grow up spiritually by being renewed in our minds. We can't become any more perfect inwardly; salvation solved that problem. We are in every way one with Christ. Our inner man, the spirit of man, was created perfect in the mold of Jesus Himself.

As you learn more and more from Him (Matthew 11:29) . . .

- dare to act in faith;
- grow up in the knowledge of who you are in Him;
- experience for yourself the awesome power of God to save, heal, and deliver.

The gospel of John is a wonderful tool to your success. It's like watching a movie. We listened to Jesus tell us wonders from His experience in heavenly things. We saw the heart of the Father as Jesus was moved time and time again with the compassion of God for the needs of the people. We can understand the attitude of righteousness that Jesus walked in versus the religious, self-centered attitudes of the Pharisees.

Jesus taught us the keys to releasing the power or life of God by continually being mindful of it and its ability. He often reminded us of our privilege of communing with the Father in prayer. His reliance upon the will of His Father showed us the commitment that is necessary to complete the will of God for our lives. As Jesus grew in dominion, we too begin to develop a sense of ownership over the problems of life.

Jesus showed us that great strength comes as we serve others with the kindness of God. Jesus then revealed that His commitment was 100 percent, even if it meant dying on the cross for the sin of the world. When the human will demanded its rights, we watched in the garden as Jesus, strong in Spirit, reveals the will of God.

What would the possibility be if we were to take the words and attitudes of the Lord verbatim and act as if He were preaching, healing, and delivering people all as training for us? Then with great resolve, what if we decided to prove His commission to be true? Would we get any results?

Why not find out for yourself.

Jesus showed us that great strength comes as we serve others with the kindness of God.

You are part of His body, the glorious church. It's time to let your life shine!

Personal Challenge

It is the will of God that everyone receives eternal salvation, and the way to receive this salvation is to call upon the name of Jesus and confess Him as your Lord. The Bible presents this exciting opportunity for eternal life in Romans, Chapter 10: 9-13. It tells you that if you confess with your mouth the Lord Jesus, and believe in your heart that God has raised Him from the dead, you shall be saved. For it is with the heart that man believes unto righteousness; and with the mouth confession is made unto salvation. It goes on to let you know that whosoever-and that really does include you-shall call upon the name of the Lord shall be saved.

God's invitation to you is an invitation to the whole world. John 3:16 says, "For God loved the world so much that he gave his only Son so that anyone who believes in him shall not perish but have eternal life" (TLB). By simply receiving Jesus as your Savior, you can experience God's love for yourself. Repeat this prayer from your heart:

Heavenly Father, I come to you in prayer to receive Jesus as my Savior. I confess with my mouth and believe with my heart that Jesus is your Son, and that he died on the Cross at Calvary that I might be forgiven and have Eternal Life in the Kingdom of Heaven. Jesus, I believe that you rose from the dead and I ask you right now to come into my life and be my personal Lord and Savior. I repent of my Sins and will Worship you all the day's of my Life! Thank you for coming into my life. Father, because your word is truth, I confess with my mouth that I am Born Again, cleansed by the blood of Jesus, A new creature in Christ! In Jesus Name, Amen

If you have prayed this prayer to receive Jesus Christ as your Savior, or if this book has changed your life, we would like to hear from you. Please write us at:

Jim Hockaday Ministries, Inc.
Post Office Box 839
Broken Arrow, OK 74013

Now that you are beginning your new life in Christ, where does God fit in? Can you see that you already qualify to live in the miraculous? Then until He comes you need to be doing the works of Jesus.

WHERE DOES GOD FIT IN?

Have things been tough lately?
Have bills been stacking up...
Car not working...
Too many trips to the doctor...
Feeling blah spiritually...
Having conflict in your relationships...
Tired of the routine of life?

Ever wonder where God fits in? Certainly He's around. God's everywhere. But when you need Him, does He often seem distant, detached and hard to reach? Something happens unexpectedly... so where does God fit in?

Is God fitting in simply a matter of you squeezing Him into a hectic day or a muddled existence? Ever wonder about these things or is your life so filled with distractions that there's not even time to wonder anymore?

The psalmist said in Psalm 46:10 "Be still, and know that I am God." A simple understanding of this verse is to avoid the trap of letting your attentions be divided and to prioritize your time with God. If you've taken time to ask the question, "Where does God fit in?" then it's time to step back from life's busyness and into God's presence. He's there; waiting patiently for you to be all that He's created you to be. Come out of the familiar and step into His presence through His Word, through prayer, and being still before God. When you fit God into all that you do and say in your daily walk; when you abide, God will fit into your life in such a way that all you are will reflect His glory! "But we all, with unveiled face, beholding as in a mirror the glory of the Lord, are being transformed into the same image from glory to glory, just as by the Spirit of the Lord" (2 Corinthians 3:18).

Jesus told a parable in Luke 19:11-28 that refers to the diligence required of those disciples who actively await the return of the Lord. Verse 13 says, "And he called his ten servants, and delivered them ten pounds, and said unto them, Occupy till I come." Simply put, Jesus said to *busy yourself in the work you have been commissioned to do.*

God the Father has a very specific and detailed plan for mankind. Jesus came to earth for the precise purpose of fulfilling His assignment. He succeeded; then He delegated His authority to the Church so His will could continue to be enforced on the earth. Never has there been such a need for the finished work of Christ to be implemented in this earth. To be sure, people's intentions have been good and their hearts have been pure; yet the work of the Lord has lacked application. Would you be proud to stand in the presence of Jesus? What about the eternal trophies—the ones that come from the souls who are touched for God and from the divine call that has been fulfilled the way it was given through the heart of God?

Jude exhorted us to *contend earnestly* for the faith (Jude 1:3). He wasn't talking about just any faith, but the faith that once was given to the saints—faith that Jesus demonstrated in His ministry. We must earnestly contend for Jesus's kind of faith to be demonstrated in our lives. We can only know God's fullness as we determine to be bold, courageous, and strong in Him. Who will rise up and be held accountable for the task at hand? Will you? You are the answer to the needs of this world. Know who you are; know what you have; and know what you can and must do... *until He comes.*

"Humanity was created for it...

The soul hungers for it...

All creation longs to understand its pulse
I'm speaking of the Supernatural pathway to the miraculous
If it could be understood, harnessed and released with purpose,
what would you be willing to do to live in it?

For all ages and all people, the miraculous is God's idea!
Why not know where you are going, know how to get there,
and know what to expect when you've arrived?

This is the time,
the hour and the day to live in the miraculous.

LET'S DO IT!?

Jim Hockaday Ministries
Post Office Box 839
Broken Arrow, OK 74013

JOHN NKJV TEXTUAL FOOTNOTES

1:5 [a]Or *overcome*

1:9 [a]Or *That was the true Light which, coming into the world, gives light to every man.*

1:11 [a]That is, His own things or domain [b]That is, His own people

1:16 [a]NU-Text reads *For.*

1:18 [a]NU-Text reads *only begotten God.*

1:23 [a]Isaiah 40:3

1:28 [a]NU-Text and M-Text read *Bethany.*

1:42 [a]NU-Text reads *John.*

1:51 [a]NU-Text omits *hereafter.*

2:17 [a]NU-Text and M-Text read *will eat.* [b]Psalm 69:9

2:22 [a]NU-Text and M-Text omit *to them.*

3:13 [a]NU-Text omits *who is in heaven.*

3:15 [a]NU-Text omits *not perish but.*

4:42 [a]NU-Text omits *the Christ.*

5:2 [a]NU-Text reads *Bethzatha.*

5:4 [a]NU-Text omits *waiting for the moving of the water* at the end of verse 3, and all of verse 4.

5:16 [a]NU-Text omits *and sought to kill Him.*

6:11 [a]NU-Text omits *to the disciples, and the disciples.*

6:19 [a]Literally *twenty-five or thirty stadia*

6:22 [a]NU-Text omits *that* and *which His disciples had entered.*

6:31 [a]Exodus 16:4; Nehemiah 9:15; Psalm 78:24

6:45 [a]Isaiah 54:13 [b]M-Text reads *hears and has learned.*

6:47 [a]NU-Text omits *in Me.*

6:55 [a]NU-Text reads *true food* and *true drink.*

6:69 [a]NU-Text reads *You are the Holy One of God.*

7:1 [a]That is, the ruling authorities

7:8 [a]NU-Text omits *yet.*

7:16 [a]NU-Text and M-Text read *So Jesus.*

7:26 [a]NU-Text omits *truly.*

7:29 [a]NU-Text and M-Text omit *But.*

7:33 [a]NU-Text and M-Text omit *to them.*

7:39 [a]NU-Text reads *who believed.* [b]NU-Text omits *Holy.*

7:40 [a]NU-Text reads *some.*

7:50 [a]NU-Text reads *before.*

7:52 [a]NU-Text reads *is to rise.*

7:53 *a*The words *And everyone through sin no more* (8:11) are bracketed by NU-Text as not original. They are present in over 900 manuscripts.

8:2 *a*M-Text reads *very early.*

8:4 *a*M-Text reads *we found this woman.*

8:5 *a*M-Text reads *in our law Moses commanded.* *b*NU-Text and M-Text read *to stone such.* *c*M-Text adds *about her.*

8:6 *a*NU-Text and M-Text omit *as though He did not hear.*

8:7 *a*M-Text reads *He looked up.*

8:9 *a*NU-Text and M-Text omit *being convicted by their conscience.*

8:10 *a*NU-Text omits *and saw no one but the woman;* M-Text reads *He saw her and said.* *b*NU-Text and M-Text omit *of yours.*

8:11 *a*NU-Text and M-Text add *from now on.*

8:38 *a*NU-Text reads *heard from.*

8:54 *a*NU-Text and M-Text read *our.*

8:59 *a*NU-Text omits the rest of this verse.

9:4 *a*NU-Text reads *We.*

9:8 *a*NU-Text reads *a beggar.*

9:9 *a*NU-Text reads *"No, but he is like him."*

9:11 *a*NU-Text omits *the pool of.*

9:35 *a*NU-Text reads *Son of Man.*

10:8 *a*M-Text omits *before Me.*

10:26 *a*NU-Text omits *as I said to you.*

10:34 *a*Psalm 82:6

10:38 *a*NU-Text reads *understand.*

11:18 *a*Literally *fifteen stadia*

11:30 *a*NU-Text adds *still.*

11:31 *a*NU-Text reads *supposing that she was going to the tomb to weep there.*

11:41 *a*NU-Text omits *from the place where the dead man was lying.*

11:50 *a*NU-Text reads *you.*

12:1 *a*NU-Text omits *who had been dead.*

12:5 *a*About one year's wages for a worker

12:7 *a*NU-Text reads *that she may keep.*

12:13 *a*Psalm 118:26

12:15 *a*Zechariah 9:9

12:38 *a*Isaiah 53:1

12:40 *a*Isaiah 6:10

12:41 [a]NU-Text reads *because.*

12:47 [a]NU-Text reads *keep them.*

13:2 [a]NU-Text reads *And during supper.*

13:18 [a]NU-Text reads *My bread.* [b]Psalm 41:9

13:25 [a]NU-Text and M-Text add *thus.*

14:2 [a]Literally *dwellings* [b]NU-Text adds a word which would cause the text to read either *if it were not so, would I have told you that I go to prepare a place for you?* or *if it were not so I would have told you; for I go to prepare a place for you.*

14:14 [a]NU-Text adds *Me.*

14:15 [a]NU-Text reads *you will keep.*

14:28 [a]NU-Text omits *I said.*

15:2 [a]Or *lifts up*

15:7 [a]NU-Text omits *you will.*

15:25 [a]Psalm 69:4

16:3 [a]NU-Text and M-Text omit *to you.*

16:4 [a]NU-Text reads *their.*

16:15 [a]NU-Text and M-Text read *He takes of Mine and will declare it to you.*

16:33 [a]NU-Text and M-Text omit *will.*

17:2 [a]M-Text reads *shall.*

17:11 [a]NU-Text and M-Text read *keep them through Your name which You have given Me.*

17:12 [a]NU-Text omits *in the world.* [b]NU-Text reads *in Your name which You gave Me. And I guarded them;* (or *it;*).

17:20 [a]NU-Text and M-Text omit *will.*

18:15 [a]M-Text reads *the other.*

18:20 [a]NU-Text reads *where all the Jews meet.*

19:3 [a]NU-Text reads *And they came up to Him and said.*

19:7 [a]NU-Text reads *the law.*

19:16 [a]NU-Text omits *and led Him away.*

19:24 [a]Psalm 22:18

19:28 [a]M-Text reads *seeing.*

19:36 [a]Exodus 12:46; Numbers 9:12; Psalm 34:20

19:37 [a]Zechariah 12:10

20:16 [a]NU-Text adds *in Hebrew.*

20:18 [a]NU-Text reads *disciples, "I have seen the Lord,"* . . . .

20:19 [a]NU-Text omits *assembled.*

20:29 [a]NU-Text and M-Text omit *Thomas.*

21:3 [a]NU-Text omits *immediately.*

21:15 [a]NU-Text reads *John.*

21:16 [a]NU-Text reads *John.*

21:17 [a]NU-Text reads *John.*